European Migration in the Late Twentieth Century

The International Institute for Applied Systems Analysis

is an interdisciplinary, nongovernmental research institution founded in 1972 by leading scientific organizations in 12 countries. Situated near Vienna, in the center of Europe, IIASA has been for more than two decades producing valuable scientific research on economic, technological, and environmental issues.

IIASA was one of the first international institutes to systematically study global issues of environment, technology, and development. IIASA's Governing Council states that the Institute's goal is: *to conduct international and interdisciplinary scientific studies to provide timely and relevant information and options, addressing critical issues of global environmental, economic, and social change, for the benefit of the public, the scientific community, and national and international institutions.* Research is organized around three central themes:

- Global Environmental Change;
- Global Economic and Technological Change;
- Systems Methods for the Analysis of Global Issues.

The Institute now has national member organizations in the following countries:

Austria
The Austrian Academy of Sciences

Bulgaria
The National Committee for Applied Systems Analysis and Management

Canada
The Canadian Committee for IIASA

Czech Republic
The Czech Committee for IIASA

Finland
The Finnish Committee for IIASA

Germany
The Association for the Advancement of IIASA

Hungary
The Hungarian Committee for Applied Systems Analysis

Italy
The National Research Council (CNR) and the National Commission for Nuclear and Alternative Energy Sources (ENEA)

Japan
The Japan Committee for IIASA

Netherlands
The Netherlands Organization for Scientific Research (NWO)

Poland
The Polish Academy of Sciences

Russia
The Russian Academy of Sciences

Slovak Republic
Membership under consideration

Sweden
The Swedish Council for Planning and Coordination of Research (FRN)

Ukraine
The Ukrainian Academy of Sciences

United States of America
The American Academy of Arts and Sciences

European Migration in the Late Twentieth Century

Historical Patterns, Actual Trends, and Social Implications

Editors
Heinz Fassmann
Austrian Academy of Sciences
and
Rainer Münz
Humboldt University, Berlin

Edward Elgar

IIASA
International Institute for Applied Systems Analysis
Laxenburg, Austria

Published by

Edward Elgar Publishing Limited
Gower House
Croft Road
Aldershot
Hants GU11 3HR
England

Edward Elgar Publishing Company
Old Post Road
Brookfield
Vermont 05036
USA

British Library Cataloguing in Publication Data

Fassmann, Heinz
European Migration in the Late Twentieth Century: Historical Patterns, Actual Trends and Social Implications
I. Title II. Munz, Rainer
304.8094

Library of Congress Cataloguing in Publication Data

European migration in the late twentieth century: historical patterns, actual trends, and social Implications / editors, Heinz Fassmann, Rainer Münz.
304p. 23cm.
Includes bibliographical references and index.
1. Europe—Emigration and immigration—History—20th century,
I. Fassmann, Heinz. II. Münz, Rainer, 1954–
JV7590.E962 1994
304.8'094'09045—dc20 94–21838
CIP

ISBN 1 85898 125 5

Printed and bound in Great Britain by
Hartnolls Limited, Bodmin, Cornwall

Contents

Foreword

We are currently witnessing a period in which actual and potential migration flows are changing the political, social, and economic map of Europe. These events cannot be seen out of their historical context because the past processes laid the basis for the structure of present and future migrations, as well as for our perception and interpretation of these phenomena. This is the focus of the present book, which aims to provide a comprehensive scientific overview of migration flows within Europe since World War II with special emphasis on recent movements.

The book is one of the outcomes of an international conference on Mass Migration in Europe organized by IIASA at its Laxenburg Conference Center, together with the Institute for Advanced Studies in Vienna and the Institute for Future Studies in Stockholm, in March 1992. The production of the present volume has been the responsibility of IIASA together with the Austrian Academy of Sciences. Heinz Fassmann and Rainer Münz planned and organized the corresponding conference workshop, selected the papers, and edited the book. We are sure it will find its firm place in the rapidly increasing literature on international migration.

Wolfgang Lutz
Sture Öberg
IIASA
Laxenburg, Austria
January 1994

Preface

Since the mid-1980s international migration has become a major issue in Europe. One reason is obvious. The fall of the Iron Curtain has led to the largest wave of migration the continent has seen since 1945–46. The sudden freedom of travel and Eastern Europe's mounting economic problems and social tensions caused by the transition to market economy have been important push factors. In many cases ethnic discrimination has also played an important role; in the early 1990s the largest single wave of emigration was caused by the wars in Croatia and Bosnia–Herzegovina. Yet in most West European countries the focus still is more on South–North migration than on East–West migration.

It is important to know about the quantitative side of these issues, but today numbers alone cannot fully explain the impacts of these migrations on public opinion and the political climate in Western Europe. The symbolic side of the issue seems to be as crucial as the quantitative one. For many people in the West migration has become a synonym for social problems, and is seen as a threat to the welfare state. At the same time we should not overlook that many problems related to migration are not caused by the migrants themselves. Some are caused by the fact that most European societies are not ready to cope with the necessity to integrate immigrants. In many cases foreigners have to serve as scapegoats.

This book contains both quantitative and policy-related information on international migration within and to Europe. It focuses on the main sending and receiving countries in the second half of the twentieth century. Originally the chapters of the book were presented as papers at a workshop organized by the editors in March 1992 within the framework of a conference in Laxenburg, Austria, on Mass Migration in Europe. The conference was organized by IIASA, Laxenburg, the Institute for Advanced Studies, Vienna, and the Institute for Future Studies, Stockholm.

The papers included in this book have been reviewed by three referees, revised and updated by the authors, and finally edited by the editors and by IIASA's publications department.

The initial workshop and this book are part of a larger research project jointly sponsored by three Austrian federal ministries: the Ministry of the Interior, the Ministry of Labor and Social Affairs, and the Ministry of Science and Research. The project is being carried out at the Austrian Academy of Science, Vienna, and at the Humboldt University, Berlin.

The editors would like to thank Andreas Andiel, Sarah James, Carmen Nemeth, Ursula Reeger, Ulrike Stadler, and all others who helped to organize the workshop and to edit this book.

Heinz Fassmann
Rainer Münz
Vienna and Berlin
January 1994

Contributors

Odo Barsotti
Professor of Demography at the Department of Social Sciences, University of Pisa, Italy. Research topics: International migration, migration models, foreign immigrants, commuting and daily movements, interactions between demographic and socioeconomic phenomena.

Daniela Bobeva
Head of the Department of Employment and Labor Market, Ministry of Labor and Social Welfare, Sofia, Bulgaria. Research topics: Foreign investment, labor market policy, migration.

David Coleman
Lecturer in Demography at Oxford University since 1980. Research topics: Demography of the industrial world, including immigration and ethnic minorities.

Zoltán Dövényi
Senior Research Fellow at the Geographical Research Institute of the Hungarian Academy of Sciences, Budapest. Research topics: Small towns, international migration, labor markets.

Han Entzinger
Professor of multiethnic studies at the University of Utrecht, the Netherlands, and Director of the Research School on Labor, Social Welfare, and Social and Economic Policy. Research topics: International migration, social integration, ethnicity, public policy and comparative studies.

Heinz Fassmann
Director of the Institute of Urban and Regional Science of the Austrian Academy of Sciences, Vienna, and Senior Lecturer at the University of Vienna. Research topics: Migration, urban development, labor markets.

Peter A. Fischer

Research Assistant at the Institute for Economic Policy Research, University of the Bundeswehr, Hamburg. Research topics: International economics, migration, population economics.

Piotr Korcelli

Professor and Director at the Institute of Geography and Spatial Organization of the Polish Academy of Sciences. Research topics: Urban change, internal and international migration, population projections, regional economic development and planning.

Laura Lecchini

Researcher at the Department of Statistics and Applied Mathematics, Professor of Social Statistics, University of Pisa. Research topics: Living arrangements and social networks of the elderly, international migration in the Mediterranean area.

Janez Malačić

Associate Professor at the Faculty of Economics, University of Ljubljana. Research topics: Demography, economic statistics, national economy, population and labor-force reproduction, migration.

Rainer Münz

Professor of Demography at the Humboldt University in Berlin and Senior Lecturer at the University of Vienna. Research topics: Population development, social policy, migration, ethnic minorities.

Hedwig Rudolph

Professor at the Technical University of Berlin and Director of the Social Science Research Center in Berlin. Research topics: Internationalization and employment, class and gender relations.

Eitan F. Sabatello

Head of the Division of Population, Demography, Health, and Immigrant Absorption, Central Bureau of Statistics in Jerusalem, Israel.

Thomas Straubhaar
Professor of Economics and Director of the Institute for Economic Policy, University of the Bundeswehr, Hamburg. Research topics: International economics, migration and population economics.

Anatoli Vishnevsky
Director of the Center of Demography and Human Ecology of the Institute of Economic Forecasting of the Russian Academy of Sciences, Moscow. Research topics: Demographic transitions in the former Soviet Union and in the world, historical demography, family evolution and family policy, social consequences of demographic processes.

Gabriella Vukovich
Demographer, Chief of Population Statistics, Central Statistical Office, Budapest. Research topics: Economic and social implications of demographic processes, population policy.

Catherine Wihtol de Wenden
Research Director at CNRS (CERI), Paris. Research topics: Immigration policies in Europe, East–West and South–North Migrations.

Zhanna Zayonchkovskaya
Head of the Laboratory of Population Migration of the Institute of Economic Forecasting of the Russian Academy of Sciences, Moscow. Research topics: International migration, demography and settlement systems.

Part I

Introduction

Chapter 1

Patterns and Trends of International Migration in Western Europe

Heinz Fassmann and Rainer Münz

1.1 West European Migration: Historical Developments since 1945

Thirty years ago, the Federal Republic of Germany welcomed Armando Rodriguez who was said to be its one-millionth "migrant worker". The Portuguese national received an official welcome in Cologne and was offered a motorcycle. The German news magazine *Der Spiegel* devoted its cover story to this event. Three decades later in most West European countries people like Armando Rodriguez are no longer referred to as "migrant workers" or "guest workers". Usually they are seen simply as "foreigners". Typically, migrants no longer come from Ireland, Italy, Spain, or Portugal but from Turkey and former Yugoslavia, from the Maghreb and the Indian subcontinent. Those who came during the 1960s and 1970s no longer ride motorcycles, but many of them drive mid-size cars. In Western Europe first- and second-generation immigrants are no longer welcome. This has not, however, reversed the basic trend toward the internationalization of European labor markets, a development also found in capital and commodity markets. In many European countries, despite widespread unemployment, the share of foreign workers and employees has stabilized at high levels, and in most countries the share of foreigners among the total population is still increasing.

This chapter presents a brief account of salient developments in international migration in Western Europe since the end of World War II, discusses the patterns that characterize the distribution of foreign resident populations in major West European receiving countries by country of origin, considers the factors that help explain those patterns, and comments on likely future developments and policy challenges concerning international migration affecting Western Europe.

Until 1945 Europe's migration history was predominantly marked by emigration. At the end of the colonial era and during the economic boom that followed World War II, the situation in Western Europe changed rapidly. At first, European settlers and colonial officers and troops returned home in the course of decolonization. In the United Kingdom, France, Belgium, and the Netherlands they were followed by migrant workers from the former overseas territories. In some cases this process created a steady inflow, in other cases the former colonial powers were confronted with large waves of immigrants. During and after the bloody war of independence (1954–62) more than 1 million former French residents of Algeria were resettled in France. Return migration from other former French colonies was of comparable size. Since the early 1950s a sizable number of people have migrated from Indonesia to the Netherlands, and since the 1970s from Suriname and the Dutch Antilles. In the mid-1970s Portugal was also confronted with a sudden surge of returnees and immigrants from its former African colonies. This kind of migration was amplified by several European countries that granted citizenship to the residents of their former overseas territories, or facilitated their immigration by granting them special legal status as quasi-nationals or privileged aliens.

It is impossible to specify who immigrated or emigrated over the last decades to or from which country in Western Europe. No precise data are available on the chronological course and the geography of all relevant migration streams. The first problems are those of definition. It is not always clear who is to be regarded as a migrant. Moreover, statistics concerning foreigners or foreign workers and employees are likely to be distorted owing to concealment.

In most West European countries nationality or citizenship is the decisive criterion for distinguishing between "locals" and immigrants. In only a few West European countries immigrants are officially or statistically divided into analytical categories. Most countries try to distinguish between European Union (EU) nationals or privileged aliens and "other" foreign residents. In the UK, immigrants with British Dependent Territory Citizenship or British Overseas Citizenship[1] and immigrants holding the citizenship of a Commonwealth country are recorded separately from "other" groups of the foreign resident population. Sweden distinguishes between foreigners and Swedish nationals born abroad, and the Netherlands between "regular" foreign nationals and the former residents of Suriname, the Dutch Antilles, and the Moluccas and their descendants. Other countries whose international boundaries changed markedly during the twentieth century and which granted preferential immigration status to former nationals, or even systematically resettled them, have frequently taken the opposite approach. If at all possible, they have avoided statistically registering these residents as immigrants once they were resettled. Above all, this holds true for Germany, which, upon application, grants citizenship to all members of ethnic German minorities from Eastern Europe, the Balkans, and Central Asia. Thus, a person's citizenship does not necessarily distinguish migrants from nonmigrants.[2] In West European countries, children of foreign immigrants are generally regarded as foreigners, although of course they are not first-generation immigrants.

The national statistics summarized in *Table 1.1* show sharp increases in the foreign resident populations of almost all West European countries during the 1950s through the 1970s, but no increase or only a minor increase during the 1980s when immigration had become a major political issue.[3] Between 1950 and 1980 the number of foreigners in countries of the present-day EU and the (former) European Free Trade Association (EFTA) tripled. In 1950 approximately 5 million foreigners were living in Western Europe; in 1982 the number was 15 million;[4] and in 1992, the number was estimated at 18–19 million. This trend clearly suggests the ongoing internationalization of Western labor markets and societies.

Around 1950, the greatest proportions of foreign residents were found in "mini-states" like Liechtenstein (20% of the total population) and Luxembourg (10%), as well as in Switzerland (6%) and Austria (5%).[5] At the same time, scarcely any foreigners were living in West Germany[6] and the Netherlands (1%). At the beginning of the 1950s France had a significant number of foreigners (1.8 million), far more than West Germany (less than 568,000) and Belgium (less than 368,000).

The picture would be quite different if we were to count not only foreigners and stateless persons but all foreign-born residents of the

Table 1.1. Foreign resident populations (FRPs) in Western Europe (FRP in thousands and share of the total population), 1950–1991/92.

	1950		1970–71		1982		1989		1990		1991–92	
	FRP	%	FRP	%	FRP	%	FRP	%	FRP	%	FRP	%
Germany[a]	568	1.1	2,976	4.9	4,667	7.6	4,846	7.9	5,338	8.2	6,800	8.4
France	1,765	4.1	2,621	5.3	3,660	6.8	3,752	6.8	3,534	6.4	3,600	6.3
UK	*	*	*	*	2,137	3.9	1,894	3.3	1,904	3.3	1,930	3.3
Switzerland[b]	285	6.1	1,080	17.2	926	14.7	1,040	16.0	1,127	16.7	1,190	17.6
Belgium	368	4.3	696	7.2	886	9.0	881	8.9	903	9.1	918	9.2
Italy	47	0.1	*	*	312	0.5	407	0.7	781	1.4	*	*
Netherlands	104	1.1	255	2.0	547	3.9	642	4.3	692	4.6	728	4.8
Austria	323	4.7	212	2.8	303	4.0	323	4.3	482	6.2	560	7.1
Spain	93	0.3	148	0.4	183	0.5	335	0.9	407	1.0	505	0.3
Sweden	124	1.8	411	5.1	406	4.9	456	5.4	484	5.6	494	5.7
Denmark	*	*	*	*	102	2.0	136	2.6	161	3.1	169	3.3
Norway	16	0.5	76	2.0	91	2.2	140	3.3	143	3.4	148	3.5
Luxembourg	29	9.9	63	18.4	96	26.4	104	27.7	109	28.0	115	29.6
Portugal	21	0.3	32	0.4	64	0.6	94	0.9	108	1.0	114	1.2
Ireland	*	*	137	4.6	232	6.7	84	2.4	80	2.3	90	2.5
Greece	31	0.4	15	0.2	60	0.7	*	*	173	1.7	210	2.0
Finland	11	0.3	6	0.1	13	0.3	21	0.4	26	0.5	30	0.6
Liechtenstein	3	19.6	7	36.0	9	36.1	10	38.5	10	38.5	10	38.5
Western Europe total[c]	5,100	1.3	10,900	2.3	14,700	3.1	15,600	3.2	16,600	4.5	18,400	4.9

[a]The German figures for 1950–90 do not include the former GDR.

[b]The Swiss figures do not include so-called seasonal workers.

[c]Interpolated figures were substituted for the missing data (*). Therefore the number of foreign residents in Western Europe is partly based on estimates (see Maillat 1987: 40).

Note: Figures for Austria, Germany, and Finland are national estimates for 1989–92. The German figures for 1991–92 include the former GDR. As a rule, stateless persons are recorded as foreigners but stationed foreign troops are not included in this table.

Sources: For 1950, 1970, and 1982 see Maillat (1987: 40), Council of Europe (1993); for 1990, OECD/SOPEMI (1992).

respective host countries. Thus, even if return migrants are ignored, a significantly larger number of people have migrated since 1945 than those listed by statistics as foreigners. Apart from naturalized refugees and migrant workers the available data usually do not include immigrants from the former colonies who came to Europe as citizens of their new home countries.

Several more or less distinct groups of migrants may be considered "immigrants" or "foreigners", their relative importance varying in the different West European countries. They include migrants from former colonies with or without citizenship of the new host country;[7] migrants with the same nationality or with ethnic affiliation from (mainly) eastern areas of settlement;[8] migrant workers and their relatives; recognized refugees and *de facto* refugees and their relatives; and "other" immigrants.[9]

1.1.1 Labor migration

Following the end of World War II, the West European economies first had to integrate refugees, displaced persons, and returnees from the colonies. By the end of the 1950s, these countries began to meet part of their growing demand for labor by recruitment in several Mediterranean countries: first in Italy, Spain, Portugal, and former Yugoslavia, and later in Morocco, Algeria, Tunisia, and Turkey. In most cases the recruitment took place on the basis of bilateral agreements. In the early 1970s the employment of foreign labor in the countries of Western Europe reached its maximum.

In terms of absolute numbers, in 1970 West Germany was already leading with nearly 3 million foreigners or 4.9% of its resident population, followed by France (with 2.6 million foreigners, or 5.3% of the resident population), Switzerland (1.1 million, or 17%), and Belgium (700,000, or 7%). Large proportions of these foreigners, often the majority, were migrant workers. In 1970, 2.1 million foreign workers were employed in West Germany, 1.6 million in France, 520,000 in Switzerland, 330,000 in Belgium, 230,000 in Sweden, and 180,000 in Austria.[10] In all these receiving countries the number of foreigners also grew as a result of family reunifications (i.e., close relatives arriving later), and because of the rising number of children born to migrant workers in their host countries. At that time the most important countries of origin of these migrant workers were Italy (820,000),

Turkey (770,000), Yugoslavia (540,000), Algeria (390,000), and Spain (320,000) (see United Nations, 1986).

In the mid-1970s, West European governments and employers reacted to the economic recession that followed the 1973 oil price shock and the reduced absorption capacity of labor markets by halting recruitment of foreign labor and by imposing restrictive immigration regulations on residents of former overseas territories. The aim was to stop virtually all further immigration. In some countries – particularly the UK and France – the deteriorating economic position of "visible" immigrant minorities and native lower classes led to the first racial conflicts.

Halted recruitment and restricted immigration in the second half of the 1970s led to reductions in the foreign resident populations in two countries – on the order of 180,000 in Switzerland (between 1974 and 1979; see Straubhaar and Fischer, Chapter 7, this volume) and 5,000 in Sweden. In Switzerland a massive antiforeigner movement gained ground at that time. Some of its representatives were elected to parliament, where they exerted political pressure by means of forcing plebiscites on issues that fanned xenophobic sentiments. The reduction in foreign labor was mainly achieved by not extending temporary residence and work permits. Similarly, in Sweden, after years of liberal immigration practices, in the mid-1970s immigration was restricted to recognized refugees. At that time other West European countries, e.g., Germany and Austria, experienced only temporary reductions in their foreign resident populations. While in some cases the return of foreigners was strongly encouraged and rewarded with premiums, the newly introduced restrictions only slowed rather than halted immigration.

Family reunions and birth rates of the foreign resident population that were higher than the national average compensated for decreased labor migration, while naturalization reduced the number of persons recorded as foreigners. These phenomena led to significant changes in the composition of the foreign population which had earlier consisted mainly of males of working age. Among foreign residents the percentage of women as well as of children and adolescents increased.[11] This entailed more than demographic consequences. The new restrictive immigration policies resulted in a marked increase in the foreign resident population's average duration of stay, while their representation in the labor force changed due to the high rate of female employment among the new immigrants. Meanwhile, closed borders led to rising numbers of illegal immigrants. The control of the foreign labor supply by administrative means (work permits, residence permits, etc.) had only limited success. The existence of informal ethnic networks and the opportunity to enter the receiving country as a "tourist" became an essential basis for illegal immigration.

No precise data on illegal immigrants are available, so we can only speculate about the magnitude of this stream. However, many of those illegal immigrants do not stay for more than a few months in Western Europe. Many new patterns of illegal seasonal work and long-distance commuting (under the cover of tourism) have emerged.

Along with these changes during the 1980s new patterns of migration have also developed. Most southern European countries became countries of immigration. This is particularly so in the case of Italy, which has nearly 800,000 legal foreign residents in 1990 (versus 300,000 in 1982) and an even larger number of illegal foreign immigrants. To a lesser extent the same holds true for Spain, Portugal, and Greece. At the same time, the membership of Spain and Portugal in the EU has caused return migration of labor from Germany, France, and the Benelux countries, and has also increased the number of immigrants from South America holding Spanish and Portuguese passports. Italy has also become a highly favored destination of the children and grandchildren of Italian emigrants to South America.[12]

1.1.2 Refugees and asylum seekers

Another group of migrants who decisively influenced the size and structure of international migration flows to Western Europe are the overlapping categories of refugees, displaced persons, and asylum seekers. Between 1945 and 1950 about 8 million displaced persons (see Reichling, 1986) moved to the territory of West Germany (within the 1949–90 borders). During the same period another 4.6 million people emigrated from the former East Germany before the construction of the Berlin Wall in 1961, while some 0.5 million West Germans moved to East Germany (see Bethlehem, 1981: 26). The establishment of the Iron Curtain and travel restrictions within the former Eastern Bloc reduced this type of immigration from Central and Eastern Europe and from the former Soviet Union. After 1955 mass emigration mainly occurred in cases of political crisis (from Hungary in 1956–57, from Czechoslovakia in 1968, and from Poland in 1980–81). But for several decades Western governments pressed their Eastern counterparts to liberalize emigration procedures. Some countries, notably the USA and West Germany, even offered trade concessions or lump sum payments to induce Communist countries to liberalize their emigration policies. Soviet Jews, Armenians, East German citizens, and other ethnic Germans profited most from this political and economic pressure.

Despite the Iron Curtain, some 13 million people were able to leave their East European home countries between 1950 and 1992.[13] Large as this flow was, the division of Europe and the Cold War undoubtedly reduced the scale of the traditional East–West migration in Europe, thus contributing to the opening of Western Europe's gates for South–North migration.

In recent years, with the division of Europe starting to dissolve and the Iron Curtain falling, East–West migration has resumed on a larger scale. This development is also clearly reflected in the number of refugees. In 1983 there were just 76,000 asylum seekers in 14 European OECD countries; three years later the figure had tripled. In 1992 some 680,000 people asked for asylum in the EU and EFTA countries; 438,000 of them in Germany (UNHCR data; United Nations/ECE, 1993).

The flow of refugees, resettlers, and asylum seekers is again playing a major role in European migration. As a result of the wars in Croatia and in Bosnia–Herzegovina in 1991–93 and ethnic repression of Serbia in Vojvodina and Kosovo, the number of asylum seekers and *de facto* refugees from former Yugoslavia in Central and Western Europe has grown rapidly and by the end of 1993 reached 700,000 (UNHCR data).

As far as asylum in general is concerned, in 1992 more than 60% of those who applied for asylum in Western Europe did so in Germany. In 1992, out of the 438,000 people who applied for asylum in Germany, less than 5% were successful. However, many other asylum seekers stay on as *de facto* refugees. In the past, repatriation was not enforced on a large scale. Since 1993 Germany's restrictive Asylum Law has led to reduced numbers of applications. Germany has also been particularly affected by the surge of ethnic Germans from the East seeking resettlement. In 1990 about 377,000 and in 1991 another 397,000 such ethnic Germans arrived in Germany, representing a tenfold increase compared to 1985.[14] In 1991 the German government imposed more restrictive procedures.[15] German citizenship now has to be claimed before moving to Germany.

As a result the number of ethnic German resettlers dropped from the peak levels of 1990–91 to 219,000 in 1993.[16] All in all, between 1945 and 1992 West Germany accepted and integrated a total of about 24 million displaced persons, refugees, ethnic Germans, and labor migrants.[17]

Although the motives of some East–West migrants are still political, a large proportion of present-day immigrants from Central and Eastern Europe try to escape from unemployment, political instability, rising nationalism, and economic deterioration in their home countries. Others, as noted above, are victims of the wars and ethnic cleansing in Croatia and Bosnia–Herzegovina or of political repression against ethnic or religious minorities in other parts of the Balkans. Most West European countries, particularly the two most affected countries, Germany and Austria, are now seeking to safeguard themselves against both kinds of immigration by means of compulsory visas, more stringent border controls, very restrictive asylum regulations, and troop deployment along the common borders with East–Central Europe. The immigration waves of so-called economic refugees from Eastern Europe, from Africa and the Middle East, and also the case of displaced Croats, Bosnian Muslims, and minority groups from Serbia have triggered discussions throughout Europe on the proper meaning and handling of the right of asylum. Since 1992–93 countries like Austria, Germany, and Sweden once known for their liberal asylum policies, do not accept applicants who had already reached a "safe country" before entering Western Europe. The fact that Poland, the Czech Republic, Slovakia, Hungary, Slovenia, and Croatia have signed the Geneva Convention and are therefore seen as "safe countries" has at least one consequence. Nowadays people entering Germany, Sweden, or Austria by land have almost no chance of being recognized as refugees whatever their backgrounds.

1.1.3 Migration of elites

The least visible group of migrants are those who are neither unwelcome nor seen as a problem by the receiving society. Migrants of this category comprise businessmen, employees of multinational companies and international organizations, artists, research personnel, students, and retirees. In many of these cases there is a gradual transition from intermittent stays for varying intervals to permanent migration. Quantitatively, such migrants do not constitute a major element of immigration in Western Europe. Nevertheless, they are often important as gatekeepers for other migrants. It is likely that the importance of these groups will increase in the future.

1.2 Geographic Patterns of European Migration

The distribution of Western Europe's foreign resident population reflects three migratory patterns (see *Tables 1.2* and *1.3*):

1. South–North migration. This pattern, reminiscent of similarly directed internal migration in several countries, can be found in movements from the southern to the northwestern part of Western Europe and from North Africa/Middle East to Western Europe.
2. East–West migration. This migration was greatly reduced for 40 years due to the political division of Europe, or it was channeled by means of bilateral political agreements (mainly between West Germany and Poland, Romania, and the former Soviet Union in the case of ethnic Germans).
3. Migration between the main countries of destination and their demographic hinterlands. European migration clearly shows "privileged" relations between sending and receiving countries, linked by cultural, economic, and/or political affinities rooted in history.

As to the third pattern, in many cases such privileged relations are obvious. Even in the postcolonial era, the former colonial ties constitute a major factor explaining migration. Immigration to former home countries is promoted by the fact that English, French, Dutch (Afrikaans), and Portuguese are still used as *linguae francae* in the former colonies, and that their economies, their transportation systems, and their cultures are still oriented toward London, Paris, Amsterdam, and Lisbon. By repatriating white settlers and importing labor from the Third World, Europe also reimported some of the social and ethnic conflicts it had created in earlier times in its colonies.

Germany, which had already lost its overseas colonies in 1914, has been playing an analogous role by serving as destination of immigration for millions of ethnic Germans from Eastern Europe, the Balkans, and Central Asia.

France enjoys privileged relations with Portugal and a number of overseas countries. It also exemplifies South–North migration. As shown in *Table 1.3*, which presents the distribution of the foreign resident

Table 1.2. Foreign resident populations (FRPs) in six major receiving countries of Western Europe. Percent distribution of the total foreign resident population within each of the receiving countries by country of origin and total FRP by country of origin and of residence, 1990.

	Country of residence							
Country of origin	Belgium	France (1985)	Germany	Netherlands	Sweden	Switzerland	Six-country (1000s)	Total FRP (%)
Austria	*	*	3.5	*	0.6	2.6	213	1.8
Finland	*	*	0.2	*	24.7	*	130	1.1
Greece	2.3	*	6.0	0.7	1.3	0.7	355	3.0
Italy	26.7	7.0	10.5	2.4	0.8	35.0	1,452	12.1
Portugal	1.8	17.9	1.6	1.2	*	7.7	841	7.0
Spain	5.8	6.0	2.6	2.5	0.6	10.5	539	4.1
Turkey	9.4	5.6	32.0	29.4	5.3	5.8	2,255	18.9
Yugoslavia	0.6	1.4	12.4	1.9	8.5	12.7	905	7.6
Algeria	1.2	17.2	0.1	*	*	*	637	5.3
Morocco	15.7	16.2	1.3	22.7	*	*	951	8.0
East–Central Europe	*	1.3	6.5	*	5.0	0.9	421	3.5
Tunisia	0.8	5.8	0.5	0.4	*	*	242	2.0
USA	1.3	*	*	1.6	1.7	0.9	41	0.3
Others	34.6	21.6	22.9	37.1	51.5	23.3	3,050	25.3
Total	100.0	100.0	100.0	100.0	100.0	100.0		100.0
FRP (1000s)	905	3,608	5,241	692	484	1,100	12,030	
%	6.9	30.2	43.8	5.8	4.0	9.3		100.0

*See *Table 1.1*, footnote (*c*).
Sources: OECD/SOPEMI (1992, several tables).

Table 1.3. Foreign resident populations (FRPs) in six major receiving countries of Western Europe. Percent distribution of foreign residents by country of origin within the total foreign population of that origin residing in the six receiving countries, and total FRP by country of origin and of residence, 1990.

Country of origin	Country of residence: Belgium	France	Germany	Netherlands	Sweden	Switzerland	Six-country total (%)	FRP (1000s)
Austria	*	*	85.2	*	1.3	13.5	100.0	213
Finland	*	*	7.9	*	92.1	*	100.0	130
Greece	5.9	*	88.6	1.4	1.8	2.3	100.0	355
Italy	16.6	17.5	37.8	1.2	0.3	26.7	100.0	1,452
Portugal	2.0	76.8	10.1	1.0	*	10.2	100.0	841
Spain	9.7	40.1	24.9	3.2	0.5	21.6	100.0	539
Turkey	3.8	8.9	74.3	9.0	1.1	2.8	100.0	2,255
Yugoslavia	0.6	5.7	72.1	1.5	4.5	15.5	100.0	905
Algeria	1.7	97.3	1.1	*	*	*	100.0	637
Morocco	14.9	61.5	7.1	16.5	*	*	100.0	951
East–Central Europe	*	11.0	81.0	*	5.7	2.3	100.0	421
Tunisia	2.6	85.6	10.7	1.1	*	*	100.0	242
USA	28.7	*	*	27.9	19.6	23.8	100.0	41
Others	10.2	25.8	39.6	8.5	8.2	8.5	100.0	3,050
Total FRP (%)	6.9	30.2	43.8	5.8	4.0	9.3	100.0	
(1000s)	905	3,608	5,241	692	484	1,100		12,030

*See *Table 1.1*, footnote (*c*).
Sources: OECD/SOPEMI (1992, several tables).

population within the six largest immigration countries of continental Western Europe by country or region of origin, almost all Algerians living in these six countries (97%) reside in France. Seven out of eight Tunisians and nearly four-fifths of all Portuguese registered in the six countries live in France, as do three out of five Moroccans. Mainland France is also the principal destination for migrants from the overseas territories it still holds.[18]

Germany, since the 1970s the European country with the largest immigrant population, is home for the large majority of immigrants from Central and Eastern Europe (see *Table 1.3*). Also, seven out of eight Greeks (89%) living in the six major continental immigration countries and nearly three-quarters of all former Yugoslavs and Turks reside in Germany.

Similar patterns prevail in the UK. As of around 1990 most of the Irish living in Europe outside Ireland, as well as almost all Indians, Pakistanis, Bangladeshis, and emigrants from the English-speaking West Indies who migrated to Europe, were living in the UK.

Other small-scale patterns of "privileged" recruitment of migrants are also discernible in *Table 1.3*. Most emigrants from Finland live in Sweden, Dutch migrants can be found mainly in Belgium, Austrian emigrants live predominantly in Germany. Also noteworthy is the high percentage of Moroccan immigrants in Belgium and the Netherlands, although the share of migrants from other North African countries is very low there. Emigration from other European countries follows less specific patterns. Migrants from Italy and Spain are distributed rather evenly among several European host countries. Of the Italians living abroad in Europe, more than one-third live in Germany, one-quarter in Switzerland, and less than one-fifth each in France and in Belgium.

Around 1991–92, with the exception of the European mini-states,[19] the highest percentage of foreigners was found in Switzerland (17.6%; see *Table 1.1*). Italian nationals alone accounted for 5.7% of Switzerland's resident population. In comparison, the largest single group of foreigners in Europe, the 1.9 million Turkish nationals in Germany (1993), accounted for only 2.3% of Germany's resident population.

When comparing the migration patterns of the 1950s and 1960s with those between 1975 and 1990 one change is most obvious. With immigration flows spreading to the northern, western, and more recently also southern parts of Western Europe, the hinterland of this labor migration expanded geographically. In the decades immediately following World War II, Italy was the most important recruitment area for labor migration to Europe's main receiving countries. For many Italians, to work in West Germany, France, or Switzerland was an attractive alternative to emigrating overseas to the USA, Canada, or Argentina. In the 1960s Spain and Portugal had become the most important European emigration countries, followed by Greece and former Yugoslavia. Non-European countries and regions sending migrants to Western Europe were above all Algeria, India, Pakistan, and the Caribbean. In the 1970s Turkey, Morocco, and Tunisia became increasingly important countries of origin for European immigration.

In the 1980s political conflicts, civil wars, and economic crises in the Middle East, South America, and Africa generated new surges of immigration to Greece, Italy, Spain, and Portugal. Some migrants profited from the "green borders" along the Mediterranean, others reactivated the Italian, Spanish, or Greek citizenship of their parents or grandparents who had emigrated overseas. In the late 1980s and early 1990s new refugee and migration movements originated both within the Balkans and Eastern Europe and from the eastern part of Europe to the West. So far, the main destinations have been Germany, Sweden, Switzerland, Austria, but also Hungary, Slovenia, and Croatia.

As noted above, in 1991–93 the war in Croatia and Bosnia–Herzegovina created the largest single wave of European emigration since the end of World War II. Of the 5 million people who were forced to leave their home towns and villages, 700,000 were able to immigrate to Western Europe and were tolerated there. It is likely that in the future Scandinavian countries will also be the target of European East–West migration, given their historical, ethnic, and geographic links with the Baltic states and northwestern parts of Russia.[20]

1.3 Explaining the Patterns of West European Migration

For the analysis of international migration patterns several approaches are of explanatory value. First, migration between countries of origin and destination can be understood as the result of geographic proximity. In this case migration flows between neighboring states would be the strongest. When looking at a map of Europe one finds, however, that in the past geographic closeness mainly played a role in cases of privileged access of neighbors to the receiving country's labor market. Examples are Finns and Danes in Sweden, the Irish in the UK, Dutch and French in Belgium, Austrians and Poles in Germany, and to some extent also Italians in Switzerland and France. In these cases cultural similarities, language, and commuting opportunities also play a decisive role.

Some migration flows are determined by economic disparities between countries. In this case, countries with flourishing economies, high demand for labor, and high wage levels become attractive for migrants from countries with high unemployment rates, low wage levels, and stagnating economies. While this approach explains why migration starts, it does not explain why certain countries become preferred destinations. For example, if economic indicators like wage differentials were the only factor, Portuguese citizens would go to Germany rather than to France. As citizens of the EU they can migrate legally to either of these countries. But despite higher wage levels in the western part of Germany, few Portuguese migrants live there. This means that cultural, political, and historical links between the society of origin and the host society can be of higher explanatory value than purely economic factors such as wage differentials.

In recent years growing differences between the standards of living prevailing in Eastern Europe as well as in North Africa and the Middle East, on the one hand, and Western Europe, on the other, motivate people to migrate even to areas with relatively well-saturated labor markets or to areas with high unemployment. At the same time, regional disparities within Western Europe have declined. In Portugal, for example, the demand for labor increased markedly when the country joined the EU, and many emigrants returned home. Also traditional regions of origin for European labor migration have lately become regions of immigration. Today southern regions of Italy and Spain are host to North African harvesters, while Polish traders and construction workers find employment in Greece.[21]

The diffusion of information on opportunities and problems existing in the labor and housing markets of potential destinations also helps to explain patterns of migration. This information is carried to geographically and culturally ever more distant regions by "gatekeepers" (returnees, nationals on home leave) and the mass media. The knowledge of a language and a specific educational background may – mainly as a colonial heritage – greatly enhance migration to the former colonial powers. With such knowledge, information on opportunities spreads more easily and turns many people who look for improvement in their material circumstances into potential migrants. Existing ethnic and social networks also provide support for new immigrants that is often decisive and facilitates their integration within host countries.

1.4 European Immigration Countries

During the last decade Europe's three most important immigration countries have been France, Germany, and the UK, although Belgium, Italy, the Netherlands, Switzerland, Austria, Sweden, and Spain also have large foreign resident populations. For the three largest receiving countries the geographic patterns of origin of migrants are depicted in *Figures 1.1, 1.2*, and *1.3*.[22]

1.4.1 The UK

Immigration to the UK clearly can be explained by the aforementioned pattern of privileged relations. In 1992 about 60% of the UK's 1.9 million foreign residents were immigrants from African or Asian countries (all of them former dominions or colonies). Immigration to the UK from other European countries is comparatively low; labor migration from former Yugoslavia or Turkey, for example, has been practically nonexistent. Almost three-quarters of all European immigrants come from Ireland, the oldest demographic hinterland of the UK. Similar patterns of geographic origin are found among foreign-born British subjects.

In 1990 about 930,000 foreign nationals were working in the UK. The labor force survey from which this statistic has been taken lists both foreigners in the UK and ethnic and visible (nonwhite) minorities. According to this survey, in 1989 some 2.6 million people, or 4.6% of the population of the UK, belonged to ethnic minorities, most of them of Indian, Pakistani, or Bangladeshi descent. With a share of 3.3% the relative importance of foreigners in the UK is smaller than in most other West European countries. However, the proportion of the foreign-born population (foreigners and British subjects) is about 7%.

1.4.2 Germany

In the decade following World War II, Germany was the destination of about 12 million displaced persons (see Reichling, 1986). Between

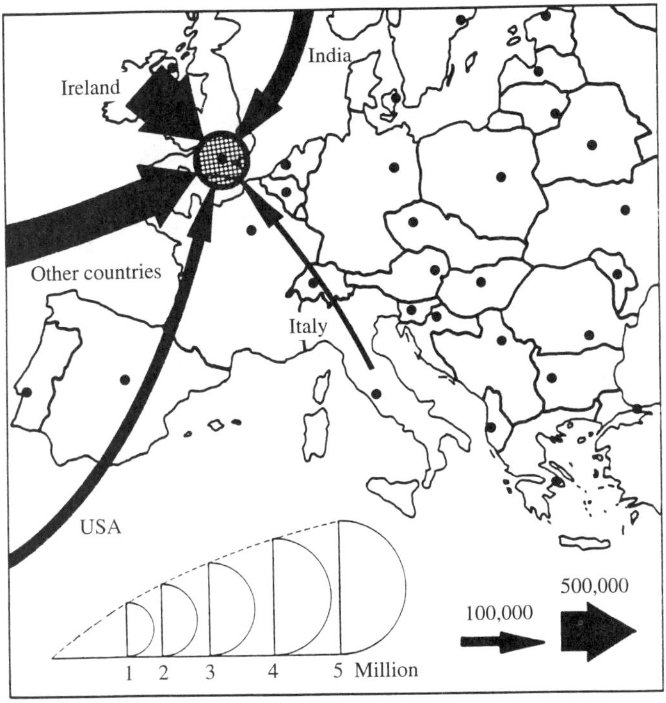

Figure 1.1. Foreign resident population in the UK, by country of origin, 1990.

1949 and 1961 approximately 3.6 million citizens of East Germany (see Bethlehem, 1981) moved to West Germany before the construction of the Berlin Wall intercepted this migration flow. Between 1955 and 1960 the number of non-German immigrants to West Germany was relatively small. After 1961 the first migrants came from Italy, Spain, Greece, and Austria.

By 1975 the absolute numbers of Italians, Spaniards, and Greeks in Germany was higher than in 1965; however, their share among the foreign resident population had declined sharply. The reason was a surge of immigration from Turkey, former Yugoslavia, and other European and non-European countries. Between 1985 and 1991 the number of immigrants from Poland, Romania, and Iran also had some impact. German reunification in 1990 did not change this picture, for the share of the foreign population in East Germany was below 1% (136,000 in 1990). Since the mid-1980s a growing number of East–West migrants have moved to (West) Germany: between 1985 and 1992 some 1.5 million

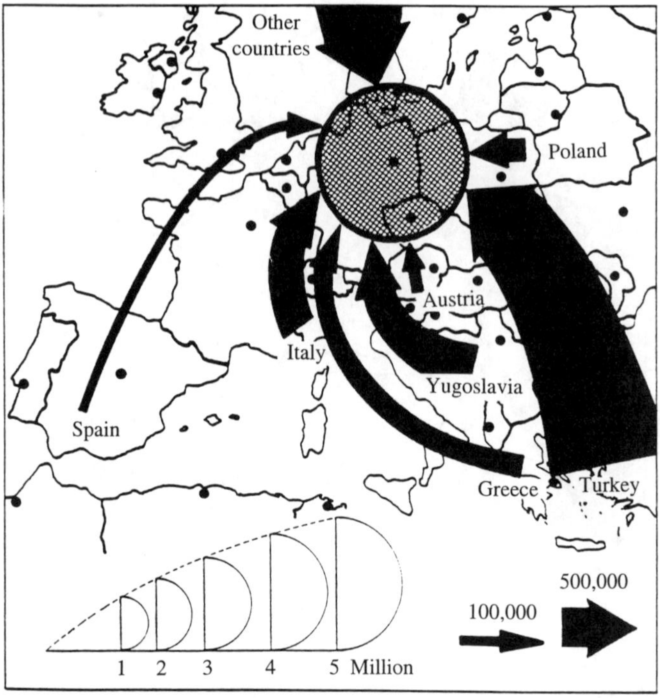

Figure 1.2. Foreign resident population in Germany, by country of origin, 1990.

ethnic Germans, more than 1 million asylum seekers, and more than 0.5 million new migrant workers from East–Central Europe (300,000 Poles in 1991; 53,000 Romanians in 1990). Currently due to family reunifications and partly due to the war in Bosnia, the number of immigrants from Turkey, former Yugoslavia, and Greece is still rising.

In 1993 the number of foreign nationals living in Germany was 6.8 million (8.4% of the total population of unified Germany);[23] among them, as noted above, were 1.9 million Turkish nationals (including some 400,000 of Kurdish origin). Some 2.3 million foreigners were working legally, representing about 8% of the country's labor force. There is also evidence of a growing proportion of illegal employment. In 1990 alone some 315,000 new cases were investigated (OECD/SOPEMI, 1992).

With a net intake of more than 20 million (1945–91/92; see Section 1.1.2) displaced persons, refugees, other foreigners, and ethnic Germans,

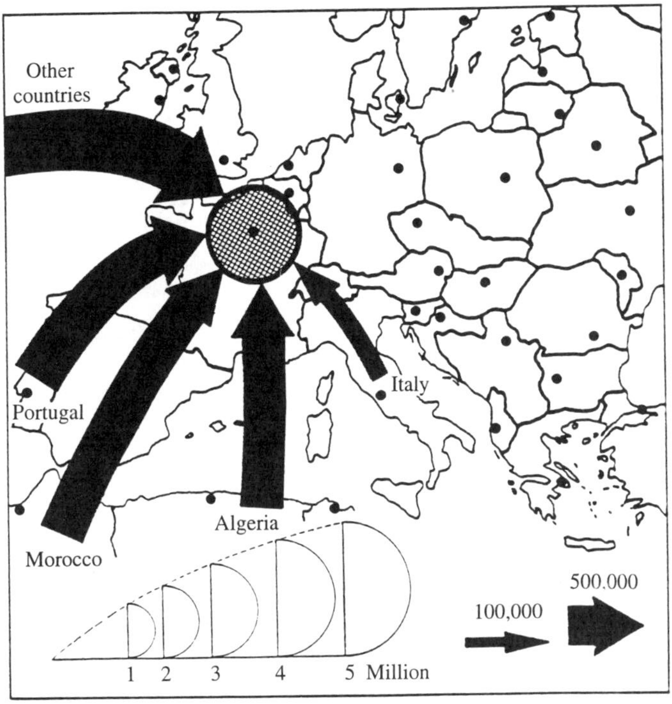

Figure 1.3. Foreign resident population in France, by country of origin, 1990.

western Germany is by far the largest country of immigration in Europe. Today (1994) some 20% of Germany's population is foreign-born.

1.4.3 France

France is Europe's second most important country of immigration. In the course of decolonization and the rapid postwar economic growth more than 2 million French overseas residents came to the country. Many of these, however, were neither listed nor treated as "foreigners". Moreover, residents of former colonies were encouraged to come to France, and emigration from Italy, Spain, and Portugal was also welcomed. Whereas immigrants to West Germany originated mainly from eastern and southern Europe, the recruitment area of French immigration comprised the entire western Mediterranean: Portugal, Spain, Morocco, Algeria, Tunisia, and Italy. The number of migrant workers from Yugoslavia has always been low.

The composition of the foreign resident population by country of origin in France has changed little over time. Since the early 1980s, however, the number of Moroccans, Turks, and immigrants from the rest of the world (identified by the category "others" in *Tables 1.2* and *1.3*) residing in France has increased, while the number and share of Portuguese, Algerians, Italians, and Spaniards have decreased, because of both naturalization[24] and net return migration. In 1992 the number of foreigners in France was 3.6 million (6.3% of the total population of France). Some 1.6 million foreigners were part of the French labor force. The proportion of the foreign-born population (foreigners and French nationals) is about 9%.

1.4.4 Belgium and the Netherlands

Belgium and the Netherlands hold a position in European migration similar to that of France. These countries have been the destination of immigrants from the Mediterranean (Italians, Moroccans, and Turks in Belgium; Turks and Moroccans in the Netherlands), as well as from neighboring countries (French and Dutch in Belgium; Germans and UK citizens in the Netherlands). Both countries also had significant immigration from their former colonies (Indonesia, Suriname, Zaire) and from overseas territories (Dutch Antilles). There are, however, two significant differences between Belgium and the Netherlands. One is the large number of Italians in Belgium; the other is the increasing number of Dutch citizens who live in Belgium (mainly due to tax reasons) but work in the Netherlands.

A comparison over time shows that in Belgium and the Netherlands the share of Moroccans, Turks, and other foreigners increased during the 1980s. In Belgium, this phenomenon must also be attributed to the expansion of international organizations (EU, NATO) with headquarters in Brussels. In 1992 there were 918,000 foreigners in Belgium (or 9.2% of the total population) and 728,000 in the Netherlands (or 4.8%). In each of the two countries there were approximately 200,000 foreign workers in the labor force.

1.4.5 Switzerland

Compared with other European countries, the distinctive features in Switzerland are the highest share of foreign residents (besides the

European mini-states) and its restrictive immigration policy. Despite this policy, of all European states with territories larger than that of Luxembourg, Switzerland has the largest percentage of foreigners in its resident population (17.6% in 1991). If seasonal workers and the employees of international organizations are also taken into account the percentage of foreigners reaches 20%.

More than one-third of the foreigners in Switzerland are of Italian origin. A much smaller share comes from the other neighboring countries (especially Germany and France). Foreign residents from other "traditional" countries of origin such as Spain, Portugal, former Yugoslavia, and Turkey account for broadly similar shares of the foreign resident population. With the exception of neighboring Italy, Switzerland has no "privileged" demographic hinterland.

In 1992 some 1.2 million foreigners were permanently living in Switzerland, of whom more than 700,000 were part of the labor force. Another 122,000 foreigners had the status of "seasonal workers", and some 180,000 foreigners were working but not living in Switzerland (mainly commuters from localities just across the Swiss border).

1.4.6 Sweden

Sweden is the most important immigration country in northern Europe. Immigrants come from a relatively large number of countries, including former Yugoslavia, Turkey, and Chile. But the largest foreign resident population is of Finnish origin. About 90% of all Finns living abroad in Western Europe reside in Sweden. With a total number of 120,000 these immigrants account for roughly 25% of all foreigners in Sweden, but their share is decreasing. Neighboring Norwegians, Danes, and Icelanders account for another 14% of foreigners, bringing the share of immigrants to Sweden from the common Nordic labor market to almost 40%. However, when comparing the periods 1955–65 and 1975–90 the most important change has been the sharp increase in the number and share of immigrants from outside this traditional area of origin.

In 1992 the number of foreigners in Sweden was 494,000 (or 5.7% of the total population), of whom 260,000 were part of the labor force. When naturalized citizens are included, the share of all foreign-born residents in Sweden accounts for 7.8%.

1.4.7 Austria

From the standpoint of the industrialized West European nations – and of many Austrians themselves – Austria remains at the periphery of the West. For them several Western countries – above all neighboring Switzerland and Germany – represent attractive labor markets characterized by higher wage levels, more advanced production structures, and often also more appealing working conditions. To some extent Austria is therefore an emigration country. From the eastern point of view Austria is the gateway to the West and is a potential immigration country.

Between 1945 and 1992 about 2.4 million people entered Austria as expatriates, asylum seekers, or refugees. Of these some 700,000 have settled there permanently, most of them from neighboring Central and Eastern Europe. Another 1.2 million people went to Austria as migrant workers or as family members. Most of them were recruited in former Yugoslavia and in Turkey. Since 1989 a rapidly growing share of foreign labor has come from Central Europe (Poland, Hungary, the Czech Republic, Slovakia, and Romania).

In 1992 the number of foreigners in Austria was somewhat above 560,000, or 7.1% of the country's population.[25] Of these, 274,000 were part of the labor force. When all displaced persons, refugees, and naturalized citizens are included, the share of Austria's foreign-born population rises to approximately 15%. The total immigrant population of 1.2 million is counterbalanced by some 500,000 people of Austrian origin living abroad, more than one-third of them in Germany.

1.5 European Emigration Countries

The main countries of origin within the framework of European East–West migration were the former GDR, Poland, former Yugoslavia, the former Soviet Union, Bulgaria, and Romania.

1.5.1 Former GDR

During the 12 years between the establishment of the two German states in 1949 and the erection of the Berlin Wall in 1961, some 3.8 million East German citizens immigrated to the Federal Republic of Germany, while 475,000 West Germans decided to settle in the GDR. During the existence of the Wall 810,000 people managed to leave the GDR. Most of them were either retired persons (who were free to travel abroad) or part of the 300,000 cases, including political prisoners, negotiated individually between the two German governments. Between 1950 and 1990–92 more than 40% of the total European East–West migration originated in the former GDR.

For the FRG this German–German migration was a strong argument in support of the market economy model and the democratic system. It was often claimed that emigrants were "voting with their feet". The erection of the Berlin Wall was, after all, an attempt by the GDR to avoid having to find a political solution to the problem by preventing emigration as such. After 1961 the continuing East–West migration became a financial matter. Both German states granted citizenship rights to migrants from the other side. The FRG even offered generous financial compensation for the release and emigration of prisoners (30,000 cases) and other GDR citizens.

In 1989 the mass emigration of some 181,000 people before the fall of the Berlin Wall and of another 218,000 thereafter largely contributed to the collapse of Communist rule in East Germany and to German reunification.

1.5.2 Poland

Between 1950 and 1992 about 17% of all European East–West migrants were from Poland. In contrast to other countries of origin, Polish emigration was ethnically heterogeneous. The largest group of migrants comprised ethnic Germans and others who could claim West German citizenship. The so-called resettlers (*Aussiedler*) came to the FRG in several waves: 1956–57 (216,000), 1976–82 (about 242,000), and since 1987 (753,000 between 1987 and 1990). Until 1990 this migration was actively supported or even promoted by the West German government and was seen as a return favor for Western economic aid to Poland.

In the late 1960s, in reaction to the anti-Semitic campaign led by the state itself, a large proportion of Jewish Polish citizens went to Western Europe, Israel, and the USA. This exodus would not have occurred without the strong practical support of Poland's ruling elite, the USA, and Israel.

In 1980–81, however, the emigration of about 250,000 Poles fleeing from the imposition of martial law to the West – especially to Austria and Germany – was spontaneous. They were much less warmly received there than were the Czech and Slovak refugees in 1968, perhaps because the Red Army did not intervene in Poland. In the following years about half of the Polish emigrants of 1980–81 returned to their home country.

From 1986, when it again became possible to leave Poland and emigrate, a larger number of Poles of non-German origin tried to gain a foothold in the West. Between 1950 and 1990–91 about 2.1 million people emigrated from Poland; more than 1 million of them in the second half of the 1980s. Since then, however, about 60% of the non-ethnic German immigrants to the West have returned to Poland.

1.5.3 Former Yugoslavia

In the 1950s and early 1960s emigration from Yugoslavia primarily involved two groups: first, Muslims of Turkish origin and Bosnian Muslims, the overwhelming majority of whom went to Turkey; and second, political opponents of the Tito regime, who headed for Western Europe and overseas. Data are available only for the first group. During the 1950s some 300,000 ethnic Turks left Bosnia, Macedonia, and other southeastern parts of Yugoslavia for Turkey.

From the mid-1960s Yugoslavia became the first Communist country to allow almost all categories of citizens to emigrate. As a result, the Federal Republic of Germany and Austria recruited 0.5 million labor migrants, who were followed by an unknown number of family dependents.

The wars in Croatia (1991–92) and Bosnia–Herzegovina (1992–93) and the repression of ethnic minorities in Vojvodina, Serbia, and Kosovo led to the largest wave of European migration since 1945–46. Between 1991 and 1993 more than 5 million citizens of former Yugoslavia became refugees or displaced persons. Only 700,000 of them came to Western Europe, of whom 355,000 to Germany, 80,000 to Switzerland, 74,000 to Sweden, and 70,000 to Austria. In most cases they were not recognized as political refugees but were tolerated as *de facto* refugees. In 1993 most Western countries closed their borders to the victims of war and ethnic cleansing from that part of the Balkans. Thus 4.3 million refugees and displaced persons are still living in the states that emerged from the break-up of Yugoslavia. In mid-1993 there were more than 690,000 of them in the parts of Croatia controlled by the Zagreb government and another 110,000 in the rest of the country controlled by Serbian militia, 560,000 in Serbia, 82,000 in Montenegro, 45,000 in Slovenia, 27,000 in Macedonia, and 2.74 million in Bosnia–Herzegovina.

Today, with 2.3 million people, former Yugoslavia is a major sending area of East–West migration (17%). Because of the political situation in the Balkans, the substantial and growing economic gap with Western Europe, and the prevailing ethnic conflicts, the successor states of former Yugoslavia are likely to remain countries with a considerable emigration potential.

1.5.4 Former Soviet Union

Between 1950 and 1992 about 12% of all European East–West migrants came from the former Soviet Union. In the 1950s and 1960s it was almost impossible to emigrate from the Soviet Union, but thereafter the USA and some West European countries pressed for an easing of the restrictive Soviet emigration policy. In 1973 the US Congress made this a precondition for the removal of trade barriers. In the CSCE Treaty (signed in Helsinki in 1976) the USA and Western Europe forced the Eastern side to recognize the principles of freedom of travel and emigration. As a consequence, during the 1970s (1973–80) some 340,000 people were in fact able to leave the Soviet Union. Following a brief revival of the Cold War in the early 1980s (Afghanistan, SDI) a second large wave of emigration took place from 1987 onward under Gorbachev. In all, some 1.5 million people emigrated from the Soviet Union between 1950 and 1991.

As already stated, almost all the emigrants belonged to ethnic or religious minorities. About half of them were Soviet Jews, almost all of whom went to Israel or the USA. More than a third were ethnic Germans whose emigration was made possible by the Federal Republic of Germany.

By far the largest migration was not oriented toward the West but took place after 1991 between the former Soviet republics that became sovereign states (now CIS member countries and the Baltic states). In the majority of cases ethnic Russians were returning from the peripheries of the former Soviet Empire. The withdrawal of the Red Army, including soldiers' family dependents, from Central and Eastern Europe also led to substantial migration.

1.5.5 Bulgaria

Another 1.2 million East–West migrants came from Romania and Bulgaria, but to a smaller extent also from former Czechoslovakia and Hungary. Between 1950 and 1952 some 155,000 ethnic Turks were allowed to leave Bulgaria. Another wave of 39,000 followed in 1969–73 under the provision of the 1968 agreement between Bulgaria and Turkey, which granted the right of emigration to a total of 95,000 Bulgarian citizens. The most recent wave began during the collapse of the Communist regime in Sofia. In 1982–92 some 350,000 ethnic Turks and Slavic Muslims fled from collective oppression, enforced "Bulgarianization", and economic problems. Most of them made their way to Turkey before the Turkish government closed the border with neighboring Bulgaria. Of these 150,000 people are reported to have remigrated to Bulgaria. The closing of the Turkish border has led to higher numbers of Bulgarian citizens trying to apply for asylum in Western Europe.

1.5.6 Romania

In 1945–46, the Romanian regime, in contrast with those in Yugoslavia, Hungary, Czechoslovakia, and Poland, did not collectively expel ethnic Germans living in the country. Nevertheless, from the 1970s the Federal Republic of Germany sought to organize ethnic German emigration based on bilateral agreements with the Romanian authorities. Between 1970 and 1989 some 230,000 Romanians of German origin took advantage of this opportunity to emigrate, in return for which the FRG gave generous financial support to the Ceauşescu regime. Since the last wave of large-scale migration organized in 1991, involving almost 200,000 people, there are hardly any ethnic Germans left in Romania who are able and willing to emigrate.

Since 1987 about 60,000 members of the Hungarian minority have left the country, most of them for Hungary. This is also a form of selective East–West migration. Between 1990 and 1993 a further 240,000 Romanian citizens applied for asylum in Western Europe, most of them of Gypsy origin. In spite of the obvious discrimination and casual pogroms they are subjected to, many of them were turned back to Romania, which, in the view of most Western governments, now qualifies as a "safe" country.

1.6 The Future of European Immigration

Since 1945 West European labor markets have become increasingly internationalized by attracting and integrating labor migrants from Europe's economic peripheries and from overseas. Historical analysis shows that this increasing spatial mobility of individuals is not only a postwar phenomenon. When Europe's industrial and service economies encounter an inelastic labor supply, they always seek to expand the recruitment areas of their labor markets, thus broadening their demographic hinterland. These tendencies can be traced back to the Industrial Revolution of the late eighteenth and early nineteenth centuries, when large cities as well as newly developed industrial and urban areas became the destinations of migrants seeking employment. In Europe the broadening of the hinterlands of migration occurred along two geographic axes: from the northwest to the east and to the south. Migratory movements along these geographic axes have sometimes been interrupted and sometimes accelerated in the course of this century by major historical events (world wars, economic crises, and the political division of Europe) or altered by migration surges related to those shocks (such as mass movements of displaced persons and refugees). The dates and origins of migration have exerted a major influence on migrants' chances of being integrated into the labor markets of the receiving societies. In most cases displaced persons and refugees of the postwar era enjoyed solidarity in Western Europe; the same held true for returnees from former colonies. They were seen as victims either of the East–West conflict or of decolonization. At the same time, the absorption of these immigrants into the labor force constituted a major contribution to the rapid postwar economic revival of Western Europe.

Refugees and return migrants of the early postwar years were soon followed by migrants from the less developed regions of southern Europe, the Balkans, Turkey, and some former colonies. For almost two decades these migrants were not regarded as "real immigrants", but as a kind of transferable and temporarily transferred work force. It was expected that these migrants would return home after a limited period of employment, but in fact the majority of migrants wanted to stay for long periods and often for the rest of their lives. The "guest workers" became immigrants. The receiving societies had to face the problems of family reunions, integration of foreign-born children into their educational systems, and finally the demands for suffrage and citizenship by immigrant workers and their relatives.

The revival of ethnocentrism, as well as the rise of xenophobia, in Europe is a reflection of the inadequacy of the solutions for these and related problems. Thus the challenge of integration has become even more acute in the 1990s than it was before. The cessation of labor recruitment in the mid-1970s and the wide range of anti-immigration measures introduced thereafter have not reduced the number of foreigners in the main receiving countries of Western Europe. The countries bordering on the northern Mediterranean are confronted with large numbers of new immigrants from North Africa. Germany, Austria, and the Scandinavian countries have become much sought-after destination points for legal and illegal immigration from Central and Eastern Europe, while Poland, the Czech Republic, Slovakia, and Hungary are – for the first time since 1945–48 – also experiencing immigration. Wars and inter-ethnic hostilities, acute or impending, in the successor states of former Yugoslavia and the former Soviet Union have added a new dimension to international migration in Europe. For the first time since the early postwar years, Europe has to cope with several million displaced persons, victims of war, and *de facto* refugees, most of whom cannot claim asylum in Western Europe under the terms of the Geneva Convention.

It seems certain that international migration will remain an essential element responding to and affecting West European labor markets. The coming decades are likely to witness the realization of an expanded single EU market, the political and economic restructuring of the eastern half of the continent, and a variety of ethno-political, ecological, and demographic changes in the eastern half of Europe, in North Africa, and in the successor states of the former Soviet Union. Some of these changes are bound to generate new migration potentials and pressures.

Even if there is no longer a high demand for additional labor in their labor markets, most West European countries are likely to remain *de facto* immigration countries.[26] It is true, of course, that with the disappearance of the Iron Curtain immigrants from the East no longer have quasi-automatic access to the status of political refugee. But large numbers of people living in these countries still have strong reasons to migrate, such as to escape from economic deprivation, political instability, and ethnic violence. The syndrome is also found, often in more acute forms, in North Africa, the Middle East, and in other parts of the developing world.

Faced with this situation, West European countries must strive for more than defensive crisis management. There is a pressing need to develop active and farsighted migration policies that rest on sound legal and institutional frameworks. Such policies must command wide domestic public support, but they must also reflect the fact that Western Europe is not an island isolated from the rest of the world.

Notes

[1] Neither category of citizen has any legal claim to the right of settlement in the UK.

[2] Between 1949 and 1990 immigration from East Germany was not even registered as cross-border migration in West Germany, as the former German Democratic Republic did not constitute a "foreign country" according to the legal viewpoint of the FRG.

[3] The analysis in this article is based on an evaluation of the SOPEMI statistics for the years 1984–90, data published by the Council of Europe (1993), the 1989 *UN Demographic Yearbook*, Eurostat population statistics for 1985 and 1990, and the annual abstracts of statistics of individual countries: the *Statistik Arsboks* for 1970 and 1978 (in the case of Sweden), the *Statistisches Jahrbuch der Schweiz* for 1955, 1970, 1975, and 1980 (Switzerland), and the *Annuaire Statistique de la Belgique* for 1973 and 1978 (Belgium). The SOPEMI database, which is the main source for this chapter, is a continuous reporting system on migration organized by the OECD. In most OECD member countries and some countries of East–Central Europe local correspondents collect and interpret available data on international migration. The aim of SOPEMI is to compile available national data, but there is no authority to impose changes in the data collection procedure or to correct government statistics. The quality of the SOPEMI data depends heavily on the quality of the national data collection procedures. In general, we can assume that in countries such as Germany or Switzerland, both of which have population registers for foreigners, the quality of the data is higher than in countries such as Austria, where estimates are based on special labor market data, work permits, and police registers (see OECD/SOPEMI, 1992: 123).

[4] The year 1982 was chosen (instead of 1980) as a reference because higher quality data were available for this year.

[5] At that time approximately 350,000 refugees and displaced persons from neighboring Central and Eastern Europe were living in Austria; the majority of them were stateless or still citizens of their country of origin.

[6] In contrast to what was done in Austria, at the time most former citizens of the Third Reich, ethnic Germans, and other refugees from the East had already been naturalized in West Germany.

[7] These host countries are Belgium, France, the UK, Italy, the Netherlands, Portugal, and Spain.

[8] These areas include Germany (which sees itself as home country for all ethnic Germans in Eastern Europe and Central Asia), Finland (Karelians), Greece (Greeks from Turkey and the former Soviet Union), Italy (Italians from Istria and Dalmatia), Poland (Poles from Lithuania, Belarus, and the Ukraine), the Czech Republic (Czechs from Volhynia and former Yugoslavia), Slovakia (Slovaks from Hungary and the Carpatho-Ukraine),

and Hungary (Hungarians from Slovakia, Transylvania, the Carpatho-Ukraine, and former Yugoslavia).

[9] This last category encompasses the significant North–South migration of older people (e.g., Britons to Spain, Germans to Spain, Switzerland, and Italy), the international migration of elites (employees of multinational companies, universities, research institutions, and international organizations), the return of descendants of overseas emigrants (of particular importance in Spain, Italy, and Greece), and the return of migrant workers from elsewhere in Europe (a phenomenon that can only partly be explained as retirement migration). As a rule, stationed foreign troops, including civilian staff and relatives, are neither registered nor counted as immigrants or foreigners.

[10] In contrast to the situation in 1950, by 1970 all displaced persons and refugees from 1945 to 1950, as well as Hungarian refugees of 1956–57 who were still living in Austria, had been naturalized by the government.

[11] Among them foreign-born children who joined their immigrant parents at a later stage of the family life cycle and "second-generation" immigrants, that is, children born to foreigners in the country of immigration. Because of the *ius sanguinis* regulations prevailing in most European countries, the children are not foreign-born but remain foreign citizens.

[12] Between 1840 and 1970 an estimated 30 million Italians emigrated, a large proportion of these to such overseas destinations as South America and the USA.

[13] East–Central Europe (including the GDR), the Balkans, and the former Soviet Union 1950–92, approximately 13 million; among them from Poland, 2.1 million (ethnic Germans, Germans-by-law, ethnic Poles); from Bulgaria, 630,000 (ethnic Turks and Pomak Muslims); from Romania, 460,000 (ethnic Germans, Gypsies, some ethnic Romanians; not including ethnic Hungarians to Hungary); from the former East Germany (1949–June 1990), 5.3 million; from former Yugoslavia (1965–91), approximately 1.5 million (labor migrants, political refugees), since 1991, 700,000 victims of recent wars; from the former Soviet Union (1950–92), 1.8 million (Jews, ethnic Germans, Armenians, ethnic Greeks) (see Bade, 1992; Basok and Brym, 1991; Chesnais, 1991a,b; Okolski, 1991b; Rudolph, Chapter 6, this volume; and Vishnevsky and Zayonchkovskaya, Chapter 13, this volume).

[14] In 1984 the number of ethnic Germans migrating to West Germany was 36,500; in 1985, 39,000; and in 1986, 43,000. Since then the number has increased greatly, rising from 78,500 in 1987 to 203,000 in 1988, 377,000 in 1990, and 397,000 in 1991.

[15] The number of asylum applications dropped from 224,000 (January–June 1993) to 98,500 (July–December 1993).

[16] In 1992–93 some 600,000 people living in Eastern Europe and the CIS countries had applied for German citizenship and for immigration to Germany.

[17] Displaced persons (1945–50), 8 million; refugees from East Germany (1949–90), 5.3 million; ethnic German resettlers from Eastern Europe (1950–92), 3 million; labor migrants and their family members, 7 million; political refugees and asylum seekers, 1 million (see Bade, 1992; Rudolph, Chapter 6, this volume).

[18] Such as the French Antilles, Guyana, Reunion, and Tahiti.

[19] Andorra, Liechtenstein, Luxembourg, Monaco, and the Vatican.

[20] The countries of East–Central Europe, Poland, the Czech Republic, Slovakia, and Hungary are also preparing for a growing number of immigrants from the former Soviet Union. In 1991 an estimated 30,000–70,000 former Soviet citizens were already working in Poland (see Korcelli, Chapter 9, this volume).

[21] Despite high general unemployment in Greece, about 40,000 Poles were employed there, one way or another, during the summer of 1990.

[22] The layout for the figures in this book was provided by Andreas Andiel (Vienna).

[23] Meanwhile the number of foreigners in Germany has grown to 7 million.

[24] According to the 1990 census the proportion of naturalized French citizens was 3.1% of the total population. This proportion was 2.6% in 1982.

[25] In 1992 Austria accepted some 60,000 displaced persons from Bosnia–Herzegovina.

[26] The realization of the concept of the single market will also influence migration within Western Europe. Legal migration barriers within the EU have been almost nonexistent since the end of the 1960s, yet social, economic, linguistic, and a series of hidden barriers still exist. These will gradually be eliminated in the future by such changes as the mutual recognition of educational qualifications, more uniform social security systems, and the opening of the public service sector of the individual EU and EFTA countries to nationals of other EU and EFTA member countries.

Part II

Migration to and from Western Europe

Chapter 2

The United Kingdom and International Migration: A Changing Balance

David Coleman

2.1 British Migration History

Britain does not, and never has considered itself to be a "country of immigration". Throughout its history it has exported population particularly to its English-speaking former colonial territories and dominions, both those that broke away – the United States and the Republic of South Africa – and those that remained within the Old Commonwealth – Canada, Australia, and New Zealand. Migration to the dominions was encouraged in the nineteenth century initially to reduce the number of poor people in Britain's rural areas and later to strengthen the Commonwealth as a multinational English-speaking power (see *Table 2.1*). Such migration peaked in 1913. It was promoted by government policy through the 1922 Empire Settlement Act and other measures in cooperation with the dominions, initially for ex-servicemen, "to promote the economic strength and the well-being of the Empire as whole and of the United Kingdom in particular." That Act to promote emigration was the basis of British emigration policy for over 30 years, being renewed as late as 1952 for a further five years with the creation of the Oversea Migration Board in 1953 (Oversea Migration Board, 1954).

Table 2.1. British populations in overseas countries by birthplace or nationality.

		Population (1000s)			UK born	UK born
Country	Year	Born in UK	All foreign born	Total pop.	as % of foreign born	as % of of total pop.
Australia	1986	1,030.0	3,491.7	15,602.2	29.5	6.6
Belgium	1989	21.8	868.8	9,937.7	2.5	0.2
Canada	1986	793.1	3,908.2	25,022.0	20.3	3.2
Denmark	1989	10.0	142.0	5,131.6	7.0	0.2
France	1982	34.2	3,680.1	54,480.4	0.9	0.1
Germany	1989	85.7	4,845.9	62,104.1	1.8	0.1
Greece	1989	17.3	225.6	10,033.0	7.7	0.2
Ireland	1989	51.7	79.3	3,515.0	65.2	1.5
Italy	1989	19.1	433.6	57,540.6	4.4	0.0
Netherlands	1990	37.4	623.7	14,848.8	6.0	0.3
New Zealand	1991	235.2	527.3	3,373.9	44.6	7.0
Portugal	1989	7.8	101.0	10,320.8	7.7	0.1
South Africa	1991	217.9	1,796.1	30,040.5	12.1	0.7
Spain	1989	73.5	398.1	38,888.3	18.5	0.2
USA	1980	584.5	14,079.9	226,546.0	4.2	0.3
Total		3,219.2	35,201.3	567,384.9	9.1	0.6

Notes: In Belgium, Denmark, France, Germany, Greece, Ireland, Italy, Netherlands, Portugal, and Spain the foreign populations are defined by their nationality and not by foreign birthplace.
Sources: Eurostat, 1991, *Demographic Statistics*, Tables B-19, H-1; National Statistical yearbooks: Canada, 1986 census; France, 1982 census; USA, 1980 census; Australia, 1986 census; South Africa, 1991 census; New Zealand, 1991 census.

With one exception, there has never been an official immigration policy to recruit or encourage immigrants, only to keep them out, starting with the Aliens Act of 1905. The UK only once recruited workers on an official basis for specific economic purposes. From 1947 to 1950, 75,000 "European Volunteer Workers" were recruited to work in sanatoria, hospitals, and the cotton and other industries. Initially, most were female Balts from displaced persons camps; later, Ukrainian prisoners of war and Germans, Austrians, and Italians of both sexes were recruited. Some stayed and became naturalized, others returned at British government expense (Tannahill, 1958). They and their descendants are now almost completely "invisible" as social groups. Such recruitment as occurred later was arranged privately by specific companies (British Railways, the National Health Service) on a relatively small scale (primarily in Barbados) and for a short time (from the mid-1950s to 1962). Less than 10% of the immigrants from the new Commonwealth who had arrived by the time control was first imposed in 1962 had been directly recruited (Jones and Smith, 1979; Peach, 1991). Large-scale immigration to

Britain since World War II was a relative novelty. Except for movement from Ireland (up to 1922 part of the UK) and of Eastern European Jewish refugees after 1880, there had been little immigration pressure.

Events since World War II cannot be understood in terms of labor recruitment; only 10% of immigrants came to a specific job. Furthermore the economic revival in Britain, although earlier than that in war-damaged Europe, was less dramatic. There was a general shortage of labor in the 1950s which immigrants helped to fill (Peach, 1979), but the scale of the demand was nothing like the same as that created by economic growth in Germany and France in the 1960s. In Britain, the migrants, most of whom were unskilled, found work in a variety of manufacturing, service, and transport occupations, in manufacturing especially in the obsolete mills and foundries of the north, many of which were soon to close. There was no concentration in assembly-line work such as was seen in Germany (Jones and Smith, 1979; Salt and Clout, 1976). The conventional wisdom was that the immigrants were mostly a "replacement" population to take the jobs the natives did not want. Unlike Germany, unemployment rates of immigrants have typically been higher than those of the native population. This immigration began much earlier than on the continent and was controlled much earlier. Its end was not provoked by the 1973 oil price shock and it was not impeded by any serious suggestion that the economy might be damaged by stopping the immigrant flow. Instead, control was imposed by the Commonwealth Immigrants Act of 1962 and more effectively by the Immigration Act of 1971 for social reasons: to avoid friction with populations perceived as being difficult to assimilate because of differences in race, religion, language, and customs. Their concentration in particular urban areas greatly accentuated the impact on public opinion and the fear that the immigrants were putting unmanageable pressure on housing and employment (see Peach, 1968; Jones, 1977).

Most of the immigrants did not come from the mainland of Europe, not even from its poorer fringes. That is another contrast with the experience of most other West European countries. Instead, the migrants came mostly from Ireland and even more from the "New Commonwealth", that is, from colonies or former British colonies in the Third World which, unlike Turkey or the Maghreb, are not even near-neighbors of Europe.

This has to be understood in terms of the unique arrangements made by the UK in relation to its former territories, in Ireland and former colonies overseas. Since the Middle Ages Ireland had always been associated with Britain in one form or another. But it did not formally become part of the UK until 1801. Irish separatist sentiment, backed by political resistance and fighting, was never extinguished and in 1922, 26 of the 32 counties left the UK to found the Irish Free State, which remained within the Commonwealth until 1948. Before 1922, residents of Ireland, being British subjects, would not have been subject to any immigration control. But even after 1922 citizens of the new Irish state have never been subject to immigration control, except during wartime, despite the fact that Irish citizens are technically "foreigners". Such freedom of movement now applies to all passengers arriving from Ireland.

Similar freedom of movement used to apply to all citizens of the British Empire and Commonwealth. British subject status, conferring the right of entry and other privileges, had been confirmed to all those owing perpetual allegiance to the British monarch by virtue of birth in the UK, a dominion, or a colony by the British Nationality and Status of Aliens Act 1914. Its provisions were continued after World War II and had effectively put an end to the dream of a multinational, decentralized world state with a common citizenship, which had been discussed up to the 1930s. In particular, the British Nationality Act 1948 continued the privileges of free entry (and of subsequent voting in all elections) for the citizens of former colonies which had become independent countries, even if they became republics (e.g., India, Pakistan in 1947), unless they actually left the Commonwealth (e.g., Burma in 1948, South Africa in 1964). In respect of these entitlements they remained British subjects or "Commonwealth Citizens", exempted from the requirements for aliens. The Act created a "citizenship of the United Kingdom and Colonies" within the category of British subject. By 1977 these privileges applied to about 950 million people (Home Office, 1977a). This meant that the push factors of poverty and population growth in the sending countries, and local disruptions which put people on the move, were likely to bring them to Britain. The mobilization of these populations was greatly helped by the temporary experience of wartime service of West Indians in Britain, cheap sea travel, especially the rise of cheap air travel from the 1950s, and, in the case of West Indians, the barrier to a preferred closer destination created by the McCarran–Walter Act of 1952, which reduced the West Indian immigration quota to the USA to 100 until its repeal in 1965 (Coleman and Salt, 1992).

2.2 Peculiarities of British Migration Data

This odd history has made data on migration to Britain and on migrants to Britain, and their patterns and trends, difficult to relate to those of continental countries (Coleman, 1987). The details are exceedingly tedious but they must be described at least in outline; otherwise it is impossible to understand even the limited messages the data can convey.

Acceptance for Settlement Statistics

Because there was no control, no official statistics were gathered on migrants from the Irish Republic or (until 1962) of movements from any Commonwealth country. Since 1914 foreigners wishing to enter had been required to state the purpose of their journey and could not enter without leave from an Immigration Officer. The grant of the right of permanent residence – effectively "immigration" although the term is not used in law – is called "acceptance for settlement" and can either be granted on arrival or after the expiry of some time limit or condition (four years in approved employment, marriage, etc.). Entry for purposes of work does not of itself constitute "settlement" and requires a short- or long-term work permit issued by the Board of Trade, latterly by its successor the Department of Employment. These arrangements remain in force for all foreigners and (since 1971) all Commonwealth citizens, except citizens of EU countries. Because there are no controls on exit, the statistics on "acceptances for settlement" refer to gross inward movements only. These controls and the statistics generated from them were only applied initially in a modified form to Commonwealth citizens in 1962 and then in a form similar to those applied to foreigners since 1971; but never to movements from Ireland.

International Passenger Survey

In addition to that, data on inward and outward passenger movements, first from shipping and then also from airlines, provided a nominally complete picture of gross flows by the 1920s, including even the Republic of Ireland but without any details on the purpose of the journey or characteristics of those entering or leaving. Such data have been overwhelmed by the growth of international passenger movement (48.2 million persons of all citizenships, not counting those from Ireland, entered the UK in 1990) and are only used in rounded figures. In addition, Immigration Officers used to keep a count of persons entering and leaving at ports of entry, which generated a theoretically complete total of gross flows and consequently of net balances. By 1976 it was becoming apparent that this procedure had become perfunctory, causing among other things embarrassing political rows about lax immigration control. Rather than reform the system, it was abandoned. For more detailed purposes the use of passenger statistics has been replaced by the International Passenger Survey, a voluntary survey of about 0.2% of all passenger movements of persons of all citizenships to and from all destinations (except Ireland).[1]

Citizenship Statistics

This strange history also causes problems for the enumeration of people of foreign origin in the UK. The creation of a "Citizenship of the UK and Colonies" together with the wider category of "Commonwealth citizen" in combination with mass immigration from the Commonwealth, made it impossible to use "citizenship" to distinguish between UK residents of British origin and many immigrant residents who were not. The category "foreigner" substantially underestimates the proportion of persons of overseas origin, or holding overseas citizenships, in the UK, since it applies to EU citizens, Americans, Japanese, etc., but to only a minority of the 1.3 million UK residents born in the New Commonwealth or the 2.7 million of New Commonwealth ethnic origin. British law permits the retention of dual nationality. Citizenship has in fact become so confused and devalued a concept that a question about it has not been asked in the census since 1961. The only routine source of data on the nationality of the British population is the Labour Force Survey. In 1991, for example, this survey estimated that there were 262,000 persons of Indian, Pakistani, or Bangladeshi nationality resident in the UK (Salt, 1992, Table 20). Commonwealth citizens who were not citizens of the UK and colonies were able until 1987 to acquire such citizenship by the simple process of registration (application on demand after a year's residence), as opposed to the more complex process of naturalization, which requires evidence of ability to speak English and other tests of suitability. In 1981 the British Nationality Act attempted to bring this confused scene back into line with reality and with immigration entitlement by defining a new, narrower British citizenship for those with some ancestral connection with the British Isles and for existing naturalized and adopted citizens. There has been a last-minute rush to make use of the registration procedures before they were ended, during the transitional period up to 1987 (*Table 2.2*).

Data on Place of Birth

Data on place of birth, however, have been recorded in the decennial censuses since 1841 and also in relation to the mother on the registration of births (*Table 2.3*), and also on the registration of deaths, and (together with citizenship) in the large-scale annual Labour Force Survey, which has a sample size of about 90,000 households.

Data on Ethnicity (Labour Force Survey)

Since 1981 this survey has also asked a question on "ethnicity", asking respondents to classify themselves according to a short list of ethnic categories effectively corresponding to major national origins, irrespective of birthplace (*Table 2.4*). This has its origins in the realization that New Commonwealth immigrants were not assimilating quickly to British life and that their UK-born children, otherwise statistically invisible (not being foreigners), remained a distinct group in society with special needs and problems associated with ability to speak English, school provision, unemployment and local authority expenditure.

On top of that, British race relations or "integration" policy has become more and more focused on officially defined groups or "minorities" on the American or Dutch mode and is increasingly using "targets" and "positive action" directed at them to achieve the ends of its equal opportunities policies. This puts an increased premium on data relating to such minorities. The collection of such data is not appropriate in the context of policies based on principles of individual equality which do not recognize "minorities" (France) or which require foreigners to retain foreign citizenship until they can show that they are fully assimilated (Germany, Switzerland). Whatever the wisdom of these policies (Coleman, in press a), the British ethnic categories make sociological and anthropological sense. But they make British data, which are increasingly being presented in this form, difficult to compare with those on Third World immigrants in continental countries, most of whom remain defined as "foreigners". Despite a decade of successful and uncontroversial use, this ethnic classification was replaced for the census

Table 2.2. Grants of UK citizenship, 1979–90 (thousands).

Previous citizenship or nationality	Citizenship of UK and colonies				British citizenship							
	1979	1980	1981	1982	1983	1984	1985	1986	1987	1988	1989	1990
All grants	24.6	27.5	48.6	76.3	60.7	74.0	53.8	45.9	64.9	64.6	117.1	57.3
Ireland, Rep. of	0.3	0.2	0.3	0.5	0.4	0.4	0.4	0.3	0.4	0.9	8.8	4.1
Commonwealth total	17.4	15.6	29.8	58.6	47.3	56.2	37.7	31.0	47.2	51.6	91.1	38.4
Old Commonwealth	0.3	0.4	0.6	0.9	0.8	1.6	1.4	1.1	1.7	1.2	3.5	1.6
Australia	0.1	0.2	0.2	0.3	0.3	0.6	0.5	0.4	0.4	0.3	0.9	0.6
Canada	0.1	0.1	0.2	0.3	0.3	0.6	0.5	0.4	0.7	0.5	1.6	0.6
New Zealand	0.1	0.1	0.2	0.3	0.3	0.6	0.5	0.3	0.5	0.4	1.0	0.5
New Commonwealth	16.9	15.2	29.1	57.7	39.6	52.5	33.3	27.7	43.0	47.4	82.6	32.7
Africa	2.3	2.1	2.9	5.1	4.3	5.7	3.8	2.7	3.1	3.3	5.3	3.7
Bangladesh, India and Sri Lanka	3.5	3.2	6.1	15.9	10.6	17.4	10.0	7.7	9.5	11.8	26.0	15.7
Pakistan	5.4	4.3	9.0	10.8	7.7	10.3	6.9	4.9	5.6	4.8	7.5	5.4
West Indies	4.1	4.1	9.1	22.2	14.7	15.6	9.6	10.0	22.0	25.0	38.1	4.9
Other Commonwealth	1.8	1.6	3.1	3.8	2.3	3.6	3.0	2.5	2.7	2.4	5.7	3.0
British overseas citizens and British dependent territories citizens	*	*	*	*	6.9	2.1	2.9	2.1	2.5	3.0	5.0	4.1
Foreign total	6.9	11.7	18.5	17.2	13.0	17.2	15.7	14.6	17.3	12.1	17.3	14.7
European Union	1.0	2.0	4.1	3.0	2.1	2.6	1.9	2.0	2.0	1.0	2.0	1.4
Other Europe	1.7	2.7	4.0	3.4	2.5	3.0	2.7	1.6	2.7	1.4	2.1	2.3
USA	0.2	0.3	0.8	0.7	0.5	0.7	0.7	0.6	0.6	0.4	0.7	0.7
Central/South America	0.3	0.4	0.6	0.6	0.5	0.6	0.6	0.5	0.5	0.4	0.6	0.4
South Africa	0.9	1.3	2.3	1.9	1.3	2.1	2.3	3.3	3.7	1.8	2.7	2.6
Other foreign	2.8	5.0	6.7	7.6	6.3	8.3	7.4	6.5	7.9	7.1	9.2	7.3

Source: *Home Office Statistical Bulletin* 6/91, 15 April 1991.

Table 2.3. Birthplace of the population, selected countries, England and Wales 1901–81 (thousands).

Country	1901	1911	1921	1931	1951	1961	1971	1981	1991
UK	32,048	35,048	35,161	38,929	41,836	43,642	45,585	45,303	45,619
Northern Ireland				70	135	188	216	209	212
Southern Ireland	427	375	365	451	492	683	676	580	552
Old Commonwealth		49	64	70	88	89	129	137	158
New Commonwealth	136	162	204	226	202	571	1,121	1,292	1,620
West Indies		11	11	10	16	172	302	294	260
India		63	74	87	111	157	313	383	326
Pakistan and Bangladesh				11	31	136	230		326
Foreign born	339	374	306	308	914	760	929	1,209	1,737
Foreigners (foreign nationality)	248	285	228	180	378	417	228	—	1,791[a]
France	31	39	33	29	30	30	35	37	
Germany	65	65	22	28	99	121	148	169	
Italy	20	22	21	20	33	81	103	93	
Poland	21	37	42	44	152	120	104	88	
Russia/USSR	93	108	62	36	76	53	46	34	
All countries	32,528	36,070	37,887	39,952	43,758	47,105	48,750	48,522	49,135

[a]Data from Labour Force Survey 1991 refers to the UK, and includes citizens of Commonwealth nations. Elsewhere, foreign nationality excludes Commonwealth.

Notes: Southern Ireland included with UK until 1931. New Commonwealth includes all Empire plus Old Comonwealth before 1921. Before 1951 almost all such persons would have been white. Pakistan and Bangladesh included with India until 1951. Poland was Russian Poland until 1921. The Russian data include Poland's totals before 1921. Census totals for New Commonwealth populations in 1961 and 1971 are known to be substantial undercounts. Since 1981, nationality is no longer asked in UK censuses.

Sources: Censuses of England and Wales. For 1991, *Census Report for Great Britain*, Part I, Volume III, Table 51.

Table 2.4. Ethnic minority populations by birthplace and ethnic origin in the UK, 1987.

Ethnic group	Number (1000s)	As % of total	% born in UK	% born abroad
West Indian	495	19.2	53	47
African	112	4.3	38	62
Indian	787	30.5	37	63
Pakistani	428	16.6	46	54
Bangladeshi	108	4.2	32	68
Chinese	125	4.9	26	74
Arab	73	2.8	14	86
Mixed	287	11.1	77	23
Other	163	6.3	36	64
All ethnic	2,577	100.0	45	55
White	51,470	—	96	4
Total	54,047	—	93	7

Source: Haskey (1990).

and the Labour Force Survey from 1991 by the new categories "Black–Caribbean", "Black–African", and "Black–Other" and abolishes the "Mixed" category, which was by far the most rapidly growing of ethnic categories. These new usages reflect the preferences of some immigrant and ethnic minority activists, as well as those of the general population.

2.3 Four Types of "Migration System"

It will be apparent from the account above that the UK today is the focal point of four different migration systems defined on the basis of geography and motivation.

1. A "settlement system" which strongly reflects old colonial ties and is centered today on the Indian subcontinent. Almost all attention is focused on this stream, which has mostly comprised nonwhite people from rural low-skilled backgrounds with different languages and religions from the host population.
2. A much smaller labor system which has been selective in the levels of skill of those involved since 1920 and which is now dominated by movements of highly skilled workers often moving between advanced economies in the EU, the USA, and Japan.
3. A refugee system, previously numerically trivial and now large, which involves a small number of countries sending an increasing number of asylum seekers to Britain.

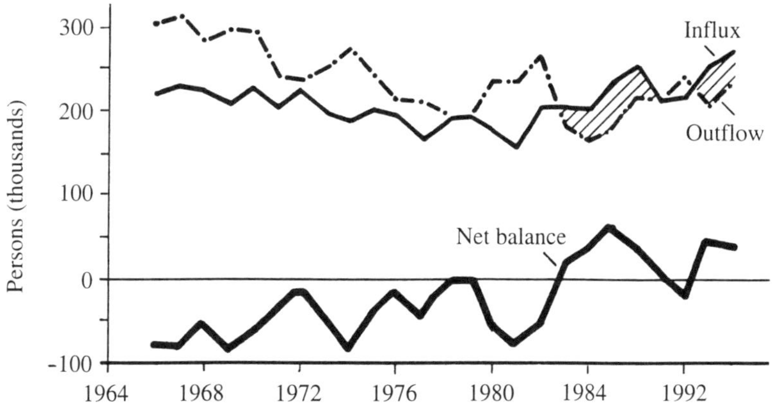

Figure 2.1. Population inflow, outflow, and net balance, UK, 1966–90 (based on the International Passenger Survey). Source: OPCS (1992, 17 Tables 2.2, 2.3, etc.).

4. Finally, overlapping with systems (1) and (3), there is an illegal migration system including physically illegal entry, false relationship claims and overstaying from New Commonwealth citizens, and bogus refugee applicants, many from non-Commonwealth countries such as Sudan and Zaire, some of whom abscond when allowed to remain in the country (see Coleman and Salt, 1992)

With this classification and with the severe limitations of the data in mind, we look first at the trends of immigration since 1945. These can be briefly summarized as follows:

- A general reduction in the gross flows of migrants into and out of the UK until the mid-1980s, since when the outflow has changed little and the inflow has increased.
- Continued net population loss by a negative migration balance (i.e., more emigrants than immigrants) from 1945 until the mid-1980s, despite New Commonwealth immigration, except for the peak years of inflow around 1962 to "beat the Immigration Bill" (*Figure 2.1*) and that arising from the exodus of 23,000 Asian refugees from Uganda in 1973.
- Most years since the mid-1980s have seen net population gains from immigration which even the economic recession of the late 1980s and the early 1990s has not ended. Since the 1960s the general trend of the net balance figure from the International Passenger Survey is

clearly gently upward. It may be that the 1980s finally saw the end of the old British tradition of exporting population.

2.3.1 "Settlement" migration system

Regarding the former colonial stream, migration flows to and from the Commonwealth, both Old and New, have weakened in favor of migration involving foreign countries without historical ties with Great Britain (*Figure 2.1*). Since the mid-1980s these have accounted for about half of the movements in both directions, although the proportion has changed a little in recent years. Net emigration to the old dominions has fallen substantially, from 100,000 in the 1950s to about 30,000 in the 1980s (*Figure 2.2*) and with actual net inflows from New Zealand since the late 1980s. That outflow of British people to the dominions, which has lasted for well over a century, appears now to be in its final phases. Canada ended free access to British settlers in 1948 and the assisted passenger scheme to Australia ended in 1983. For decades now both countries have welcomed immigrants from all countries; more than half of their new immigrants come from Third World countries. In connection with these immigration policies, ambitious multicultural policies have also been developed, partly to foster a new, non-British national identity, although not without some domestic opposition (see Citizens' Forum, 1991; Birrell and Birrell, 1990; Castles *et al.*, 1990).

However, net migration to the USA, which may be regarded as part of the same emigration stream, continues although at a low level. Its outflow was temporarily reversed during the draft-dodger era toward the end of the Vietnam War and also by the immigration of skilled US personnel into the UK during the economic recovery of the mid-1980s.

In the past, South Africa was also a favored English-speaking destination and migration from the UK continued to be encouraged by the South African government. The reversal of the emigration from South Africa, usually about 10,000 per year, in the 1970s and late 1980s, corresponds with periods of unrest and disturbance.

Europe has never been a major destination or source of population in the UK, except for about 100,000 poor Ashkenazi Jewish refugees from 1880 up to 1905 who were the ancestors of most of today's British Jews. During most of the twentieth century, the net balance of migration with Europe has been negative, generating a small net loss of population, reflecting Britain's relative economic weakness and the existence of

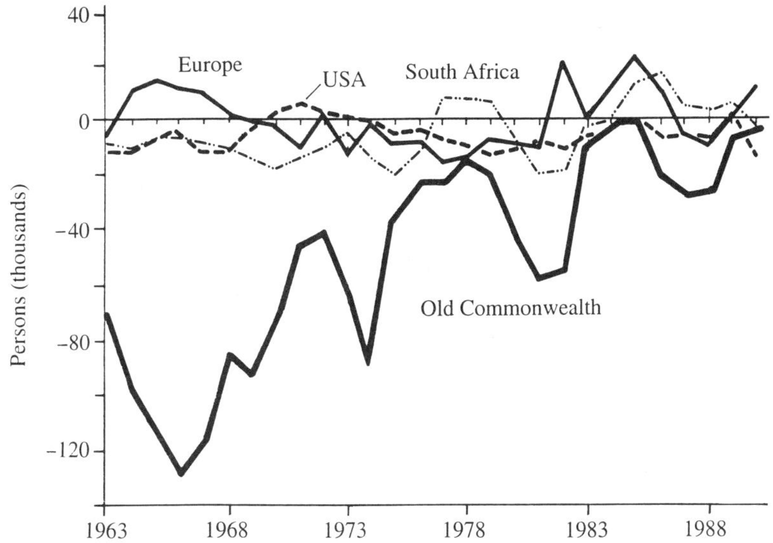

Figure 2.2. Net migration to the UK, 1963–90 (based on the International Passenger Survey). Source: OPCS (1992, Tables 2.2, 2.3, etc.).

traditional migration streams independent of mainland Europe. But in the 1980s a new pattern emerged closer to a net balance with EU countries (whose member states have of course increased in number).[2] This is connected with the revival of the UK economy in the mid-1980s and the scarcity of skilled labor in the southeast of England (where most international migrants settle). It is not possible to say anything about the detailed composition of such EU migrants, but the numbers are clearly modest. Similar, higher-grade labor migration is behind the heightened migration exchange with Japan and the narrowing gap with the USA.

Despite complaints about the "Arabization" of Knightsbridge and the turning of Harrod's into an upmarket corner of the souk, net migration has been to Arabia, not from it – mostly short-term highly skilled labor migration. There is not much permanent settlement in either direction, although male Arabs living in the UK have a particularly high propensity to marry British women (Coleman, 1985). British expatriate workers in the Gulf States, mostly highly skilled manual, professional, or technical workers, on relatively short-term contracts, have become known as the "new nomads" (Findlay and Stewart, 1985).

The longest running substantial migration stream, that from the Republic of Ireland, still escapes effective contact with official statistics.

It is an invisible migration because the flow is neither controlled nor directly measured. The relative lack of data and of controversy makes Irish immigration one of the most neglected corners of British migration study. It can be regarded partly as a component of the former colonial stream and partly as an informal equivalent of the 1960s movement into northwest European countries of workers from Spain, Portugal, Italy and Finland. Many of the migrants would not be accepted if work permits were required for entry; nonetheless Irish immigrants provide a substantial proportion of building workers in Britain, especially in the south, although people of Irish origin are widely distributed socially and geographically.[3]

Enough can be assembled from the censuses of the UK and of Ireland, the Labour Force Survey, National Insurance, and other sources to say that migration from Ireland has been positive and substantial throughout most of the period, notably in the 1950s and 1960s. The peak Irish-born population (all parts) in England and Wales was 880,000 in 1966, 2% of the population and a larger number than any New Commonwealth group (O'Grada, 1985). Irish immigration still proceeded vigorously when immigration from the New Commonwealth was restricted.

Irish migration in the 1950s was substantial. In the late 1970s Irish economic growth, stimulated by EU membership and tax incentives, during a time of deep economic crisis in the UK, reversed the flow (Kirwan and Nairn, 1983). There was an annual net loss of 11,000 Irish from the UK in 1974–79. The emigrants were mostly return migrants, rather than UK citizens migrating to Ireland. By the early 1980s this was all over. Ireland's youthful and growing population, once bravely advertised as an asset to investors, is once again an economic embarrassment, and large-scale emigration to the outside industrial world has re-established itself: to the UK, to other EU countries, and to the USA. The rate of migration to the UK may be as high now as in the 1950s, although other EU countries and the USA are preferred destinations.

New Commonwealth migration belongs almost entirely to the "former colonial" system. Net immigration has remained positive throughout the period, with immigration exceeding emigration by a factor of three or four (*Figure 2.3*).[4]

Even though mass primary labor migration has ended, the British government remains committed to the reunification of families in Britain. Thus, even after looser control of immigration was attempted in 1962 and 1971, there has been an apparently never-ending stream of

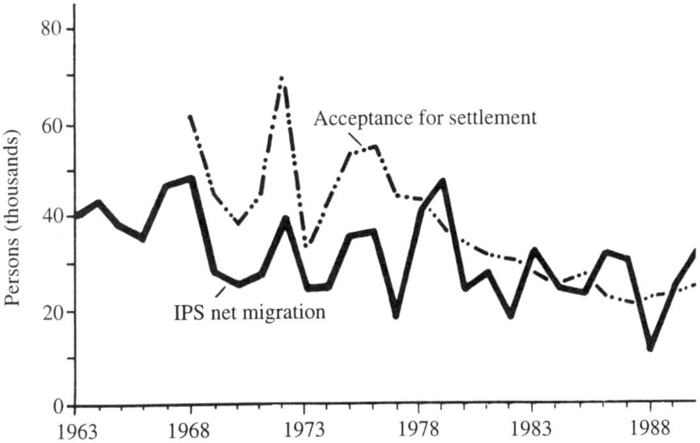

Figure 2.3. New Commonwealth work permit immigration, 1963–90. Source: OPCS (1992, Tables 2.2, 2.3, etc.); Home Office (1991).

dependents, which has consistently exceeded all forecasts (Eversley and Sukdeo, 1969).

Considering each region separately, only net migration from the West Indies and from Africa has ever been negative, and that for a few years only. The dominant countries of origin have shifted substantially: first the West Indies, then Pakistan and India, the East African refugees of the 1970s, and the increasing preponderance of Bangladeshis, now the fastest-growing New Commonwealth immigrant minority. Labor migration continued after the 1962 Act. Employment vouchers that were not linked to specific jobs were still offered in limited numbers, but were ended by the 1971 Immigration Act which required would-be labor migrants from the New Commonwealth to satisfy the identified needs of employers through the Department of Employment and acquire work permits, on the same basis as workers from foreign countries. There are now only a very few unrestricted categories (ministers of religion and entertainers); those of dentist and medical doctor were abolished in 1985.

As in the rest of Europe, which dropped the shutters on Third World labor migration a decade later in 1973, large-scale labor migration to the UK has been replaced by equally substantial and continuing migration of dependents and of spouses, punctuated by occasional irruptions of refugees and increasing pressure from asylum seekers and illegal immigrants. The government can claim that uniformly applied work permit rules make it impossible for New Commonwealth immigration to threaten British employment prospects. It claims success in having reduced overall New Commonwealth immigration to a minimum as promised (this seems to be generally accepted, even if some may deplore it), but in fact the restrictive immigration policy has only been partially successful. There are several loopholes and exceptions; immigration has hardly declined from the levels of the early 1970s. Most New Commonwealth (NC) immigrants in the UK, especially from the Indian subcontinent, and almost all Africans and Chinese, have arrived after the ineffective controls of the 1962 Act thanks to its originally generous employment voucher provisions and the broad definition of dependents then adopted. Since the 1971 Act over 600,000 New Commonwealth immigrants including the majority of Bangladeshi immigrants have been accepted for settlement; marriage migrations due primarily to the provisions for family reunification and exceptions made for refugees have played a significant role. The cumulative net balance of immigration from 1971 to 1987 calculated from the International Passenger Survey (IPS) was almost 500,000, more than one-third of the total NC-born population. In confirmation of this the 1984 Labour Force Survey showed that about 900,000 of 1.3 million NC-born residents entered after 1962, and over 450,000 since 1971.[5]

2.3.2 Labor migration

Only one in seven – about 30,000 – of the 200,000 or so immigrants to the UK each year enter to take up a specified job under the work permit system. This does not include EU workers, who do not require work permits. This is the lowest number of organized labor migrants in the EU, but it is also the most specialized; the jobs involved are predominantly managerial and professional; more so than in any other OECD country (Salt, 1991). Work permits were not required by Commonwealth labor migrants before the 1971 Act (vouchers were required after the 1962 Act). Work permits ceased to be necessary for EU migrants after accession in 1973 and of course the numbers of persons so exempted has grown as the number of EU member states has increased, so trends are not easy to analyze.

In 1969, the first year for which data are available, 75,405 permits were issued, falling to 52,699 in 1972. Rule changes account for a large drop to 36,536 in 1973. Permits declined progressively to a low

Table 2.5. Long-term work permits and first permissions issued by country, 1984–90, countries with over 500 issues in one year.

	1984	1985	1986	1987	1988	1989	1990
USA	2,493	2,504	2,414	2,639	3,432	4,187	4,998
Japan	1,028	1,246	1,402	1,490	2,053	2,190	2,583
Australia	342	361	359	400	620	878	1,007
Malaysia	35	354	126	94	531	680	678
Hong Kong (Br.)	429	416	287	263	495	656	840
India	250	332	293	272	541	635	816
Sweden	283	274	293	260	418	454	473
China	42	42	53	108	207	453	616
Canada	271	234	302	268	392	408	511
All long-term permits	6,800	7,100	7,900	8,100	10,400	13,300	16,100
Short-term permits	6,200	6,600	8,000	9,400	11,800	12,200	13,800
Trainees	2,700	2,900	2,800	2,900	3,800	4,200	4,800
Total	15,700	16,600	18,700	20,400	26,000	29,700	34,700

Source: Salt (1991, Table 28).

point of 15,454 in 1982, from which they increased to 20,348 in 1987 and have since risen steeply by about 20% per year to 34,627 in 1990 (*Table 2.5*). Of these permits, 16,055 were for long-term work, 13,760 for short-term work, and 4,812 for trainees. Over 80% of the long-term permits were for professional and managerial work. In 1987 the majority were in insurance, banking, and finance (27%), professional services (25%), metals manufacturing (15%), and other services (14%). This migration involves much movement between the companies of multinational corporations. Only 13% of the short-term permits fell into these managerial categories, most of them (84%) were for literary, art, and sports workers. Over 80% of these workers and their dependents were from non-Commonwealth countries (Salt, 1991).[6]

However it can be seen that in aggregate, the percentages of migrants in the two streams who are employed is converging. In 1977 some 50% of immigrants were in employment, compared with 55% in 1990 (with lower levels in all intervening years). In 1977, 61% of emigrants were employed compared with 57% in 1990. In recent years the proportion of professional and managerial workers has grown both in inflows and outflows. In 1990 they comprised 63% of employed immigrants and 57% of employed emigrants.

In 1990 therefore, and in half the years of the previous decade, the UK gained through immigration more "professional and managerial

Table 2.6. Occupational distribution of immigrants to and emigrants from the UK, 1986 (thousands).

	Immigrants	Emigrants	Balance
All persons	250.3	213.4	+36.9
Professional/managerial	76.2	76.8	–0.6
Manual/clerical	46.1	38.5	+7.6
Students	47.1	28.2	+18.8
Housewives	28.5	23.3	+5.2
Others	4.3	8.3	–4.0
Children	48.2	38.2	+10.0

Source: OPCS (1988, Table 6).

workers" than it lost by emigration (*Table 2.6*). Given the heterogeneity of the categories the real balance of advantage may be different: the category includes scientists, executives, schoolteachers, and managers. Immigration also brings a surplus of students, wives, and children. Most of the wives and children and less skilled workers were from the NC, entering as spouses or dependents. This is counterbalanced by the highly skilled streams, numerically smaller, from the USA and Japan and the EU. Hardly any long-term work permits are issued to persons from New Commonwealth countries (*Table 2.5*). They are not, of course, required for entry by EU citizens in search of work or other purposes.

2.3.3 Refugees and asylum claimants

There has been a considerable increase in the number of applications for refugee status or asylum, with a roughly corresponding increase in the much smaller number of admissions. In 1979 there were only 1,563 applications to the UK from all sources. By 1985 there were 5,444, by 1990 22,000, who with their dependents number over 30,000 (Salt, 1991). The figure for 1991 was 44,745 (Home Office, 1991; Salt, 1992).[7]

Nationals of different countries have predominated in applications to the UK in different years. Some of the increases have been linked to specific political events: Iran (2,280 applications in 1982), Sri Lanka (2,306 applications in 1985), and Poland (494 applications in 1982), but others have shown a more progressive increase in the absence of any dramatic new political developments (Ethiopia, Ghana, India, Pakistan, and Uganda). In 1991 the biggest category of applicants was from Zaire (3,650 applicants) followed by Angola (3,300); two countries with no historical connections with the UK. There were 145 and 45 applicants

Table 2.7. Applications received for refugee status or asylum, selected countries, 1988–91 (more than 100 in one year).

Country	1988	1989	1990	1991
Afghanistan	25	85	200	—
Angola	45	220	1,030	3,300
Bangladesh	10	10	55	—
Bulgaria	5	30	130	240
Ivory Coast	0	15	50	625
Ethiopia	225	560	1,840	1,035
Ghana	170	325	790	1,595
India	290	630	1,415	1,085
Iran	390	345	335	290
Iraq	165	210	915	465
Lebanon	150	175	1,035	590
Nigeria	10	20	90	—
Uganda	410	1,240	1,895	1,110
Pakistan	330	245	1,295	1,830
Poland	70	45	20	20
Romania	10	15	295	280
Somalia	305	1,845	1,850	1,225
Sudan	20	110	220	260
Ceylon	405	1,785	3,325	2,410
Turkey	335	2,360	1,100	1,260
USSR	5	30	93	115
Zaire	145	490	1,490	3,650
Others	465	720	>2,250	2,410
Total	3,755	11,280	>20,608	23,795
Dependents	1,715	5,070	>8,000	—
Overall total	5,700	16,580	>29,718	—

— No data available.
Source: Home Office (Salt, 1991, Table 12).

in 1988 from these countries, respectively, when the civil war in Angola was still in full swing. There has been a general underlying increase in applications from all parts of the world, beyond these exceptional cases (*Table 2.7*). In demographic terms the impact on the UK population is relatively small, but applications to other countries from 1984–87 amount to between 0.5% and 0.75% of the national population; over 400,000 to Europe as a whole in 1990.

Most applications to the UK are rejected. In 1979 only 525 grants of refugee status or asylum were given, rising to a maximum of 1,727 in 1982 (mostly to Iranians). The total in 1989 was 2,220, Somalians now being the biggest single contingent with 820 and Ethiopia next with 410. These figures are almost doubled when dependents are included. In addition, a further 5,920 grants of exceptional leave to remain were given in 1989, a large increase on the 215 given in 1979. But in 1991 fewer grants of asylum were made (420), and a further 1860 were granted "exceptional leave to remain" (49% of decisions); this is permission to enter while asylum applications are sorted out. It is most unlikely that these persons will ever leave. On top of that, very few of those who are neither granted asylum nor exceptional leave to remain are repatriated by force.

2.3.4 Dependents, fiancées, and spouses from the Indian subcontinent

Early forecasts of the inflow of dependents, such as that made by Eversley and Sukdeo (1969), have been substantially overtaken by events.[8] The reduction in the numbers making entry clearance applications from the Indian subcontinent, particularly the numbers of children (*Figure 2.4*), suggest that the pool of dependents is slowly being emptied. The number of New Commonwealth children accepted for settlement relative to the number of wives has declined in recent years. That was expected to occur because the number of work permits issued to Commonwealth citizens has fallen to just a few hundred per year by the early 1980s – 627 in 1980 to the whole Indian subcontinent (Home Affairs Committee, 1982). But new sources of dependency are always arising. An increasing proportion of the wives are recently married women with no children who would previously have entered as fiancées.[9]

The sex/age structure of the New Commonwealth population made from the Labour Force Survey shows sex ratios of 138 males per 100 females among persons born in Bangladesh, 126 for those born in the Far East, and 122 for those born in Pakistan. This suggests that to produce a balanced sex ratio from reunification of families would require further substantial immigration. However, new applications for entry clearance have declined since the 1970s for children but there is no clear downward trend for wives in the 1980s.

Until the rise of asylum seekers in the late 1980s, the marriage patterns of persons settled in the UK from the Indian subcontinent were seen as a major potential threat to the policies of control. Arranged marriages are customary in Asian society. Asian parents in Britain are often keen to ensure that their children marry spouses from the correct religion and caste (Jones and Shah, 1980). Pakistani Muslims strongly prefer marriages between cousins. Many Asian parents do not approve

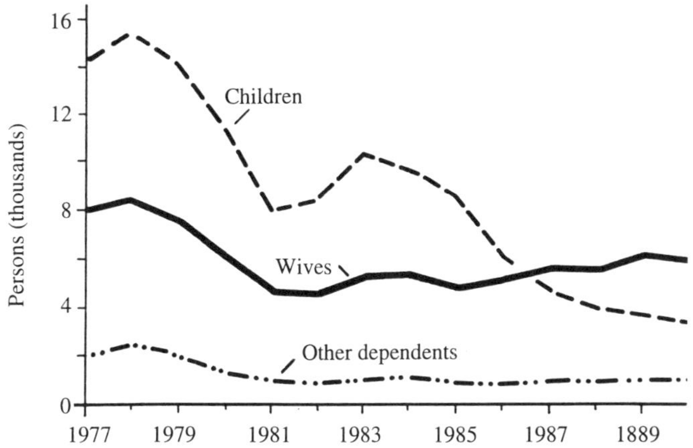

Figure 2.4. Entry clearance applications from the Indian subcontinent, 1977–90. Source: Home Office (1991).

of British society, considering it to be immoral, so that they seek spouses for their children in the country (often the village) of origin, where there is much demand for spouses already settled in Britain as such a marriage removes the barrier to immigration. Such marriages have maintained primary migration for some years (Jones, 1982). Even under the existing rules the rapidly expanding age structure of the UK Asian population would, other things being equal, produce a corresponding increase in the importation of fiancées and spouses from the Indian subcontinent. At the moment there are about 40,000 South Asian females aged 20–25 born outside the UK, and about 10,000 born in the UK. In 20 years' time these will have changed to a couple of thousand and over 80,000 respectively. A substantial proportion of the marriages of Asians resident in the UK are thought still to be arranged and to involve intended spouses from the country of origin.[10]

Changes in the immigration rules which extended the right of settlement to husbands of all female British citizens irrespective of birthplace (1983) and then to husbands of all women settled in Britain irrespective of citizenship (1985) has caused much discontinuity in the statistics. Entries of husbands and male fiancés have sharply increased. The introduction of a requirement for a probationary year to elapse following entry before settlement is granted greatly increased the category "given limited leave to enter" (*Figure 2.5*). They would previously have been

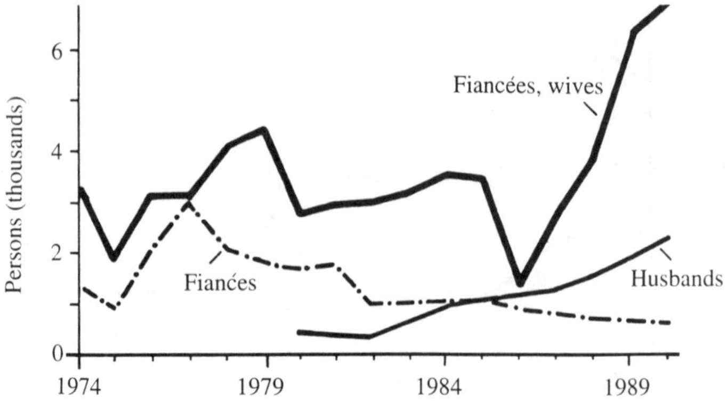

Figure 2.5. NC fiancés, fiancées, husbands, and wives given limited leave to enter, 1974–90. Source: Home Office (1991).

given settlement on arrival, and this category has correspondingly declined. It is now more sensible for women, too, to apply as wives rather than as fiancées, since that helps to satisfy the "primary purpose" rule.[11]

Despite these erratic trends there does not appear to have been a dramatic increase in the numbers of fiancées and wives over the 1980s. If the propensity of Asians in Britain to import fiancées or spouses from Asia had remained constant, then the irregular age structure of the Asian population would create a reduction of up to 10% in such spouses in the 1980s followed by a similar increase in the early 1990s and a more substantial increase at the end of the 1990s assuming marriage between the ages of 20 and 24. Therefore if the number of such spouses remains roughly constant in the early 1990s, marriage preferences must be changing. Data on current marriages from the Labour Force Survey suggest that in the 1980s a high proportion of UK-born Asians married Asians of British origin and up to 20% married outside the Asian communities altogether (Coleman, 1992b), but these are still a small proportion of each marriage cohort.

2.4 British Immigration Policy

British immigration policy is simple. For 20 years or more it has been, in the words of the Conservative party's manifesto of 1974 "to reduce and keep new immigration to a small and inescapable minimum" subject to the rights of dependents and the needs of the economy dealt with through the work permit system (p. 27).[12]

Minimizing immigration is thought to be essential for the successful development of harmonious race relations. There is no disposition on the part of the present Conservative government to change it; no likely opposition dares to promise to do so. Even as early as 1950 the Labour government under Attlee considered proposals to stop immigration from the West Indies because of its supposed undesirable social consequences. Such proposals were considered from time to time by the Conservative government that succeeded Labour in 1951. No action was taken until 1962 after acrimonious debates between the parties and within Conservative ranks. Backbench MPs reported that their constituents were strongly against continued immigration; others claimed the controls were racist and betrayed the ideal of free movement in a multiracial Commonwealth. Freedom of movement had long ceased to apply to British people seeking to settle in most other Commonwealth countries. Such was the strength of public opinion that the Labour party, although it voted against the legislation, did not repeal it when they came to power in 1964. Instead they strengthened it in 1965. In new legislation in 1968 the Labour government introduced additional immigration controls on East African and Asian UK passport holders[13] and in 1969 required persons seeking to enter as dependents from the Indian subcontinent to apply for "entry clearance" from British officials there rather than on arrival. An operational consensus has been reached but a consensus on sentiment has not. In compensation, the Labour government introduced a series of Race Relations Acts (1965, 1976) progressively outlawing racial discrimination and paving the way for what has become in effect a minorities-based "multicultural" policy. This in turn has had to be accepted by the Conservatives even though they originally opposed it. Immigration controls are still opposed by the Left but not by the Labour party, even though particular aspects of the laws are denounced as racially discriminatory, a charge that the government strongly rejects.

Immigration policy in the UK has been defined by the 1971 Immigration Act.[14] Since then it has been described by the government as a "firm but fair" immigration policy, intended to "control immigration from all sources on the same basis as an essential prerequisite for satisfactory race relations." Its explicit aim was to limit immigration, particularly from the New Commonwealth, and to place the control of Commonwealth and foreign migration on the same defensible footing.

It established the same procedure for labor migration for all migrants, regardless of origin. It enshrined the principle, established by the Labour government's legislation in 1968, that the right of abode should be enjoyed automatically only by persons who had a personal connection with the UK ("patrials"). It took a further ten years before the wide-ranging definition of British citizenship was reformed in 1981 to bring it into line with the practices of immigration control.

The Labour governments of 1974–79 (Wilson, Callaghan), which had opposed the 1971 Act, nonetheless did not repeal it. They did not challenge its basic principles and passed no primary immigration legislation of their own. But among a number of changes they did alter the Immigration Rules on fiancés (1974) and changed administrative procedures. These speeded up entry clearance, accepted for settlement persons resident on 1 January 1973 after five years' residence, and increased the UKPH (UK passport holder) quota from 3,500 to 5,000. This made the entry of fiancés and husbands and other relatives easier, with consequent increases in acceptances. But from 1977 newly married husbands were no longer accepted for settlement on arrival, but instead were given "limited leave to enter". That was intended to reduce illegal immigration through bogus marriages of convenience.

Immigration policy is conceived in the context of a belief in a strong "pressure to migrate" to the UK from the Third World. This provokes a kind of hydraulic analogy, with constant repairs and additions being made to a basically sound structure in order to stop water slopping over the top or finding its way through new or previously undetected leaks. On the whole, the government feels that the present policy is right and is popular. It does not wish to change it. It will only impose new legislation in order to protect the status quo from new threats or challenges, not to change it. In these areas, governments want a quiet life.

That is the main reason why the government has never made any effort to promote the return migration or "repatriation" provisions of the 1971 Immigration Act. These operate on a trivial scale – about 100 per year – to provide a low level of highly conditional financial help to immigrants who wish to return to their countries of origin. The work is subcontracted to a private agency and receives no publicity. Any emphasis given to it would be thought to prejudice "good race relations". There is therefore no return migration program in the UK. Britain acquired its Commonwealth immigrant population in a fit of absence of mind. There was no plan to start the immigration and no intended purpose for it. Consequently there was no plan to return it whence it came. Of course, as in all migration streams, there are some return migrants, permanent and temporary, who move at their own initiative, whose numbers can be estimated from the International Passenger Survey (IPS).

There is no measurable popular support for any increase in settlement and general support for its further reduction. In the British Attitudes Survey of 1984, 65% of respondents called for less settlement from the New Commonwealth, as did up to 45% of ethnic minority respondents (Airey, 1984). Most who favor free entry are moral and intellectual critics from the churches and the Left, including some of the Black and Asian voters who predominantly support the Labour party. They denounce the immigration policy as racist. In fact its provisions apply strictly to all persons, but the majority of those who are thereby excluded are nonwhite people from the Third World. That is where most of the pressure for immigration comes from. So the government sees itself as holding a neutral position, causing minimal political problems, capable of being sustained indefinitely, reactive rather than part of any national "immigration" plan, the lack of which often bemuses transatlantic and antipodean visitors accustomed to inhabiting a "country of immigration".

During the 1980s immigration almost disappeared from view as a topic of public controversy in Britain. Immigration was not an issue in the 1983 general election nor in 1987, despite the Conservative party's manifesto promise, amplified during the election, to tighten the existing law limiting immigration. Neither was it prominent in the 1992 election. In 1983 and 1985 only 5 and 11 motions on immigration were submitted to the Conservative party conferences, for example, compared with 59 motions on social services. The Labour party manifesto for the 1987 general election even adopted the Conservatives' "firm but fair" slogan. The National Front (extreme right wing, British National Party) declined to field a single candidate.[15]

The 1988 Immigration Act – the first major legislation since 1971 – created little interest outside race relations circles. Most major challenges come from immigrant groups and race relations and civil liberties interests. Government could point to the substantial decline in the numbers accepted for settlement from the New Commonwealth in the 1980s, even though other figures show no trends for a decade. Control is felt to be as tight as it can reasonably be made, even though many government supporters would like to see it tightened further. But in a policy of containment, part of whose justification is better race relations, further steps need new challenges. Such challenges have not been lacking since the late 1980s – from refugees and illegal immigrants, especially from Africa – and the resumption of the upward movement in New Commonwealth immigration. The Asylum and Immigration Appeals Act 1993 is the latest legislative response to the new pressure.

Press reports of court cases suggest that illegal immigration from Nigeria and other African countries, using false passports, bogus marriages, or illegal overstaying, is now organized on a large scale (in 1993 it was estimated that there were 100,000 illegal immigrants in the UK). Such a problem is too difficult to quantify, but there has been (unofficial) discussion of the desirability of identity cards and appropriate legislation, to deter the employment of illegal immigrants. There is no official identity document in Britain.

A consensus therefore appears to have been established based on the following propositions: Britain has no general need for more people or for further immigration, but there is a pressure to emigrate from areas of low wages and living standards to the UK and other countries. The high rate of unemployment in the UK makes a labor market free-for-all with low-wage countries unthinkable. Special labor needs can easily be managed by the work permit system, and renewed large-scale immigration would be unacceptable to the British people and would be bad for race relations. Settlement should therefore be limited to those with existing close personal connections with the UK, or who come for clearly specified work purposes, or for defined family reasons such as spouses or dependents. This restrictive immigration policy is shared, more or less, with most other European industrialized countries.

2.5 Outlook

The increase in refugee claimants in recent years reflects pressures to migrate and the easier mobilization of populations following the spread of information about immigration control and refugee procedures and how to use them to best advantage. The British government believes that most of the new refugee pressure is conventional betterment migration which cannot be met in other ways.[16]

The government's restrictive policy on asylum claimants attracts much criticism from political opponents and the churches. In its defense, the government points to the 20,000 Vietnamese "boat people" accepted since 1979. It points to the failure to substantiate claims that Tamils returned to Sri Lanka, for example, are actually at risk. Contrary to its own previous promises, it has extended the right of settlement to 50,000 Hong Kong heads of household in addition to the 15,000 British passport holders already estimated to be in Hong Kong. Serious trouble in South Africa may also spell serious trouble for British immigration policy. It has been estimated that up to 800,000 people entitled to hold UK passports live there.

Because of its mediocre economic growth Britain has not attracted much migration from other EU countries (except Ireland), although there is a long but little publicized postwar immigration stream of workers from the Iberian peninsula for work in the holiday and catering services. If the current economic differential remains, Irish emigration to Britain and elsewhere will continue. There are no controls and there are unlikely to be any. Even though the Irish birth rate is falling close to the replacement rate, demographic inertia will ensure that cohort size continues to increase for some years beyond the capacity of the Irish economy to absorb it.

A radical increase in immigration to Britain from the poorer EU countries is unlikely. British wages are still much lower than those in Germany or the Netherlands, for example. Future labor demand will be for the managerial and skilled occupations. For the present, unemployment is the dominant concern. Therefore the single European market and further steps toward European integration are unlikely to make much difference to movement of EU citizens across what is already a fairly open labor frontier. But by making qualifications interchangeable, and by stimulating economic growth, it should accelerate higher-level manpower transfers, which are already the characteristic and dominant feature of British work permit labor movement. The crucial point is whether freedom of movement applies to non-EU residents in other EU countries and whether entry into one EU country permits entry into them all. The British government is determined to maintain its border controls, especially in the light of illegal immigration in southern EU countries and the pressure to migrate from Eastern Europe and the former Soviet Union. So far there has been little migration or asylum application from Eastern Europe to the UK, although there has been an increase, from a tiny base, in work permit applications.

It has been suggested that a resumption of higher levels of immigration will be necessary in order to remedy the shortage of teenagers, to provide the more youthful working population to support the growing number of pensioners. In general this does not seem to be a serious option. First, the comparison of the present birth deficit is with the highly unusual years of the baby boom. The low skills of most Third World immigrants are not much in demand in modern economies, the level of immigration needed to rectify age-structure imbalances would be substantially higher than that experienced in the past. Furthermore, there is considerable capacity to expand the work force in Britain, as in the rest of the EU by bringing work force participation rates up to the level of the highest of the member states, and by retraining the unemployed. In the UK, which in 1993 had over 2.4 million unemployed and one of the highest birth rates in Europe, and whose population is not expected to start to decline until 2030, there is little imminent need for such measures. But they are sometimes favored by liberal opinion as arguments to relax immigration controls (see *The Economist*, 15 February 1992: 17–20). Meanwhile, British public opinion, and British policy, aims to keep the doors closed and the windows shut for as long as possible.

Notes

[1] Almost from its beginning the IPS has applied to Commonwealth citizens, whose entry began to be controlled after 1962. Most of the 200,000 interviews in each direction are naturally of tourists and business visitors, but in 1990 1,510 intending immigrants and 864 of intended emigrants were interviewed. Here the international definition of migration is used, that of a person resident abroad for at least a year who enters with the intention of staying for at least a year and vice versa. The data are substantially incompatible with those derived from the Home Office Control of Immigration procedures. The trivial sample size and voluntary nature of the enquiry has been much criticized as leading to uncorrectable errors (Peach, 1981). For example, for 1990 the 35 interviews with intended immigrants from the Caribbean and the 19 interviews with intended emigrants were grossed up to estimated migrant flows of 6,700 persons in and 3,800 out, with a net balance of 3,800, with a standard error of 2,500 (OPCS, 1992, Table 3.17). Immigration estimates from the entire EU were based on 127 interviews (grossed up to 65,900 persons).

[2] The data in *Figure 2.2* exclude movements from Ireland.

[3] There have always been people from Ireland in Britain, although the numbers greatly increased after the potato famine in 1845–46, which helped to institute a permanent "emigration culture" that has continued more or less ever since. Most of the approximately five million Roman Catholics in Britain have at least some Irish ancestry.

[4] For clarity, the separate data from Home Office acceptance for settlement statistics and from the International Passenger Survey are also presented separately.

[5] Certainly the government can no longer claim, as it frequently used to do, that immigration from the New Commonwealth is rapidly declining. Even in the mid-1980s that

claim depended on whether the Home Office (Britain's Ministry of the Interior) or IPS figures were used to support the argument. The Home Office figures, used exclusively in government speeches for obvious reasons, show a continuous decline from 1975 to 1985 but a sharp increase since then. The net IPS figures showed no downward trend since the late 1960s and also show a sharp upward trend in the late 1980s. According to IPS data, about 40% of the annual 5% increase in the NC ethnic group population is still accounted for by immigration. The upturn in net NC migration measured by the IPS and some categories in the Home Office data are partly due to changes in the Immigration Rules in 1985 imposed by the European Court, which made family reunification easier.

[6] The characteristics of the working population lost or gained by migration are poorly known; this is a consequence of the very small sample size of the IPS as applied to migrants, which precludes detailed employment categories for analysis; the negligible official analyses of Home Office data; and the lack of any outflow counterpart to work permit data, which of course only apply to the incoming high-level work force. This means that it is almost impossible to answer the perennial question of the extent to which Britain is suffering from a serious problem of "brain-drain". Unofficial sources claim that it is (Royal Society, 1987), although these claims apply to senior people near the tops of their professions, a flow that is never likely to be detectable in official routine statistics. The crude occupational categories used in the published IPS data combine all workers into either professional and managerial (including doctors, shopkeepers, and smallholders) or "clerical and manual" (unskilled laborers and clerks).

[7] But this is still relatively small compared with the 256,000 applications to Germany in 1991.

[8] Past Home Affairs Committee Reports have urged the creation of a register of dependents (Home Office, 1977b) or of a quota system. The 1979 Conservative party manifesto promised the introduction of both, a promise that has never been implemented or repeated.

[9] Furthermore, following the Kessori Khatun case, from 1986 certain categories of people, who formerly would have applied for entry clearance but who might in fact have had the right of abode, now apply for certificates of entitlement to right of abode and no longer appear in acceptance statistics as they are not subject to control. Some of the post-1985 increase may follow from the new rules extending entry clearance to "new" wives.

[10] Government statistical sources have so far been unable to give a figure to the Select Committee on Race Relations and Immigration (SCORRI). In fact the number of fiancées from South Asia did not increase much from 1975 to 1985, while the number of fiancés did increase. The requirement that fiancés serve a probationary year and satisfy the "primary purpose" test has made it more sensible for them to apply as husbands. That makes it easier to satisfy the requirement that the couple must have met before their marriage although they are still given "limited leave to enter" rather than "accepted for settlement on arrival", being later "accepted on removal of time limit". In 1992 4,690 fiancés and husbands were given "limited leave to enter" from the NC, 540 fiancées, and 6,290 wives. These are separate from the 20 husbands and 430 wives "accepted on arrival" as dependents and the 5,980 husbands and 9,120 wives "accepted on removal of time limit" in 1992, having entered earlier for purposes of marriage. While most of this movement is from South Asia, immigration through marriage is increasing rapidly from African Commonwealth countries, a process in which a certain degree of fraud is apparently involved.

[11] Applications from prospective spouses have dropped sharply – by about 2,000 applications per year. Instead, applications from recently married women have increased

and are expected to mirror the loss of fiancées. The 1985 requirement that prospective spouses obtain entry clearance before arrival has delayed the process and depressed the figures dramatically from 4,200 female fiancées admitted in 1985 to 1,000 in 1986 and 540 in 1992.

[12] In rather more detail it can be stated as follows:

1. "To allow genuine visitors and students to enter the United Kingdom."
2. "To give effect to the free movement provisions of European Community law."
3. "Subject to the above, to restrict severely the numbers coming to live permanently or to work in this country, but to continue to admit spouses and minor children of those already settled here, provided they satisfy the requirements of the Immigration rules."
4. "To maintain an effective and efficient system for dealing with applicants for citizenship" (Home Office, 1991).

[13] These are Asians, originally residents in Kenya and other East African Commonwealth countries, who were given UK passports at the granting of independence to these countries. Fears of large-scale immigration prompted the then Labour government in 1968 to impose an annual quota on their entry to the UK.

[14] The Home Secretary claimed that "The 1971 Act was the first comprehensive immigration statute and established a new system of immigration control for both Commonwealth and non-Commonwealth citizens. It sought to bring primary immigration by heads of households down to a level which our crowded island could accommodate. The Act was introduced in the belief that there is a limit to which a society can accept large numbers of people from different cultures without unacceptable social tensions. That remains our view" (Douglas Hurd, House of Commons, 16 November 1987).

[15] For many years UK immigration policy has attracted almost no attention from policy journals such as *Public Policy*. Neither is it given much space in the journals of demography and geography, not even those specializing in immigration such as the *International Migration Review*.

[16] For example, Tim Renton, MP, former Minister of State at the Home Office, said in a speech on 15 April 1988 that "The government also has to tackle the new challenge posed by abuse of the international agreements to protect refugees. Television, radio and travel agents inform people in the Middle East or Far East that there are other places, in Western Europe and North America, where life is more orderly and more prosperous than in their homelands. Cheap international air travel makes it possible for these 'economic refugees' to travel to Germany, or Canada, or Britain. We will never shirk our international obligations to shelter genuine refugees who have fled abroad because of a well founded fear of persecution. But neither we nor our European neighbors will admit people who come simply because of their wish to enjoy a more secure and richer life than was available at home. This wish is understandable enough, but by itself it does not provide a passport to settlement in Western Europe."

Chapter 3

The French Debate: Legal and Political Instruments to Promote Integration

Catherine Wihtol de Wenden

3.1 Introduction

For a century and a half, France has been an immigration country, but this demographic reality has not become an integral part of French national identity and of the definition of citizenship *à la française*. Today immigration is one of the main topics of French political debate. Gates of entry, illegal immigration, second-generation immigrants of North African origin, and their concentration in neglected urban areas are at the center of the controversies. The situation is characterized by discrepancies between demographic realities and political perceptions or common knowledge. Other dilemmas arise in the use of legal and political instruments to promote the integration of immigrants: Equal rights or positive discrimination? The right to be different or the right to assimilate? A wider access to nationality and citizenship or a right to retain collective identities based on ethnicity or religion? The choices are not clear. This chapter examines the evolution of these debates and of French policies and looks at the viewpoints of immigrants and their children.

3.2 From Foreign Workers to Populations of Immigrant Origin

From 1850 to World War I France was confronted with several successive waves of immigration. The number of foreigners living in France was first established in 1851, when the question of "citizenship" was included in the census. This suggests that before 1850 citizenship and immigration were not important issues. According to census results 380,000 foreigners were living in France in 1851. At the beginning of the twentieth century the number had already reached 1 million.

During this period, France faced an influx of foreigners who were employed in industrial development. Besides they also made up for the falling birth rate. At the same time, the concept of nationality was enlarged. Changes were made to the legal definition of nationality in 1867 and 1889. The conflict at the time was between liberals and protectionists. For the protectionists, the purpose was to reduce the growing number of foreigners who could profit from economic growth without having to serve in the army. In view of the worsening relations with Germany, nationalist opinion was convinced that it was urgent to increase the number of Frenchmen, whereas liberal economists and industrial leaders were in favor of using the immigrants as a labor force only. The political choice was to be made between depopulation or denationalization.

The philosophy of assimilation prevailed, at both individual and collective levels. In 1889 access to French nationality was made easier, and in 1884 secular school became compulsory and free of charge. The situation began to change with World War I. In 1916, in order to replace industrial workers serving in the army France recruited colonial workers from the Maghreb and from Asia. Most of them returned to their regions of origin in 1918, but some stayed. The war casualties also aggravated the labor shortage. New waves of Italians and Poles arrived from 1918–20. In 1924, some industrial leaders decided to transfer the recruitment of foreign workers to the "Société Générale d'Immigration". The period was characterized by the lack of an explicit immigration policy. In the meantime, assimilation by naturalization continued: the law of 1927 enlarged access to French nationality. But in 1929, when the world economic crisis started to hit France, the public began to become more xenophobic.[1] In 1930 France had 3 million foreigners. For the first time, a restrictive immigration law was adopted in 1932. It linked residence to employment and introduced a hierarchy of residence permits. This system remained largely unchanged until 1980.

The period 1929–39 was characterized by the creation of the first State Secretary for Immigration (1937) by the left-wing government of Léon Blum. New waves of asylum seekers arrived from Spain, Italy (*fuorusciti*), Germany, and East–Central Europe, fleeing from fascism and the Nazis. At the same time the right-wing press became extremely racist. Some theories on race suggesting a hierarchy of nationalities fueled the public debate on the social costs of immigrants, who were viewed as a collective burden and a danger to the French nation (through disease, delinquency, political threat, or social conflict). World War II played a role in assisting assimilation: through their membership in trade unions, the Communist party, and the French anti-Nazi movement, many foreign workers acquired a new legitimacy after the war.

3.2.1 1945–74

In 1945 the Office National d'Immigration (ONI), was created to recruit foreign workers. In the same year a new law on citizenship was adopted in the context of a liberal immigration policy, to determine which foreigners would be eligible for naturalization and which would remain a temporary labor force. The public authorities tried to select "good" immigrants and their families for permanent settlement and possible naturalization. The Italians, who had not been very welcome between the wars, had become desirable in terms of population policy, but because they arrived in fewer numbers than expected other nationalities were rapidly recruited: Spaniards in the 1950s, Portuguese in the 1960s,[2] Yugoslavs in the 1960s and 1970s, Tunisians and Moroccans in the 1970s, as well as Turks and black Africans. The Algerians who had settled in France since World War I began to bring in their families around the end of the Franco-Algerian war in 1962. In fact the dynamics of immigration were largely independent of the public authorities: recruitment was managed by companies who directly employed forces, rather than labor through the ONI. In 1968, the ONI scarcely recruited 18% of all entries. The other 82% entered as illegals and were legalized in subsequent years.

In 1966 France unsuccessfully tried to give its immigration policy a new institutional frame. A Directorate of Population and Migration was created in 1966 within the Ministry of Labor. In 1972 a first attempt to halt illegal entries was made by the Fontanet–Marcellin circular, by refusing to legalize those who had entered France after 31 December 1971. In 1973, following racial riots in Marseilles, Algeria halted labor emigration and in July 1974 the new State Secretary for Immigration, appointed by Valéry Giscard d'Estaing, suspended further recruitment of foreign workers.

In the mid-1970s, 3.4 million foreigners were living in France, one-third from North Africa (Algeria, Morocco, and Tunisia), another third from Portugal (the largest single immigration group) and Spain, and the rest from Italy and other countries. During the 1980s this geographical pattern of origins changed. The number of migrants from Portugal and Spain fell sharply, while those from Morocco and Tunisia increased.

3.2.2 1974–81

The period 1974–81 was a turning point for immigration in France. A population that was regarded as a labor force of single men, essentially socially and politically marginalized workers, progressively became part of French society. Because of the ban on new recruitments, the inflow of foreign labor was replaced by family reunions. New questions arose from the unexpected side effects of this measure. Conflicts arose from the policy of linking residence and employment.[3] The halt of recruitment and the shift to family reunions led to a new social phenomenon: the "second-generation" immigrants. More and more illegals were demanding the legalization of their status in France. Despite the increasing number of family reunions, two State Secretaries for Immigration, Paul Dijoud and Lionel Stoleru, believed that repatriation would be effective. In 1977, a policy providing lump sum payments for those willing to return was implemented, inspired by the West German model, but this policy failed except in the case of some Spaniards and Portuguese. The overwhelming majority of Algerians refused the offer.

At the same time, the concept of integration, while safeguarding the links with the countries of origin, became more popular while the model of total assimilation lost its appeal. The economic and social costs and benefits of immigration were discussed at the highest level (Le Pors report, 1976). The links of immigrants with their countries of origin were officially recognized by transferring the responsibility for teaching the languages and cultures of these countries in French schools

Table 3.1. Stock of foreign resident populations in France by nationality (thousands).

	1975	1982	1990
Portugal	758.9	767.3	645.6
Algeria	710.7	805.1	619.9
Morocco	260.0	441.3	584.7
Italy	462.9	340.3	253.7
Spain	497.5	327.2	216.0
Tunisia	139.7	190.8	207.5
Turkey	50.9	122.3	201.5
Poland	93.7	64.8	46.3
Yugoslavia	70.3	62.5	51.7
Other countries	397.8	592.6	780.7
Total	3,442.4	3,714.2	3,607.6
Of which EU	1,869.9	1,594.8	1,308.9

to representatives from the countries themselves. That decision raised many debates on the legitimacy of this practice.

But the demand for equal rights was increasing: equal social rights for industrial workers were obtained in 1972 (representation within firms) and in 1975 (union representation). The law of 1972 condemned racism in public life. Another law, adopted in 1980 (the Bonnet law), further restricted entries and the periods of residence of foreigners. This law ended a long period (1945–80) in which immigration "policy" had been implemented as part of administrative measures.

3.2.3 1981 to present

The inflow of foreigners to France peaked in 1982, but then began to diminish. In 1986 only 38,000 regular immigrants came to France. By 1993 their number was increasing again to 63,000. However, the number of asylum seekers has continued to increase: from 18,800 per year in the early 1980s to around 50,000 per year in the early 1990s, but since 1992 it has decreased (see *Tables 3.1* and *3.2*). Some of this decrease was due to changes in statistical calculations. But there has also been a political shift reducing the number of asylum seekers.

The years 1981–86 were characterized by a change in the status of the issue. The increasing centrality of the issue of immigration in French politics led decision makers to insist on the symbolic dimension of legislation and on the enunciative effect of the measures adopted. Until 1981, the emphasis had been on laws dealing with labor, and later with the equal treatment for foreigners and French nationals, but in the

Table 3.2. Stock and inflow of foreign population (thousands).

	Stock of foreign population	Annual inflow of foreign population	Annual inflow of asylum seekers
1980		59.4	18.8
1981		75.0	19.8
1982	3,714.2	144.4	22.5
1983		64.2	22.3
1984		51.4	21.6
1985		43.4	28.8
1986		38.3	26.2
1987		39.0	27.6
1988		44.0	34.3
1989		53.2	61.4
1990	3,607.6	63.1	54.7
1991			50.0

first years of the Socialist Mitterrand government (1981–83) the emphasis shifted to human rights: expulsions of young immigrants illegally living in France were suspended and the rights to family reunification and freedom of association for foreigners were reaffirmed. The main measures took the form of laws to encourage the self-expression of first- and second-generation immigrants. This policy had two dimensions, the second conditional upon the first: to limit illegal immigration and to improve the living conditions of legal immigrants already established in the country. Such aims were not without contradictions, and had some unanticipated effects: the moves to control the flows of immigrants degenerated into increased policing of frontiers (with limited success). And the regularization of illegals in 1982–83 simply attracted more new arrivals. These matters are still far from being resolved. What has changed in the political debate in France during 1981–83 is the significance of immigration in the social imagination and political mythology: the success of the extreme right-wing National Front in the March 1983 local elections revealed to what extent immigration had become a central political issue.

In 1983 stricter border controls and internal controls were introduced to convince the public that the repression of illegal immigrants was given high priority. Other measures adopted in 1984 against illegal migrants involved family reunifications and asylum seekers.

At the same time, various social movements (such as the marches of 1983 and 1984), encouraged by the freedom of association granted to foreigners in 1981, gave an impetus to new forms of political participation and intervention on the part of the second-generation immigrants in French society. A ten-year residence card was introduced in 1984, renewable automatically, thus severing the link between employment and residence. As a result of their successful integration some activists entered the professions and gained access to the middle class. Others started to participate in local politics. New "elites" emerged and became mediators between their ethnic or immigrant group and elected politicians.

In 1986, the change of majority in the National Assembly (from Mitterrand's Socialists to allied Liberals and Conservatives) led to several important changes partly inspired by proposals made by the extreme right. The "Pasqua law" of September 1986 (which dealt with the entry and residence of foreigners), the expulsion of 101 Malians (which received wide media attention), the emphasis placed on French identity, security, and the so-called threat of Islam. The proposed reforms to the Law on Citizenship concerned the right to acquire French nationality by children (foreign nationals) who were born in France and who were living on French territory. These children automatically acquired French nationality at age 18 if they had been living in France for the preceding five years. Both the Conservatives and the extreme Right wanted to withdraw this possibility, arguing that such people were French on paper only, or even French by default. It was also argued that the so-called Franco-Maghrebis (immigrants from Algeria, Morocco, and Tunisia and their children) did not deserve to become French (because of their adherence to Islam, memories of the Algerian war, but also because of suspicions about their civic behavior and their motives for acquiring French citizenship). Therefore the proposed reforms sought to reject the principle that citizenship depends on place of birth (*ius soli*), which had been an important tool of integration since the end of the nineteenth century. Consequently, the debate on immigration was transformed into one on nationality and came to focus on complex legal arguments that were of little interest to the public, not least because they were not understood. A special commission, appointed in June 1987, recommended that the Law on Citizenship should not be changed. At the end of 1987 the reforms were postponed, and the question of immigration was avoided during the presidential campaign of 1988, except when François Mitterrand stated that he was not hostile to extending voting rights to foreigners at the local level. Following Mitterrand's re-election, the Pasqua law (1986) was abolished after certain hesitation. In 1989 the "scarves affair" rapidly turned into a national debate on secularity and multiculturalism, and was resolved by the Constitutional Court (Conseil d'Etat), the Ministry of National Education, and a speech by the king of Morocco on French television. A new policy of integration was implemented with the appointment of Hubert Prevot as chairman of a new High Council on Immigration (Haut Conseil à l'Intégration, 1990) consisting of nine personalities. At the same time nine "sages" appointed in 1990, with a Muslim representative structure (the *Corif*) was installed. The government also decided to tighten measures against illegal entries and to promote local integration of immigrant populations living in neglected suburbs. In late 1990 and early 1991, the Gulf War raised new questions of allegiance and legitimacy, illustrated by debates about the place and loyalty of Franco-Maghrebis and other Muslims serving in the army. With the changes of prime minister in 1991 and 1992, integration policy tended to become more concerned with the social problems leading to ethnic tension, conflicts, and riots. In 1993 allied Liberals and Conservatives won the parliamentary election and formed a government led by Prime Minister Edouard Balladur. In early 1994 this government established a new administrative body in charge of immigration and the control of illegals (DICILEC).

3.3 Immigrants or Citizens?

During the past few years French political debate on immigration has mainly been dealing with the discrepancies between images of immigrants in public opinion (focused on the *beurs* – slang for Arabs or second-generation immigrants of North African origin – who are viewed as delinquents, drug dealers, a reserve army for urban violence, illegals, asylum seekers, and Islamic terrorists) and the socioeconomic, cultural, and demographic reality. This reality was and is marked by integration in daily life, by an immigrant population which is French by birth or becoming so by naturalization, by middle-class immigrants and asylum seekers from the south, by the structural need for illegal workers in some sectors, by the competition between migrants from the south and the east, and by the public demand for stricter controls. The political decision makers tend to fear those in their constituencies who fear immigrants. Thus political decisions became heavily influenced by an agenda set by the extreme Right.

The debate on integration centered on unemployment, the reassertion of collective identities (which sometimes resemble tribalism), and the need to build a secure Europe that excludes non-Europeans. The stronger the exclusion of foreigners, the stronger the claims for exclusive identities, either ethnic or religious. The proclamation of integration as an official political goal led to some controversial questions, such as the enforcement of equal rights or positive discrimination by law. But the question at the core of this debate is still that of citizenship.

3.3.1 The debate on citizenship

In recent years, the presence of long-term residents of immigrant origin in France has provoked new political debates. As a result, discussion within French society has focused on questions such as the definition of the social contract and dual citizenship, which has arisen from the political demands of second-generation Franco-Maghrebis. These demands include the negotiation of collective identities and the unlinking of nationality, citizenship, and local voting rights.

The classical definition of the citizen refers to membership in a state, and is expressed in terms of political rights and duties. Today citizenship *à la française* is on trial alongside immigration. Among the three terms defining the achievements of the French revolution, *Liberté, Egalité, Fraternité*, it is the last, brotherhood, that best defines the French concept of citizenship. In the present context of de-industrialization, the weakening of the working class, unemployment, and the large number of foreigners and persons with dual citizenship, this concept is questioned through the changes within the French population and society. While the classical idea of citizenship is mainly linked to universalism and to the national framework, the new idea of citizenship that emerged in 1986 proposed other criteria for political membership and participation. This new idea was initiated largely by those who are more or less at the periphery of the French political system – namely, the *beurs* – who aim to dissociate citizenship and nationality at the local level to claim voting rights for their parents' generation. The new idea of citizenship is viewed as an answer to the crisis of participation, and is based more on local than on national life, and on residence rather than on nationality and affiliation within an emerging multicultural society where all those who live together can be citizens. The rise of the so-called association movement, which received considerable impetus among the *beurs* with the law of October 1981 (which granted foreigners freedom of association) played an important role in the new claims. In 1987 the legal definition of nationality was changed again. Groups mobilized around the theme of a citizenship based on residence, participation in local life, socialization through the French education system, and integration into daily life. Since then, however, each year has brought new suspicions about the allegiances and citizenship of people from North Africa. Such debates arose around the Salman Rushdie affair, the scarves affair, and the Gulf War.

All of these affairs have brought the issues of French nationality and European identity to the center of the political discussions among Franco-Maghrebis. As they have to prove each day that they are integrated (an integration that increasingly looks like individual assimilation), they try to present an image of themselves as good French citizens and good Europeans while using the traditional tools of collective solidarity and clientelism to do so; the 200 *beurs* elected mainly on an ethnic ticket in the 1989 municipal elections are an example of such contradiction.

Official French political discourse is not so clear. On the one hand, the three reports of the High Council on Integration (Haut Conseil à l'Intégration, created by Prime Minister Michel Rocard in March 1990) of February 1991, November 1991, and February 1992 insisted that "the logic of equality (among citizens) must prevail over that of (protection and special treatment of) minorities." Although the three reports of the High Council on Integration officially eliminated the concept of a multiracial and multicultural society, thus ending 20 years of promotion of the "right to be different", both the political language and local policies show that "minorities", "ethnic communities", "cultural mediations", and "ethnicity", are still more in line with public opinion than the old assimilationist and individualist model of Ernest Renan (the "contrat d'intégration" hinted at in the third report of February 1992).

Another question about citizenship is raised by urban life. In the context of the declining class-based society that has defined citizenship in France for a century, many traditional social links have collapsed. Political, economic, and social involvements were simply the tools of integration. Today it is more at the local level (district, town, or region) that citizenship can be expressed, but at the risk of creating new exclusive identities that will be hostile to changes within the population. Another contradiction exists among Franco-Maghrebis. For most of them, identities are rebuilt or shaped in France. Nationality has ceased to be the main formal dividing line between socioeconomic exclusion and promotion. At the same time the countries of origin no longer offer a possible future. "Localism" has served as an identification point for many immigrants, and has been the base for political, social, and cultural actions, although the young generation now faces a crisis of involvement, high unemployment, and a larger degree of marginalization than their parents.

3.3.2 Legal promotion

Since the mid-1980s integration policy has both matured and become more contradictory in France. Most *beurs'* associations and political decision makers are conscious of the risks of promoting the right to be different. This right can be seen as a prerequisite of preserving cultural or religious identities but also as a means to exclude immigrants from the main stream of society. In the recent past more emphasis was put on political action against ethnic segregation, e.g., by preventing urban ghettos (a Ministry of Towns was created in 1991), by defining 70 pilot areas for integration in 1991, by taking action against school closures (*zônes d'éducation prioritaire*), and by improving the chances of immigrants and their children to become professionals.

Such positive discrimination to achieve equality of rights raises a number of questions. First, for the 3.7 million inhabitants of France who do not have French nationality, there is no equal legal status with those who have acquired citizenship by birth or by naturalization. Even if discriminations are very few in the social sector, this does not go for the political sphere and everyday life. Foreigners not coming from another EU member country are still excluded from voting and other rights considered traditional attributes of citizenship, such as access to the civil service and the right to participate in the exercise of justice. But some rights that were formerly regarded as "political" have progressively come to be viewed as social rights (such as trade union representation in industry in 1975), so there is no basis for denying them to foreigners. Another such example is the right to be appointed at universities or research institutions.

We can expect that rights already granted to EU citizens will have an influence on the future rights of non-EU foreigners in France, such as access to employment in the civil service. The new role of the highest administrative court (the Conseil d'Etat) and of the constitutional court (the Conseil Constitutionnel) will also tend to enlarge the rights granted to non-EU citizens living in France. But the European single market also introduced a new hierarchy among EU citizens, citizens of other West European EFTA countries, and others. For the last group the rights to acquire work and residence permits are restricted which makes it more difficult for them to take up certain jobs that require mobility.

Second, one may believe that equality of rights must be coupled with equal duties, such as respect for secularism, the priority of individualism, universality of collective goods, and the limitation of cultural and religious traditions in the private sphere. But this debate is far from settled.

The report of the High Council on Integration (February 1992) illustrates such debates on legal promotion. Devoted to the theme of the legal and cultural conditions of integration, it focuses on conflicts between law and cultures (questions of personal status, polygamy, sexual equality, military service which in France should include males with dual citizenship, contrary to some bilateral agreements, e.g., between France and Algeria of December 1983). If more social equality can be achieved by measures of positive discrimination (consisting mainly in fighting against the marginalization of immigrants and the emergence of ethnic "ghettos") this sometimes reduces the discourse on immigration to problems of the urban poor. A good example of this is the fact that in the official documents of France's state planning commission (the Commissariat au Plan) the chapter on "Immigration" has been replaced by chapters on marginalization and urban life.

3.3.3 Political promotion

For immigrants and their children, the suburbs of Paris, Lyons, and Marseilles have become new political arenas. Since 1981, these suburbs have been characterized by lower than average rates of participation in local and national elections, the rise of an extreme right-wing party (the National Front), the formation of new neighborhoods shared by French families and immigrant families, and sometimes a cultural vacuum.

During the 1980s, these urban suburbs served as a birthplace for Franco-Maghrebian identity. But the political and social forces having their bases in the suburbs now face a crisis.

For the actors who gained legitimacy in local life, and also in the rapid popularization through the media, are confronted with some contradictions rooted in the game they played. These include the reassertion of the symbols of the French revolution (citizenship, equality, and democracy) but with an accent on collective values of the immigrant groups represented, such as being Muslims in France, ambiguous feelings toward Europe and the Mediterranean (particularly if the single European market means a closure to the south), identification with the American way of life while being proud of the Arab heritage, and mediation with the authorities while building local collective identities as means of protest.

At the same time, ethnicity – not just Arab – becomes an unavoidable category in the French political game. One can see a lack of overall enthusiasm for integration into French society and political life. It is not even clear whether the elected and other representatives of the immigrants still represent the political interests of the second generation.

3.4 Conclusions

Which integration are we dealing with? The French model was built with reference to the state and to citizenship, but today this model must deal with a lack of networks, of leaders, of integrative social structures, and of local mediators. It seems important to create these and to include new citizens, even if they are not nationals, because the lines that were used to distinguish between nationals and foreigners, immigrants, and refugees have now become blurred. But such a dynamization of integration through citizenship cannot be achieved without a very strong political commitment.

Integration has little to do with the new migratory waves, with asylum seekers and illegals, or with the all-European debates. In the French model, the object is mostly a population that is or will become French, and for whom the legal instruments appear to be more useful long-term tools than do the promotion of collective identities within French politics, where there is no room for ethnic votes or for long-term political strategies built on partial identities.

New internal frontiers are appearing. Since summer 1993 there has been a new legal framework (the law on nationality of June 1993 and on residence and entry – the Pasqua law – of July 1993), under which the access of Franco-Maghrebis to French nationality has been restricted to:

- Children born in France after 1 January 1963 to parents born in Algeria before that date (when parts of Algeria had the same status as mainland France) who benefit from the so-called dual *ius soli*, if their parents had been living in France for five years prior to their birth.
- Children of *harkis* (Algerians serving as volunteers in the French armed forces between 1954 and 1962) and of other Muslims repatriated to France since 1962 and whose parents were already French or had the right to apply for French citizenship until 1967.
- Other foreigners (i.e., Tunisians and Moroccans) if they were born in France and resided there without interruption between the ages of 13 and 18. Since June 1993, they can only become French citizens if they willingly apply for French nationality between the ages of 16 and 21; however, this is denied if they have received prison sentences of more than six months.

In the French situation one can presume that such measures correspond more to imaginary frontiers in French minds than to socioeconomic realities and urgent administrative needs. The effects of the new laws are therefore largely symbolic.

Notes

[1] Especially against Italians, Poles, Jews from Central Europe, and refugees from the empires that had collapsed at the end of World War I.

[2] The Portuguese came particularly in 1968–74 to escape from the military service and colonial wars.

[3] The most famous one was a strike between 1976 and 1980 in the office of housing for foreign workers.

Chapter 4

Social and Economic Aspects of Foreign Immigration to Italy

Odo Barsotti and Laura Lecchini

4.1 Italy as a Country of Immigration

Since the mid-1970s most Western European countries have halted or restricted labor recruitment from the Mediterranean countries. At the same time, Italy, then Spain, Greece, and Portugal started to become immigration countries as some of those who had been recruited during the 1950 and 1960s or who had settled in Latin America remigrated. These countries also became destinations for an increasing number of immigrants from Africa and the Middle East. This shift in European migration patterns partly reflects a gradual improvement in the economic situation and the living conditions in Europe's southern peripheries, but it is also an unintended side effect of the restrictive measures taken by the UK, France, Germany, and Switzerland. While those countries closed their doors to non-EU citizens, southern Europe – which was not expecting any mass immigration – only started to regulate this process in the late 1980s.

Recent estimates indicate that a total of about 1.5 million non-EU immigrants are living in Italy (ISTAT, 1990). In relative terms, the number of foreigners living in Italy (less than 5% of total population) is still less than in most other West European countries, yet immigration from Eastern Europe and the Third World to Italy has become a public issue and a source of concern. While in the past many Italians themselves

Table 4.1. Foreigners in Italy from developing and East European countries (the 20 most important flows).

Countries	1985	1986	1987	1988	1989	1990
North Africa						
Morocco	2,634	2,903	15,705	23,549	26,752	77,971
Algeria	1,331	1,403	1,899	2,190	1,757	4,241
Tunisia	4,352	4,928	11,953	14,596	14,145	41,239
Libya	4,030	4,033	5,223	5,510	2,196	2,604
Egypt	6,958	7,183	11,016	12,585	10,209	19,614
Sub-Saharan Africa						
Ethiopia	7,196	7,479	10,528	12,150	7,900	11,946
Somalia	1,843	2,012	3,361	4,211	3,744	9,443
Nigeria	3,844	3,995	3,851	5,298	3,575	6,855
Senegal	316	335	5,719	7,397	8,191	25,107
Cape Verde	3,528	3,614	4,924	5,224	3,814	4,991
Middle East						
Iran	13,025	13,317	16,581	18,023	11,827	14,630
Iraq	1,917	1,939	2,516	2,586	1,594	2,062
Asia						
India	5,307	5,698	7,997	9,142	7,168	11,282
Sri Lanka	2,540	2,372	4,337	5,392	5,117	11,454
China	1,618	1,824	5,382	7,761	8,531	18,665
Philippines	7,621	8,064	15,050	18,075	16,131	34,328
Latin America						
Brazil	4,670	5,347	7,581	9,702	8,716	14,293
Argentina	5,267	5,645	7,018	8,270	6,980	12,839
Eastern Europe						43,432
Poland	10,303	14,005	16,874	10,091	—	
Yugoslavia	13,862	14,525	19,018	21,839	17,124	—
Total	102,162	110,621	176,533	203,591	165,471	366,996

Notes: These data are based on residence permits (1985–90). The 1989 data show a noticeable decrease connected more with a rearrangement of the archives than to an effective decrease on these permits. The noticeable increase in the 1990 data is in part a consequence of the *ex lege* regularizations of 1989.
Sources: CENSIS (1990), for 1985–89 data; Ferruzza and Ricci (1991), for 1990 data.

took the opportunity to emigrate, a growing share of Italian society now fears that immigrants might compete with the national labor force and that the already fragile social and infrastructural systems might not be able to cope with the additional task of integrating the new arrivals. The analysis of recent immigrant flows shows the difference between this relatively new phenomenon and traditional labor migration toward northern Europe (see *Table 4.1*):

- The immigrants come not only from the geographic vicinity and from countries with which Italy has maintained "privileged" relationships in the past (former colonies such as Libya, Eritrea, and Somalia), but also from areas which until now have been only slightly involved in immigration to Europe (e.g., sub-Saharan Africa and East Asia).

- Female immigrants no longer come as dependents but as actors in the migratory process.
- The new migrants use a number of strategies to enter local labor markets or rather they are able to interact with local labor markets that appear to have no apparent need for them. They are frequently adept at inventing work while awaiting better opportunities.

When not taking remigrants and retired EU citizens into account we can clearly see that immigration to Italy is still at the stage where the labor force component prevails. Therefore the average age of the new immigrants falls distinctly within the first categories of active age, and the composition according to sex is definitely asymmetrical within the different national groups, with a varying predominance of males and females (*Table 4.2*) according to the occupational fields and the gender-specific structure of the Italian labor market. So far, only a marginal proportion of all migrants consists of entire family groups; the process of the family reunions is still at the embryonic stage.

Nevertheless the mechanisms of ethnic bridgeheads and chain migration are already becoming visible. Networks of families and friendships appear to be fundamental in promoting the migratory phenomenon, and are even more important than they were for previous immigrants to Europe. The demands of the labor force, in fact, no longer play a direct role in international migrations by means of the direct recruitment of labor in the sending countries. Nowadays, however, the decision to migrate appears to be linked more than before with the migrant's access to information and the backing of some relative or friend who has emigrated before him.

Immigration to Italy seems to be based on individual rather than on collective (e.g., family or clan) decisions (Barsotti, 1988). However, before their departure about 90% of the immigrants obtained some kind of information regarding work possibilities, living arrangements, and how they would be received by the Italians.

If migration from the Third World to Italy is interpreted as labor migration, then part of it might be temporary. It is likely that the original intentions of many migrants, particularly when there is a large distance, physically and culturally, between the country of destination and that of origin, were to stay only for a short time in Italy and to save money for a new start back home. But such biographical intentions may

Table 4.2. Composition by sex and age of the 20 most important flows of foreigners in Italy from developing and East European countries, on the basis of residence permits (1990).

Countries	% Female	% <30 years old	% >60 years old
North Africa			
Morocco	9.4	46.6	0.7
Algeria	18.2	47.6	0.4
Tunisia	11.0	67.0	0.3
Libya	24.0	25.8	13.1
Egypt	14.1	32.6	1.4
Sub-Saharan Africa			
Ethiopia	59.2	41.4	2.7
Somalia	57.5	55.0	1.2
Nigeria	36.0	41.4	0.2
Senegal	3.1	47.5	0.1
Cape Verde	87.5	32.1	0.8
Middle East			
Iran	30.0	22.1	5.1
Iraq	16.5	27.0	2.0
Asia			
India	42.0	38.6	2.0
Sri Lanka	32.9	39.7	0.6
China	37.1	45.2	1.1
Philippines	69.7	36.3	0.6
Latin America			
Brazil	66.8	50.9	3.5
Argentina	49.5	39.0	7.9
Eastern Europe	56.0	38.4	9.0
Total	42.8	40.4	8.0

Source: Ferruzza and Ricci (1991).

fail or undergo transformation. In any case Italy's economic system has reacted to and has tried to glean advantages from the new situation.

4.2 Types of Immigration

4.2.1 Seasonal immigration

Seasonal immigrants come to Italy to join the work force during periods of peak demand, generally in the agricultural sector during harvesting. These are usually male migrants from North Africa, particularly from Morocco and Tunisia. They often hold similar jobs in the opposite seasons in their country of origin. The migration is naturally temporary, repeated from season to season, with the aim of supplementing incomes in the home country from jobs held there during the remainder of the year. For these migrants there is little intention to integrate.

This immigration is extremely useful to the Mediterranean type of agriculture practiced in the south of Italy, which requires a low level of technology, and which may be performed with large numbers of unskilled and highly flexible workers. To a certain extent this agricultural system is part of Italy's hidden economy. The conjunction of this supply of seasonal labor and this particular demand produces a form of immigration that might be called "invisible", since it rarely tends to become explicit on the labor market. Socially it is also scarcely visible, since it is confined to the countryside, it does not touch the social services, and public opinion only becomes aware of it when there are documented acts of violence or disputes among immigrants and Italian workers who are part of the irregular labor market. This type of immigration is hard to control. The provisions made by immigration policies have little effect on it.

4.2.2 Temporary immigration

The "invisible" migration mainly involves people for whom the main purpose of their stay in Italy is to accumulate as much capital as possible in order to reinvest it in activities or to finance the subsistence of family networks in their respective home countries. These immigrants, usually males from sub-Saharan countries, remain strongly attached to their countries of origin, which they left to escape from poverty and long-term unemployment. Many of these migrants show little interest in settling permanently in Italy as they feel distant from both a cultural and a religious point of view. By taking advantage of their skills as merchants and of the solid networks of relatives and friends which, due to the effect of the migratory chain, they have gradually formed in Italy, they have invented their own jobs and found their economic niches. In some cases "street-selling" has become a definite choice, whereas in others it is only accepted while awaiting other situations that the market might offer. In effect, the demand in certain industrial sectors has very quickly adapted to the availability of an increasing mass of young unskilled workers to fill jobs that the local labor force has either snubbed or avoided.

This process of professional mobility toward more stable and guaranteed occupations at the fringes of the formal labor market lays the ground for the stabilization of this foreign labor in Italy and for a different model of integration with the receiving society. Several attempts to regularize the status of these immigrants have contributed to this change. In this process many migrants have modified their original intentions.

4.2.3 Temporary immigration that becomes permanent

Female migrants from the Philippines provide a good example of this process. The migratory intentions of such women, whether married or not, are almost always "family" oriented, primarily to contribute to the "income pooling" of the family at home. Back in the Philippines, the family of the female migrant, which actively participated in her decision to migrate, takes on the burden of rearing her children; in exchange they expect regular transfers of money. This financial backing is used for everyday needs to save the family from poverty and in some cases it even helps the family reach levels of consumption similar to those in the West. Most of the Filipino women in Italy, just like the majority of female immigrants, do full-time domestic work in family homes; 40% of them already had the job before arriving in Italy.

The fact that these female migrants maintain strong ties with their families back home and choose to interrupt their roles as wives and mothers, would suggest that this migration could be classified as temporary. But soon after arrival in Italy most of these women seem to abandon ideas of a quick return to their country of origin, for two reasons:

1. Because many of the traditional channels for Filipino male labor migration (such as the Persian Gulf) have been closed, many of these women became indispensable to their families. In countries like Italy, the types of jobs traditionally given to women in the personal and social services sector seem to be on the increase.
2. Although such work entails a waste of the educational qualifications these women acquired at home (60% have had at least 12 years of education), it provides them with relatively stable jobs and, because they live in their employers' homes, allows for greater savings.

In this situation the final return to the home country is often postponed, and instead at least some of the family are brought to Italy. In this respect the migration intention gradually loses its temporary character, and the Filipinas (and other foreigners living and working under similar conditions) become long-term immigrants.

4.2.4 Structured immigration

Structured immigration concerns those who are already established in stable social environments in Italy. The majority of Iranian and Chinese migrants belong to this category.

Iranian immigrants are among the least recent. The first Iranians arrived in the early 1970s as either political exiles or students, and many of them have received either high school or university education in Italy. Their forced stay in Italy, together with the relative tolerance of their host society at a time when it was not yet suffering from an immigration "invasion", led to a great number of Iranians settling down. Evidence of this stable immigration intention may be seen in the number of mixed marriages, estimated at around 25% of all Iranian marriages in Italy, and in the dynamic social and professional mobility that allowed many of these immigrants to acquire positions appropriate to their level of education. After Khomeini's Islamic revolution this group served as a bridgehead for the next wave of immigrants from Iran.

Chinese immigration is linked even closer to ethnic and other business and economic niches. Unlike other groups, however, Chinese immigrants usually come with their entire families. In most cases this feature also indicates a stable decision to stay and remain in Italy.

4.3 The Labor Market and Immigration

4.3.1 Workers employed in production sectors

In the areas where the Mediterranean type of intensive agriculture is practiced, there is a high demand for large numbers of workers during the harvesting and crop-picking seasons. Farmers and agricultural entrepreneurs are thus forced to rely periodically on immigrant workers. For farmers it is a good bargain. Immigrants, especially if they are working illegally, have to accept both salaries that are well below official contract levels and unattractive working conditions.

On the other hand, the work itself does not "need long periods of training" nor does "the employer look for signs of continuity or professional upgrading" (Bruni and Pinto, 1990). The entrepreneur finds it more convenient, therefore, to choose foreign labor rather than local, since he can easily avoid restrictions, state regulations, and trades union control over working conditions, and thus manages to have extremely flexible and elastic production.

Undoubtedly, this choice could lead to competitive situations in the labor market, particularly in areas with high levels of unemployment, such as southern Italy. However, competition has only rarely caused direct friction between immigrants and local workers competing for the same jobs. As Calvanese (1989) has pointed out, in southern Italy plenty of noncontract, irregular, and underpaid work is also carried out by Italian citizens, and regular and fully paid work is rare for both foreigners and nationals alike. In areas where salaries are normally low and where many locals are already being forced to accept poor working conditions (Pugliese, 1990), the presence of many foreign workers causes salaries and working conditions to deteriorate even further and the younger local workers to abandon agriculture; the latter are no longer willing to accept "indecent" working conditions, even in temporary jobs. For many of them internal migration to northern Italy has become the main alternative. A generation ago immigration to Germany, France, or Switzerland was also common.

Fisheries is another sector which, in some areas at least, employs large numbers of immigrants. It is well known that the number of Tunisian immigrants in this sector is particularly high in western Sicily (Vizzini, 1983; Vaccina, 1983) and in the ports of the Marche and Puglia regions (Vicarelli, 1990; Di Comite *et al.*, 1985). In this manner, the demand side has at its disposal a labor force that is not only cheaper than the locals, but which is also "well trained" to this work under even harder conditions in the country of origin.

In contrast with the agricultural and fisheries sectors, the process of absorption of immigrant labor into industry has only begun to take effect since the late 1980s. This is because it was not directly activated by demand, but was rather the result of the fact that entrepreneurs and firms in the industrial and service sectors have only recently begun to take advantage of the labor force available for particularly heavy, dirty, and underpaid jobs. The integration of foreigners into the industrial production and services sectors is now reaching considerable proportions in the more developed areas in central and northern Italy and appears to be very dynamic. Employment opportunities have opened up for immigrants in those sectors where there is high demand for unskilled work, such as the tanning industries in the Veneto and Tuscany regions, the foundries, the steel, resin, and ceramic works, and the agro-industry in Emilia–Romagna, Lombardy, and Piedmont.

Considering the degree to which the immigrant workers have been absorbed into the vast area of the hidden economy, it may be said that they play a role in the transformation of productive processes, since they seem to slow down structural change (Venturini, 1990). Illegal immigration might cause capital to shift toward the informal sectors of the economy (Dell'Aringa and Neri, 1987), it might bring support to hidden activities, helping them to spread, and it might lower the level of technology (Furcht, 1989; Bruni and Pinto, 1990). The informal economy, "encouraged" by immigrants, might give rise to an element of pressure against the local labor force and supplant Italian nationals working in the formal sector of the economy. On the other hand, when immigrants are given jobs with regular contracts and they officially become employed, as happens in certain sectors in northern Italy, then their role in the jobs market might be complementary to that of the locals and of immigrants from southern Italy. In situations where there are gaps between labor demand and supply, foreigners are employed at short notice to overcome bottlenecks in the production process. They therefore contribute to increases in the level of production and allow local workers to enter or to shift toward higher professional qualifications or hierarchical positions.

The largest share of foreign workers are employed in the labor-intensive, underpaid, and low-prestige segments of the tertiary sector (e.g., small trading businesses, restaurants and hotels, domestic services). In regions with high levels of unemployment and widespread concealed activities, the immigrants might find themselves not only in competition but also in conflict with the local labor force over jobs; whereas in areas with a highly structured labor market and a decidedly seasonal demand for additional labor the role of the immigrants might be considered complementary, especially in regions with low levels of local unemployment.

4.3.2 Domestic workers

Large numbers of immigrants are absorbed by Italy's households. In most cases jobs in domestic services cannot be filled by Italian nationals or would not even be offered, if minimum wages had to be paid. Thus it appears that these jobs were created specifically for the immigrants. As long as the situation remains this way, the role of the immigrant labor force will add to rather than compete with the Italian labor force.

4.3.3 Self-employed workers

As already mentioned, a large number of immigrants from developing countries have established themselves in Italy as self-employed street vendors. Most of them are Maghrebi and Senegalese who take this opportunity while trying to obtain better positions. In this case, the migrants create their own jobs. They are therefore additional jobs which, at the macroeconomic level, can scarcely be considered competitive with similar jobs done by locals. This does not exclude the possibility, however, that the work of these non-EU workers might be seen as a form of unfair competition by people who do not have to bear the same financial and fiscal burdens as the locals.

Although the street vendor is the most common type of self-employed worker and a sort of emblem of the non-EU immigrant, in specific districts and in the larger urban areas in central and northern Italy, more independent and structured activities are taking root. Three examples are: the import and sale of carpets by the Iranians, the production of leather goods, and restaurant-keeping, the two last activities by the Chinese. These forms of business have developed from a favorable mixture of the specific talents of the immigrants themselves, the characteristics of the Italian socioeconomic environment, the possibility of using privileged channels of supply in their home country, and their particular family or group organization.

Several Iranians have managed to create a sort of "slot" for themselves in the production and service market by selling, promoting, and dealing in Persian rugs, a role considered natural and suitable for oriental immigrants by the receiving society. They are therefore appreciated and are only marginally considered to be undesirable competitors.

The businesses run by the Chinese are organized in extremely efficient productive units, based on a burden of work that is shared by the entire family, and which in many cases can be considered as a form of self-exploitation. They have therefore become highly competitive with local entrepreneurs and with noninstitutional forms of work. In some parts of the country, such as on the outskirts of Florence, the production of leather goods even seems to have been "monopolized" by some Chinese.

4.4 Outlook: The Growing Foreign Population

Recent estimates indicate that a total of about 1.5 million non-EU nationals have immigrated to Italy. In comparison with immigration levels to other European countries this number is relatively low, yet the phenomenon is a source of concern. It occurs in an economic system that is already undergoing immense structural modifications, in which the role of the industrial system is being reassessed, and there is a strong tendency toward tertiary sector growth. The Italian economy is also experiencing a chronic excess of labor supply, an increasing qualitative imbalance between labor demand and supply, plus a deterioration in the traditional gap (in terms of employment) between the north and south of the country.

The ability of many migrants to establish themselves in Italy will in the near future encourage an influx of family members and will therefore lead to a change from labor migration to migration settlement. There is no doubt that there will be an increase in the stock of immigrants because of family reunions.

As far as the arrival of new labor forces is concerned, recent regulations in Italy, which conform with EU migration policies, have been introduced to ensure that the flows are planned and regulated according to market requirements and in relation to the strength and capacity of the social system. We shall have to see, however, whether this policy of restricting arrivals will be effective or whether it will increase clandestine and thus unregulated immigration. Such an increase in clandestine arrivals certainly cannot be excluded, because of three factors:

- The deterioration in the balance in terms of differential demographic pressure between the southern and eastern shores of the Mediterranean and the northern shores.
- The particular geographical position of Italy within the Mediterranean and the impossibility of controlling all its frontiers and shores.
- The interaction between the informal economy and immigration, particularly of clandestines.

Although there is no doubt that the first two factors will cause the influx of immigrants to continue, the influence of the informal economy on migration flows is not so evident. One wonders whether the informal economy – which is an ancient practice in the Italian economic system – will grow in the near future as a response of the productive sectors to Italy's structural crisis or whether, due to the crisis itself, it will be reduced.

Second, one must determine whether the informal economic sector as the first area entered by immigrants is also a first step to entry into the formal economy. If so, then the hidden economy might function as a pull factor to attract new immigrants to fill the gaps left by successful old immigrants (Tapinos, 1991). Such substitution might be aided by the mobility of immigrants from the south of Italy, where the concealed economy is widespread, to the industrial areas of the center and north – where the immigrants might find employment in formal sectors of production.

As a likely combined effect of these three factors, we believe that clandestine immigration from Third World countries is likely to increase. Forecasts for 1991–95 made by EUROSTAT (Muus and Cruijsen, 1991) show that of all EU countries, Italy, behind Germany, will have the second highest net immigration.

Chapter 5

Shifting Paradigms: An Appraisal of Immigration in the Netherlands

Han Entzinger

5.1 An Overview of Dutch Immigration History

The Netherlands has a long history of both immigration and emigration. Its geographic location, its maritime tradition, its colonial past, as well as its open borders with neighboring countries, have all shaped this history. During the past few centuries inward and outward flows have alternated, but, above all, the country has been a safe haven for refugees from all over Europe, persecuted because of their religious beliefs. On the other hand, part of the Dutch population left to settle in the colonies or in the New World. In 1700 some 40% of the population of the city of Amsterdam were foreign born, compared with only 25% today (see *Table 5.1*). Overviews of old and new immigration to the Netherlands can be found in Entzinger (1985), Lucassen and Penninx (1986), Social and Cultural Planning Office (1986), and Entzinger and Stijnen (1990).

It was only during the first half of the twentieth century that migration in both directions was relatively unimportant. As a result of this, popular belief in the Netherlands sees immigration and emigration as exceptions rather than the rule. After World War II, migration again gained momentum. The independence of Indonesia in 1949, until then the most important Dutch colony, led to the departure of between 250,000 and 300,000 Dutch citizens, colonizers of European descent, as well as people of mixed origin. Most of them settled in the "mother

Table 5.1. Non-Dutch residents in the Netherlands, in absolute numbers and as a percentage of the population, 1899–1992 (selected years, 1 January, except for 1899–1971).

	Total population	Non-Dutch residents	Non-Dutch residents as percentage of the total population
1899	5,104,100	53,000	1.0
1930	7,935,600	175,200	2.2
1947	9,625,500	103,900	1.1
1960	11,462,000	117,600	1.0
1971	13,060,100	254,800	2.0
1976	13,733,600	350,500	2.6
1981	14,208,600	520,900	3.7
1986	14,529,400	552,500	3.8
1987	14,615,100	568,000	3.9
1988	14,714,900	591,800	4.0
1989	14,804,300	623,700	4.2
1990	14,891,900	640,600	4.3
1991	15,010,400	692,400	4.6
1992	15,138,100	732,900	4.8

Source: Central Bureau of Statistics, The Netherlands.

country", which many had never visited before. In that same period about 400,000 Dutch citizens left their country to settle in immigration countries such as Canada and Australia. It was not until 1961 that the migratory balance of the Netherlands became positive for the first time, later than in most other West European countries. Since then the migration surplus has continued; the year 1967 is the only exception.

Like elsewhere in Northern and Western Europe, during the 1960s and early 1970s unskilled workers were recruited from a number of countries around the Mediterranean. The Netherlands had a rather late start, and this is why relatively few foreign workers came from southern Europe and rather more from more distant countries, particularly Turkey and Morocco. The share of foreign workers in the labor force in this century has never been as high as in neighboring countries, largely because there is little heavy industry and no coal mining in the Netherlands. Moreover, the relatively high birth rates of those days kept the domestic labor force at a satisfactory level. As in other European countries, and contrary to the original idea, many foreign workers did not return to their home countries, but remained in the Netherlands and in many cases they have been joined by their families.

This immigration flow has continued up to the present (see also *Table 5.2*). Many members of the so-called second generation now find their

Table 5.2. Non-Dutch residents in the Netherlands, by selected categories, 1976–92 (1 January, selected years).

		EU[a]		Turkey		Morocco	
	Total	No.	%	No.	%	No.	%
1976	350,500	112,700	32.2	76,500	21.8	42,200	12.0
1981	520,900	134,000	25.7	138,500	26.6	83,400	16.0
1986	552,500	135,000	24.4	156,400	28.3	116,400	21.1
1991	692,400	168,400	24.3	203,500	29.4	156,900	22.7
1992	732,900	176,200	24.0	214,800	29.3	163,700	22.3

[a]EU member states: Belgium, Denmark, France, (West) Germany, Greece (from 1986), Ireland, Italy, Luxembourg, Portugal (from 1991), Spain (from 1991), and the UK.
Source: Central Bureau of Statistics, The Netherlands.

marriage partners in the country from which their parents came. This phenomenon is particularly evident among Turks and Moroccans who, with 230,000 and 190,000 members, respectively (citizens plus naturalized Dutch born in Turkey or Morocco), constitute the two largest immigrant communities. In 1991 alone, about 22,000 Turks and Moroccans settled in the Netherlands. Return migration to these two countries is almost negligible, and acquiring Dutch citizenship has become more popular in recent years. The number of Turkish and Moroccan citizens residing in the Netherlands is now growing more slowly than the number of those whose ethnic origins lie in these countries.

A third major immigration flow of the last decades stems from the Caribbean. For a long time there had been limited migration between the Netherlands and its overseas territories of Suriname and the Dutch Antilles. In the past two decades, however, Suriname, which was a part of the kingdom until it acquired independence in 1975, has seen more than one-third of its population leave for the Netherlands. At present, the number of people of Surinamese descent in the Netherlands is estimated at 240,000, nearly all of whom hold Dutch citizenship. There are also about 80,000 people from the Dutch Antilles (Curaçao and some smaller islands) and Aruba living in the Netherlands. These two small states are autonomous parts of the kingdom; their inhabitants all have Dutch citizenship and are free to settle in the Netherlands.

5.2 Recent Developments

In the early 1980s immigration stagnated for a short period, probably because of the economic situation, but since then it has been rising again. In 1991 immigration of foreign citizens reached a peak of almost 85,000.

Table 5.3. Arrivals and departures of non-Dutch citizens in the Netherlands, 1980–91.

	Arrivals	Departures	Balance	Corrected balance[a]
1980	79,820	23,633	56,187	+50,600
1981	50,416	24,979	25,437	+14,200
1982	40,930	28,094	12,836	−1,100
1983	36,441	27,974	8,467	+2,600
1984	37,291	27,030	10,261	+4,600
1985	46,166	24,206	21,960	+20,200
1986	52,802	23,563	29,239	+26,500
1987	60,855	20,872	39,983	+35,400
1988	58,262	21,388	36,874	+27,800
1989	65,385	21,489	43,896	+17,300
1990	81,264	20,595	60,669	+48,700
1991	84,337	21,330	63,007	+50,000

[a]This column represents the migration balance minus the administrative corrections that relate to non-Dutch citizens (mostly departures that have not been formally registered).
Source: Central Bureau of Statistics, The Netherlands.

The migration balance in that year stood at 63,000 (50,000 if the so-called administrative corrections are accounted for; see also *Table 5.3*). A major difference from previous periods is the greater heterogeneity of the countries of origin, even though one-third of all new arrivals still come from only three countries: Turkey, Morocco, and Suriname, countries with substantial established immigrant communities in the Netherlands. Another important distinction from previous periods is that only a small proportion of the new arrivals find employment shortly after they arrive. Many of the current immigrants are family members of those who have been residents for some time and they are not always sufficiently qualified for the Dutch labor market.

As in many other European countries, the number of asylum seekers has been increasing sharply, although in the last three years it has stagnated at some 20,000 per annum. Only a small percentage of these are actually granted the status of refugee under the Geneva Convention. A considerable number, however, succeed in obtaining another residential status. The category of "tolerated people" created in 1992 includes asylum seekers whose claims have been rejected, but who will not be sent back to their countries (*non-refoulement*). After a waiting period they are allowed to attend courses and take up employment. It is estimated that roughly half of all asylum seekers eventually succeed in acquiring some formal status and subsequently remain in the Netherlands. Of the other half, some may stay illegally. Recent estimates put the number of illegal immigrants at roughly 100,000. They are concentrated in a few sectors of the economy (horticulture, catering, cleaning, clothing industry), where they do the least attractive work for which no other workers appear to be available.

At the opposite end of the labor market there has been a slow, but gradual increase in immigrants from other EU member states. At present, 175,000 citizens of other EU countries reside in the Netherlands, which is relatively few in comparison with most other member states. The largest single groups are the Germans (47,000) and British (41,000). In general, these are people with high qualifications, many of whom are professional workers, and their families. In public opinion these immigrants, and those from other Western countries, are clearly seen as distinct from the other immigrant communities because their social situations and cultural backgrounds are similar to those of the original population of the Netherlands.

5.3 Some Questions of Terminology

The observations given in Section 5.2 already refer to some rather complicated questions of terminology and definition that emerge from any international comparison of migration and its social and political effects. In the Netherlands, immigrants are seldom referred to as foreigners or as foreign citizens, as is the case, for instance, in Germany, Switzerland, or Austria. A major reason for this is that, mainly as a result of the colonial past, there is a substantial number of Dutch citizens from overseas among those who take up residence in the country. The term immigrant, although mentioned frequently in this article, is also rarely used in common Dutch vocabulary in this field. This is in contrast to what is the case in, for instance, France. In the Netherlands, most people of immigrant origin are referred to as ethnic minorities, in line with the Anglo-American use of this term. The concept of ethnic minority not only reflects the minority situation of many immigrants, numerically as well as socially, but it also refers to the fact that their ethnic origins lie outside the Netherlands. More than in most other continental European countries, the public perceives immigrants on the basis of their social, economic, cultural and religious characteristics rather than in legal terms that would reflect their relationship with the state.

The significance of this distinctive approach may be illustrated with some statistical data (see also *Table 5.4*). On 1 January 1990, the number

Table 5.4. Major immigrant groups in the Netherlands, by country of origin and by different criteria, 1 January 1990.

Citizenship/ country of birth	Non-Dutch citizens	Foreign-born Dutch citizens	Total[a]
Belgium	23,300	42,000	132,400
Germany	41,900	127,500	444,000
Indonesia	7,900	187,700	472,600
Morocco	143,700	115,500	168,600
Dutch Antilles/Aruba[b]	—	56,100	84,400
Suriname	16,200	157,100	244,200
Turkey	185,500	141,300	207,000
Total immigrants	641,918	1,166,803	2,232,000

[a]This column includes all persons who fulfil at least one of the following three criteria: non-Dutch citizens, born outside the Netherlands, one or both parents born outside the Netherlands.
[b]The Dutch Antilles and Aruba are autonomous parts of the Kingdom of the Netherlands; their inhabitants are Dutch citizens.
Source: Prins (1991).

of non-Dutch residents in the Netherlands stood at 642,000. By mid-1992 it had increased to 750,000, corresponding to almost 5% of the population of 15.2 million. In early 1990, almost 1.2 million citizens, however, or another 8% of the population had been born abroad, and would therefore logically qualify as immigrants. Many of these were foreign citizens who had become naturalized; others originated from the (former) overseas territories. Finally, around 2.25 million inhabitants either were foreign citizens or had themselves been born outside the Netherlands or had at least one parent for whom this had been the case. No new data have become available since 1990, but in view of the trend in immigration statistics one may assume that at present roughly one out of every six persons (around 18%) living in the Netherlands has direct roots in another country. Who said that the Netherlands was not a country of immigration?

5.4 The Multicultural Approach to "Temporary" Immigration

In spite of substantial immigration, until 1980 official public policy was characterized by the idea that the Netherlands was not a country of immigration. A major argument put forward to support this approach was the country's already dense population. Besides, many immigrants themselves were convinced that one day they would return home. Rotation, in fact, was the idea behind the foreign worker policy as adopted by the Netherlands and other West European countries. Also, for those who had come from (former) colonies – with the exception of most migrants from Indonesia – the principle of return remained valid, often upon completion of their basic education in the "mother country". In reality, growing numbers of the latter were no longer coming for educational purposes, while the former often postponed their return indefinitely. It took a while before the Dutch, including the government, understood that in immigration the return myth might have an important ideological function for immigrant communities, but that it might always remain a myth.

Although the Netherlands did not consider itself a country of immigration until 1980, a policy was designed that aimed at promoting the "well being" of the "temporary guests". As in many other countries, the 1960s and 1970s were years of rapid expansion of the social security system and years of professionalization of social work and social services. Social work agencies, fully subsidized by the state, played the most important role in the reception and counseling of immigrants. In line with the idea of temporariness, migrants were cared for in accordance with rules and habits of their own culture. It was expected that this would facilitate their reintegration upon return. With this same idea in mind, mother tongue teaching was introduced in primary education in 1974, when family reunification had begun to gain momentum.

These efforts to preserve the immigrants' cultural heritage reflect the tradition of the Netherlands as a multicultural society with its institutionalized social and religious diversity. Since the late nineteenth century this has been an important Dutch characteristic. All major cultural and religious communities have had their own associations, trade unions, political parties, schools, and other institutions such as hospitals, housing corporations, social work agencies, and even broadcasting associations for radio and television. This variety of institutions enabled the members of each community to spend most of their lives among themselves, cooperating only at the public level. None of the major communities – Roman Catholics, several Protestant denominations, and Socialists – would ever reach majority status, so they needed each other for legitimate democratic decision making.

When describing this typically Dutch system the metaphor of a classic Greek temple is often used. The public sector is its roof, which is supported jointly by the pillars that represent the various religious and cultural communities. Although this "pillarization" system has lost some of its rigidity since the secularization process that started in the 1960s, it is still easy to distinguish pluralist structures with long-standing traditions in the Netherlands. The Dutch are used to thinking in terms of cultural heterogeneity. They are not unfamiliar with the phenomenon of minorities getting together to work out a compromise that reflects a variety of interests (the classic study of pillarization is Lijphart, 1975).

It is against the background of this tradition of pillarization that Dutch efforts to cope with immigration and its social effects should be interpreted. For a long time, many Dutch, as well as the authorities, held the view that immigration would lead to the establishment of yet another pillar, or rather a number of very small pillars, in a traditionally multicultural society. Thus, public policy was based on the idea that the temporary immigrants' cultural identity should be preserved inside their own, relatively closed institutions.

As the 1970s came to an end, it became increasingly clear that a substantial number of immigrants would not return to their countries of origin. A political debate on forced return migration was quickly abandoned with the argument that immigrant workers had contributed so significantly to the development of the Dutch economy that it would be immoral to send them home against their will. Those who had come from former colonies could not be forced to return either, not only because of their Dutch citizenship, but also because of some feelings of guilt shared by many Dutch over the colonial past. During this same period there was a clear increase in the number of immigrants, primarily as a result of family reunification, and immigrants became more visible in daily life. More or less simultaneously, their labor market situation deteriorated. As a result of economic restructuring and selective dismissals, unemployment among immigrants rose much more steeply than among the native population. Moreover, some terrorist acts, including two train hijackings carried out by young Moluccans, a relatively small group from the former Dutch East Indies, forced the authorities to take immigration and its social consequences more seriously.

In 1979 the Scientific Council for Government Policy (WRR), an independent advisory body to the Prime Minister, recommended that the fiction of temporary residence should be abandoned and that an integration policy on behalf of the immigrants be developed (WRR, 1979). The aim of such a policy would be to promote their participation in social and economic life, as well as to develop good interethnic relations. The council believed that promoting equal opportunity and avoiding discrimination should be the basis of any integration policy. In Dutch history, the concept of egalitarianism has played as predominant a role as the concept of multiculturalism, although at times the two may seem contradictory.

5.5 Minority Policy

The report of the Scientific Council marked an important change in the way of thinking concerning immigration, not only in public opinion, but also in official policy. In 1980 the government formally admitted that the idea that most immigrants would return should be abandoned, and a stricter admission policy was announced. Moreover, the government set up a coordinated policy for the ethnic minorities. It was at that time that this concept began to enter into public speech, although the new "minority policy" was not formally launched until 1983. The Minister of the Interior was given special coordinating competence for this policy, even though all ministers remained responsible for its application in their own respective fields (Minderhedennota, 1983).

In official usage, the concept of ethnic minority is a synonym neither for immigrant nor for foreigner. Minority policy, according to the government, applies to those immigrant groups "for whose presence the government feels a special responsibility [because of the colonial past or because they had been recruited by the authorities], and who find themselves in a minority situation" (Minderhedennota, 1983: 12). The following groups are affected by minority policy: Surinamese, Antilleans and Arubans, Moluccans, Turks, Moroccans, Italians, Spaniards, Portuguese, Greeks, (former) Yugoslavs, Tunisians, Cape Verdians, Gypsies, recognized political refugees, and tinkers (an indigenous semi-nomadic group that had already been subject to special government policy for many years). When the minority policy was designed in 1980 these groups together totaled 450,000 people; since then their number has roughly doubled.

The main elements of minority policy are only partly in line with the recommendations of the Scientific Council. Rather, they represent a mixture of the Council's vision and the multicultural approach of the 1970s:

- Promoting multiculturalism as well as emancipation of ethnic communities.

- Promoting equality before the law.
- Overcoming social deprivation by improving the minorities' economic and social situation.

Thus, the situation of the ethnic minorities was defined simultaneously in social, economic, cultural, and legal terms. The attempt to improve their situation should take all these aspects into account, while a group level approach seems to have been preferred over an individual approach. Minority policy does not apply to those immigrants or foreigners who do not belong to any of the groups mentioned, with the exception of certain legal measures that apply to all non-Dutch citizens residing in the Netherlands.

5.5.1 Multiculturalism

It is this first element in particular that emphasizes the group rather than the individual approach in Dutch minority policy. Initially, the policy of the 1970s, which aimed at preserving and developing migrant cultures, was continued. Mother tongue teaching, for instance, was given a legal basis and was intensified in both private and public schools. More recently, however, as doubts have grown about its effectiveness, its emphasis has been slightly reduced again (Lucassen and Kubben, 1992).

It should be mentioned that, irrespective of minority policy, Dutch law allows for the setting up of private schools of any religious denomination, entirely subsidized with public money. In the past five years about 20 Muslim schools have been established in various parts of the country on the basis of this law, as well as some Hindu schools. Their status is equal to that of Roman Catholic, Protestant, and Jewish schools. In those schools, all of which are of primary level, teaching is in Dutch and the curriculum is in accordance with the directives prescribed by the authorities. It should be noted that only a small minority of Muslim and Hindu immigrants (the latter mainly from Suriname) send their children to these schools.

Another relevant measure in this context is the establishment of consultative councils for each major ethnic minority. Such councils have been created at the national level, by the Ministry of the Interior, as well as at the local level, particularly in cities with substantial immigrant concentrations. Like almost everywhere else in Europe, the largest immigrant concentrations are to be found in the metropolitan areas: 45%

Table 5.5. Ethnic breakdown of the populations of the four major cities of the Netherlands, 1 January 1991.

	Amsterdam	Rotterdam	The Hague	Utrecht
All inhabitants (A)	702,731	582,242	444,181	231,570
Turkish citizens	24,128	28,449	16,798	7,840
Moroccan citizens	33,902	17,202	12,950	13,101
All non-Dutch citizens (B)	108,861	72,579	53,609	27,869
Origins in Suriname/ Dutch Antilles/Aruba (C)	61,679	45,533	34,564	6,876
B as % of A	15.5	12.5	12.1	13.4
(B+C) as % of A	24.3	20.3	19.9	15.0

Source: Muus (1991: 29).

of all ethnic minorities live in the four major cities (Amsterdam, Rotterdam, the Hague, and Utrecht), against a mere 13% within the population as a whole (Muus, 1991; see also *Table 5.5*). The members of these consultative councils are delegates of the main immigrant associations. The authorities are obliged to consult them on any measure that affects the minorities.

In more general terms, the authorities attempt to promote the creation of ethnic associations and organizations at the local, regional, and national levels. Such associations may pursue a variety of aims, ranging from sports activities, social counseling, language courses (both Dutch and mother tongue), to the production of radio and television programs. Subsidizing religious activities is legally forbidden. Certain publicly subsidized activities, however, such as language courses, may take place in mosques.

5.5.2 Equality before the law

An important part of this second element of minority policy is to combat racism and discrimination, for which the penal code has been amended and reinforced. In the Netherlands there is no specific legislation that aims to promote better interethnic relations, as is the case in the UK, the USA, and some other countries. The impression is that existing antidiscrimination legislation is adequate, although not always easy to apply in concrete cases.

A more characteristic element of Dutch minority policy, where it aims to achieve equality before the law, is to grant to all foreign citizens with residence records the same rights and obligations that apply to

Dutch citizens. In the 1980s a number of rights for non-Dutch citizens were gradually extended. First, several pieces of legislation relating to cultural and religious practices were altered to be able to accommodate certain non-Christian or non-Jewish rites, e.g., in funerals or in slaughtering. Foreign residents are now also allowed to enter Dutch public service (with some minor exceptions such as the police and the armed forces).

Perhaps the most interesting example is the granting of active and passive voting rights to foreign residents with residence records of at least five years. The right to vote and to be elected, however, is limited to the municipal and, in some of the larger cities, to the district levels. Participation in provincial and national elections is reserved for Dutch citizens. In the 1986 and 1990 local elections a few dozen foreigners were elected to municipal councils, particularly in the larger cities and in border regions. In both years the participation rate among foreigners remained below the overall average. The large majority of those who voted did so for one of the established Dutch parties and not for immigrant parties.

It is interesting to note that, in spite of this policy of promoting equal treatment of Dutch and foreign citizens, the number of naturalizations has risen substantially in recent years. In 1991, 30,000 foreign citizens obtained Dutch citizenship, corresponding to 4% of the entire foreign population of the country. Many foreign citizens have a rather practical reason for their applications: a Dutch passport generally guarantees uncomplicated travel in Europe and other parts of the world. The naturalization procedure is relatively uncomplicated and not very expensive (ECU 170 as a maximum). The main requirement is five years of uninterrupted stay in the Netherlands; less strict requirements apply to spouses and partners of Dutch citizens. Recently, the government decided to allow dual citizenship, which means that foreigners who have become naturalized no longer have to abandon their old citizenship.

5.5.3 Improving the economic and social situation

This third element of minority policy, to combat social and economic deprivation, has been considerably less successful than the two others. The aim is to promote the minorities' participation in the principal fields and institutions of society up to a level that corresponds to their share in the total population, at the local, regional, or national levels. This idea of proportional representation reflects the typically Dutch idea that ethnic origin, culture, or religion should not affect the possibility of participating in economic and social life. Here multiculturalism and egalitarianism find themselves united!

In reality, developments have been a lot more varied, and also rather differentiated by sector and by minority group. In the field of housing, for instance, the situation of most immigrants has improved substantially over the past ten years. The quality of minority housing is now practically the same as that for the Dutch population of a similar social and economic background. This improvement has been enhanced by the essentially non-discriminatory distribution system for social housing, which in the largest cities includes the majority of all housing.

In education and employment the situation is much less positive. Although school achievements for the second generation are considerably better than they were for the first – in particular for the Surinamese, Antilleans, and Moluccans – the gap between minority and other children remains wide. High school dropout rates, an insufficient knowledge of Dutch, as well as discriminatory practices by employers, constitute major obstacles to the successful entrance of these youngsters to the labor market. It is precisely in the labor market where the situation is worst. The unemployment rate among Turks and Moroccans (depending on the definition chosen) stands at between 21 and 36% of the labor force. For the Surinamese and the Antilleans the corresponding figure is between 17 and 31%, whereas only 7% of the nonimmigrant population is unemployed (Social and Cultural Planning Office, 1992: 66). In recent years, the last number has gradually declined, while minority percentages have remained high, despite numerous efforts to promote integration into the labor market.

Obviously, this difference between minorities and the majority is explained partly by differences in the average level of training and education. It is interesting to note that this aspect of different starting positions is sometimes overlooked by the authorities when they compare the social situation of different communities (Delcroix, 1991). Nevertheless, even when the statistics are corrected for such differences, the employment rate of ethnic minorities remains well below that of the Dutch with corresponding educational levels. More than ten years of minority policy have not led to any improvement in this crucial area, even though this can partly be seen as a result of continuing immigration of people who are insufficiently qualified for the Dutch labor market. It must be concluded, however, that instruments such as improved vocational training, intensified employment services, special job programs, etc., have not been very successful. Moreover, in the past ten years the number of unskilled jobs has diminished as a result of a fundamental restructuring of the Dutch economy. Most minority groups are faced with a wide gap between supply and demand in the labor market, and their employment prospects are not very hopeful.

5.6 The New Turn: More Emphasis on Integration

For a long time, the negative long-term social effects of persistent high unemployment among ethnic minorities have been insufficiently acknowledged. The minorities' full entitlement to social security benefits was considered an acceptable alternative that enabled those affected by unemployment to live a decent life. As in the 1970s, many Dutch still see minorities as objects of welfare-state care rather than as a labor-market potential. Only in recent years has awareness grown that such an approach is not only paternalistic, but that it may also encourage the process of marginalization among certain minority communities. A considerable number of immigrants, for instance, still do not speak Dutch, even after 20 years of residence. Many have hardly ever met a Dutch person, and withdraw into their own communities. Many are not in a position to structure their lives, because the daily routine that a regular job imposes upon the individual is lacking. Under such circumstances the challenges offered by fundamentalism or by crime may serve as substitutes in cases where there are no other opportunities that would enable ethnic minority members to familiarize themselves with the society that surrounds them.

At the same time, this surrounding society is not always aware of the cultural bias that is inherent in any system through which goods and services are distributed. The school system, the labor market, and social and cultural services all tend to disadvantage those members of a society who are less familiar with the rules and regulations that govern such institutions and their functioning. In the literature, this phenomenon is known as discrimination. A distinction can be made between conscious or deliberate discrimination, on the one hand, where differential treatment and disadvantaging of certain groups or individuals is an explicit aim, and nondeliberate discrimination, on the other. Here, differential treatment is not an aim, but an effect of the application of existing rules.

There is growing awareness in Dutch society, as well as among the authorities, that the cumulated effects of nondeliberate discrimination against ethnic minorities can be quite strong, and that this accounts to a large extent for the persistent unemployment. Therefore, it is now felt that the search for policy measures to counter these effects must be intensified.

This rather gloomy analysis of the situation of ethnic minorities is largely based on the second report of the Scientific Council for Government Policy to the government in 1989, ten years after the Council's first report (WRR, 1989). In this second report the Council argued that not only the immigrants' presence would be permanent, but also immigration itself had become a permanent feature in West European societies. Immigration, according to the Council, would continue as long as the gap between the poor and the rich persists at the global level. Besides, immigration is enhanced by the presence of substantial immigrant communities in Europe. In the Council's view, introducing more restrictions in immigration policy would have only a marginal effect.

As regards future minority policy, the Scientific Council recommended putting more emphasis on economic and social integration, particularly in the labor market, in education, and in vocational training. A country that admits immigrants should also offer them an opportunity to further develop their capacities, so that they can be self-supporting, rather than rely on the social-security system for the remainder of their potential professional lives. To achieve this aim, the Council proposed a number of policy instruments, including, for instance, a major intensification of language training (in some cases even compulsory), a "welcome policy" for newly arrived immigrants, as well as an improvement of teaching methods of Dutch as a second language in primary education.

The Council also recommended the introduction of certain forms of positive action in the labor market, including a legal obligation for employers to report publicly on their efforts to recruit members of ethnic minority groups. Such a law would be similar to the Canadian Employment Equity Law introduced in the mid-1980s, which does not prescribe quotas; it is meant to encourage employers to be more conscious about the possible negative effects for ethnic minorities of their traditional recruitment practices and personnel policies. The Council suggested that changing some of their procedures and making some additional effort would give them better access to the immigrant potential in the labor market. If this potential is neglected, the general employment situation will worsen, particularly among the large numbers of young people of immigrant origin in the larger cities. Positive action should be distinguished from positive discrimination: entry requirements should never be lowered, as this will soon backfire to all members of the group concerned.

There can be little doubt that, during the three years since the publication of the Scientific Council's second report, the appreciation of immigration and the political discourse in this area have changed (Nederlands Gesprek Centrum, 1992). Some of the measures proposed by the Council have already been implemented, although mostly in an experimental form. At present, no less than two bills on employment equity are on the parliamentary agenda, one proposed by the coalition government and one by the opposition.

A review of the three elements of minority policy indicates that there has been a general shift toward the third element, the promotion of social and economic integration. All major measures to improve the immigrants' legal position have already been put into practice. It is the multicultural aspect of public policy that has lost some of its importance over the past ten years. In fact, subsidies for social and cultural activities of ethnic minorities have been reduced or discontinued, mother tongue teaching has become more disputed, and establishing ethnic and immigrant organizations as well as encouraging other initiatives among these communities is now largely seen as the responsibility of the immigrants themselves, and no longer of the authorities.

Since the autumn of 1991 the public debate on immigration and the future of ethnic minorities has intensified. The issues are much higher on the political agenda than ever before. The debate was provoked by Frits Bolkestein, parliamentary leader of the VVD, the Conservative-Liberal party (Bolkestein, 1991). He made some comments on the subject without the usual reserve, which, until then, had been so typical of the public debate in this field full of taboos. Since then, attitudes toward immigration and minority cultures appear to have become harsher – some would say more realistic – among certain segments of the population. The tone of the public discussion on illegal immigrants that took place in the aftermath of the Amsterdam air crash in October 1992 reflected a degree of xenophobia that had hitherto been almost unknown in the Netherlands.

Yet, it would be an exaggeration to argue that the tone of the debate on immigration in the Netherlands is now similar to those in countries like France, Germany, or Belgium, all of which have strong right-wing anti-immigrant movements. The Netherlands also has its anti-immigrant party (the Center-Democrats) that has occupied one seat out of 150 in parliament for most of the past ten years and that also has a few seats on the largest city councils. Yet, with the exception of some regrettable, but relatively minor attacks against homes for asylum seekers and Muslim institutions, there have been no violent clashes so far between minorities and the majority or between minorities and the police.

It is evident that the immigration issue and, above all, the future of multi-ethnicity are currently being re-evaluated. To most observers and politicians it is clear now that a strategy of achieving equality before the law and respect for immigrant cultures has not prevented processes of social marginalization from taking place. The provisions of the welfare state, traditionally well developed in the Netherlands, have prevented "ghettoization" and large-scale poverty among immigrants. At the same time, however, these provisions have enhanced their dependency on the state, and have discouraged them from familiarizing themselves with the demands of modern Dutch society.

Today, as in 1980, the Netherlands is confronted with a change in the approach to the integration of its immigrants. It appears that the "minority model" is slowly being replaced by the "integration model", at least in public policy. It is beyond doubt that ethnic and religious pluralism, insofar as it remains within the limits imposed by the law, will continue to be recognized in the future, as it has been recognized in the past. For historical reasons the degree of pluralism that the law permits (in education or in broadcasting, for example) is greater than in most other European countries. It seems likely, however, that future appeals on such facilities for institutionalized pluralism will have to come from the ethnic communities themselves, rather than from public authorities, as has often been the case until now. The title of a recent publication that summarizes the recent debate, *Opinions on Immigrant Compatriots: Integration or Assimilation?* (Meningen over Medelanders, 1992), is indicative of this trend.

5.7 Conclusions

For a long time, the Dutch approach to immigration was based on the assumption that most of the immigrants would eventually return to their countries of origin. Since 1980 official policy has acknowledged that the immigrants are here to stay. Nevertheless, despite an immigration surplus of over 60,000 in 1991, and its continuing upward trend, the Netherlands still does not consider itself a country of immigration. In this respect, past and current Dutch immigration policy can be compared with those in Germany, Switzerland, and Austria.

A second characteristic of the Dutch approach is its strong reliance on welfare-state provisions as a means of accommodating immigration. This should be seen as an attempt to promote equal opportunity, irrespective of an individual's legal situation and of the actual contribution of that individual to the economy. The idea has been that immigrants should not be treated as second-class citizens, an approach that is also characteristic of the Scandinavian countries, especially Sweden, which is often regarded as a model for the welfare state. In recent years, however, this approach has hardened somewhat, mainly because of a more general reappraisal of the role of the state in social and economic life.

The third and final characteristic of Dutch policy is cultural pluralism. This characteristic stands in sharp contrast to the assimilationist approach in France, while there are certain similarities with the UK and Sweden. The tradition of pluralism in the Netherlands, however, is stronger than in the latter two countries, and it is against the background of that tradition that Dutch multiculturalism in the field of immigration as well as the concept of "ethnic minority" should be understood. In this field too, however, certain changes are taking place. Public awareness is growing that equal opportunity and multiculturalism cannot be pursued simultaneously in all circumstances.

Do these recent shifts imply the end of the ethnic minority concept? The answer to this question is both yes and no. No, because any policy that aims to integrate immigrants into a new society is doomed to failure if it does not take sufficient account of different cultural, legal, linguistic, and other conditions. In the "reception policy" for newly arrived immigrants that is currently being developed, this awareness has certainly been preserved. On the other hand, it should be noted that implementing a multiculturalist policy becomes more difficult, if not more archaic, as the immigrants become better integrated into the main sectors of society. It is not always easy to determine what a third-generation Surinamese immigrant has in common with one who arrived only yesterday. Current policy, however, denies the relevance of such differences. Schools, for example, receive an additional subsidy for every student who belongs to one of the recognized ethnic minority groups, without taking into account individual and group differences. Such a policy does not account for the rather rapid changes that often occur in the cultural orientation of immigrants. Even under conditions that favor the recognition and acceptance of immigrant cultures, such as those in the Netherlands, the third generation has little in common with the first, as is shown in the rich immigration history of the USA. Besides, the growing importance of intermarriage, a classic sign of integration, makes it more difficult for the authorities to define the criteria for minority membership.

It should also be remembered that, even at the moment of arrival, the immigrant population is much more heterogeneous than the receiving society may think. Authorities tend above all to see what immigrants have in common and what distinguishes them from the rest of the population: their immigrant status, their unfamiliarity with the new country and its language, and sometimes their religion. On that basis they are defined as one ethnic or national community. They often see themselves forced to overcome old political, regional, or other attitudes which they have brought with them from their country of origin. As time goes by, the immigrant population becomes more, rather than less diverse, particularly in the second and third generations. The relevance of a shared parental origin decreases, whereas other criteria for social classification may become more important.

It is still uncertain whether what has just been said about shifting criteria for classification is also valid for the role of religion. For certain members of the second generation, in the Netherlands and elsewhere in Western Europe, religious affiliation tends to replace ethnic or national origin as a criterion for organization. It is interesting to note that, even in the Netherlands, where minorities are traditionally classified by country of origin, the role of Islam is now slowly gaining importance, not only as a basis for institutionalization of certain initiatives among people of immigrant origin, but also in the public debate on immigration. Other members of the second generation, however, are going through a process of secularization and are distancing themselves from the religious beliefs of their parents.

We may conclude that the current shift of public policy in the Netherlands will leave less room for multiculturalism, and put more emphasis on the need for integration, particularly in social and economic life. The predominant role of the concept of "ethnic minority" in the Dutch approach to immigration in the past two decades will slowly disappear. Nevertheless, given the long Dutch tradition of multiculturalism and the degree to which pluralism has been institutionalized in Dutch society, it can be expected that the forces of assimilation in the Netherlands will remain less strong than those in most other countries in Western Europe.

Chapter 6

Dynamics of Immigration in a Nonimmigrant Country: Germany

Hedwig Rudolph

6.1 Germany as a Country of Immigration?

Germany has a long history of considerable influx of both foreigners and foreign-born people. Most political and scientific discussions differentiate between foreign labor, refugees, asylum seekers, and people of "German origin" living abroad. As a rule people in the last category are not regarded as migrants. However, the last group has by far outnumbered the others in the period since World War II. Although more than 20 million people have come to the country during these 46 years (see Fassmann and Münz, Chapter 1, this volume), Germany insists on defining itself as a nonimmigrant country. No immigration law exists. The basic pattern of German political discourse strongly defends the nation-state and a concept of nationality based on *ius sanguinis*. The contradiction between the demands of economic rationality and the ideological position remained the characteristic feature of German nonimmigration policies.

As early as 1880, political regulations and administrative institutions were introduced to recruit labor from neighboring countries (Herbert, 1986). During the following decades the figures and structure of foreign labor in Germany clearly reflected which economic branches were experiencing difficulties in attracting an adequate work force under prevailing conditions, especially wage rates.

Over time, a set of instruments and regulations was developed that allowed a fairly flexible use of foreign labor. The basic "invention" has been the legal concept of a "foreigner", that is, a person who can claim only limited civil rights and whose right to stay and access to gainful employment are restricted (Dohse, 1981). The main aspects of the weaker status for foreigners are:

- The principle of priority for Germans over foreigners concerning access to the labor market.
- Temporally limited employment permits for foreigners.
- Restricted regional mobility for foreigners.
- Additional systematic discrimination against foreign women.

Obviously, the room for maneuver by the labor market authorities is considerably increased if part of the work force has to accept a marginal status as it is characterized by these restrictions. The existence of some type of "reserve army" improves the functioning of the labor market without too much strain on the incentive system – especially the level and structure of wages.

The situation becomes more complex to the extent that a country wants or has to come up to the norms of civil society. This would demand striving for a balance between national economic needs, on the one hand, and civil as well as social rights of foreign labor, on the other (Hollifield, 1992). West German politics entered this stage in the early 1970s indicated by legal improvements concerning permits to stay for foreign labor.

For decades, the German labor market took advantage of the fact that levels of economic activity were lower in neighboring countries. This gap in the structure of opportunities provided plenty of volunteers looking for employment even in hard, relatively low-paying, contingent jobs. During World War II, economic incentives were replaced by repressive measures and violence. Large numbers of people from the countries occupied by the German army were forced to work in German industry and agriculture. In the summer of 1944, this compulsory foreign work force amounted to 5.7 million, one-third of them women. It need not be stressed that no one ever regarded them as migrants.

6.2 German Refugees, *Übersiedler*, and *Aussiedler*

After 1945, the huge migration flows to and within Germany made clear how fundamentally the war had changed the geopolitical landscape and the balance of power in Europe. The majority of these migrants were German citizens who had been expelled from the former Eastern provinces of the country and ethnic Germans from countries in Central and Eastern Europe. The forced exodus of millions of Germans had been decided by the allied powers as a collective punishment. Moreover, the expulsion seemed to be justified by a logic of ethnic segregation that was expected to solve once and for all the nationality quarrels in these countries. Three subgroups of postwar migration to Germany corresponding to three periods can be differentiated.

Between 1945 and 1950, 12.5 million refugees arrived in Germany. Most of them (60%, or about 8 million) settled in the western part of Germany (the later FRG), 40% (or 4.6 million) in the Soviet military zone (the later GDR). An unknown number of German refugees in the GDR became part of the migration from the GDR to the FRG in the following decades (*Übersiedler*).[1] Between 1950 and 1961 the migration flows between the FRG and the GDR were quite asymmetrical: 3.6 million going West, 0.5 million going East. After the Berlin Wall was built, the migration flow from the GDR did not stop completely; between 1961 and 1989 the net migration flow comprised more than 600,000 people (see *Table 6.1*). The number of German refugees from the GDR outnumbered those from Eastern Europe between 1950 and 1960. At the end of this period almost one out of four German inhabitants in the FRG was a refugee. In the period 1950–92, 2.9 million people of German origin (*Aussiedler*) settled in Germany; 50% from Poland.

At the time when the "guest-worker" policy was officially ended political initiatives had already been taken that secured an additional influx of people into Germany from the East. Early in the 1970s, bilateral treaties were signed by the federal government with Central and East European countries as part of the "new policy" *vis-à-vis* the East. An important issue was to achieve freedom of exit for the minorities of "ethnic Germans" who could expect special support in the FRG: financial aid, priority for housing, (re-)training programs, and language courses. However, the treaties did not have a substantial impact on the

Table 6.1. Migration between the FRG and the GDR (thousands).

Year	GDR to FRG	FRG to GDR	Net flow
1950	302.8	40.0	262.8
1951	251.3	29.3	222.0
1952	214.4	25.3	189.2
1953	518.9	22.1	496.8
1954	334.3	43.3	291.0
1955	439.5	42.5	397.0
1956	448.1	40.4	407.7
1957	418.6	47.0	371.6
1958	259.8	33.1	226.7
1959	182.7	32.1	150.6
1960	247.8	25.4	222.3
1961	236.4	19.7	216.7
1962	21.5	8.8	12.7
1963	47.1	4.7	42.4
1964	39.3	4.9	34.4
1965	29.5	5.6	23.9
1966	24.3	4.3	20.1
1967	20.7	3.6	17.0
1968	18.6	2.9	15.7
1969	20.6	2.5	18.1
1970	20.7	2.1	18.6
1971	19.9	1.8	18.0
1972	19.7	1.8	18.0
1973	17.3	1.7	15.6
1974	16.2	1.5	14.6
1975	20.3	1.4	18.9
1976	17.1	1.3	15.8
1977	13.9	1.2	12.7
1978	14.4	1.2	13.2
1979	15.4	1.4	14.0
1980	15.8	1.6	14.2
1981	18.3	1.7	16.5
1982	15.5	1.5	14.0
1983	13.4	1.3	12.1
1984	42.3	1.6	40.7
1985	28.4	2.0	26.4
1986	29.5	2.6	26.8
1987	22.8	2.4	20.4
1988	43.3	2.5	40.8
1989	399.4	5.1	383.3
1990	395.4	36.2	359.2
Total 1950–90	5,275.2	511.4	4,752.5

Note: The numbers of migrants between 1950 and 1956 do not include migration to and from the Saarland. The numbers of migrants for 1950 and 1951 do not include migration between the two halves of Berlin. Due to rounding errors the net flow may differ from influx minus outflow.
Sources: Statistisches Bundesamt; Bundesverwaltungsamt; Bundesinstitut für Bevölkerungsforschung.

number of *Aussiedler* before the second half of the 1970s; a kind of explosion took place late in the 1980s. Another 1.4 million arrived in 1988–92. *Table 6.2* illustrates the correlation of the size and structure of the influx with periods of political crisis in the countries of origin.

There was a drastic reorientation of the policies concerning ethnic Germans in mid-1990. Priority was going to be given to improving the economic, social, and political situation of ethnic German minorities in their East European home countries. The political intention to "persuade" them to stay was enforced by changes in administrative procedures and financial regulations that made the transfer to Germany much more cumbersome and less attractive. This reappraisal of policies was influenced by increasing problems of economic and social integration of the ethnic Germans in the united Germany. Even after a decade a gap concerning social status and economic standards between resident Germans and ethnic Germans could not be ignored (Malchov *et al.*, 1990); female ethnic Germans were even more disadvantaged (Elzner *et al.*, 1992). Being Germans, the ethnic Germans could not simply be relegated to the lowest segments of the labor market where vacancies persisted. On the other hand, the structure and level of their vocational skills as well as their poor German language abilities were considerable handicaps to employment. The decisive event that triggered a change was the process of German unification and the perspective that the necessary restructuring of the East German economy would create a considerable internal "reserve army".

The revisions of the judicial specification of "German origin" and of the privileges attached to it illustrate that the concept of nationality is politically constructed and can be reshaped under varying political or economic circumstances.

The successful integration of millions of refugees from the East during the first decade after World War II has sometimes been referred to as the genuine economic miracle of Germany. However, there was no magic at all. The specific framework for this growth scenario was a perfect matching of the structure of opportunities and economic incentives, on the one hand, with the skills and attitudes of individuals, on the other. In contrast to popular views, the production capacity of West German industry that had been enlarged enormously during the war was only marginally reduced by bombs. The most serious bottleneck in the early postwar period was labor, and in this situation the German refugees were an important economic resource. Because they had lost most, if not all,

Table 6.2. *Aussiedler* returning to the FRG, 1950–92 (thousands).

Year	Total	Former USSR	Poland	Former Czecho-slovakia	Hungary	Romania	Former Yugoslavia
1950	47.2	0.0	31.8	13.3	0.0	0.0	0.2
1951	21.1	1.7	10.8	3.5	0.2	1.0	3.7
1952	4.0	0.1	0.2	0.1	0.0	0.0	3.4
1953	8.3	0.0	0.1	0.1	0.0	0.0	8.0
1954	10.4	0.0	0.7	0.1	0.0	0.0	9.5
1955	13.2	0.2	0.9	0.2	0.1	0.0	11.8
1956	25.3	1.0	15.7	1.0	0.2	0.2	7.3
1957	107.7	0.9	98.3	0.8	2.2	0.4	5.1
1958	129.7	4.1	117.6	0.7	1.2	1.4	4.7
1959	27.1	5.6	16.3	0.6	0.5	0.4	3.8
1960	18.2	3.3	7.7	1.4	0.3	2.1	3.3
1961	16.4	0.3	9.3	1.2	0.2	3.3	2.1
1962	15.7	0.9	9.7	1.2	0.3	1.7	2.0
1963	14.9	0.2	9.5	1.0	0.3	1.3	2.5
1964	20.1	0.2	13.6	2.7	0.4	0.8	2.3
1965	23.9	0.4	14.6	3.2	0.7	2.7	2.2
1966	27.8	1.3	17.3	5.9	0.6	0.6	2.1
1967	26.2	1.1	10.9	11.6	0.3	0.4	1.9
1968	23.2	0.6	8.4	11.9	0.3	0.6	1.4
1969	29.9	0.3	9.5	15.6	0.4	2.7	1.3
1970	19.1	0.3	5.6	4.7	0.5	6.5	1.4
1971	33.2	1.1	25.2	2.3	0.5	2.8	1.2
1972	23.6	3.4	13.5	0.9	0.5	4.4	0.9
1973	22.7	4.5	8.9	0.5	0.4	7.6	0.9
1974	24.3	6.5	7.8	0.4	0.4	8.5	0.6
1975	19.3	6.0	7.0	0.5	0.3	5.1	0.4
1976	44.2	9.7	29.4	0.8	0.2	3.8	0.3
1977	54.2	9.3	32.9	0.6	0.2	11.0	0.3
1978	58.1	8.5	36.1	0.9	0.3	12.1	0.2
1979	54.8	7.2	36.3	1.1	0.4	9.7	0.2
1980	52.0	7.0	26.6	1.7	0.6	15.8	0.3
1981	69.3	3.8	51.0	1.6	0.7	12.0	0.2
1982	48.0	2.1	30.4	1.8	0.6	13.0	0.2
1983	37.8	1.4	19.1	1.2	0.5	15.5	0.1
1984	36.4	0.9	17.5	1.0	0.3	16.5	0.2
1985	38.9	0.5	22.1	0.8	0.5	14.9	0.2
1986	42.7	0.8	27.2	0.9	0.6	13.1	0.2
1987	78.5	14.5	48.4	0.8	0.6	14.0	0.2
1988	202.6	47.6	140.2	0.9	0.8	12.9	0.2
1989	377.0	98.1	250.3	2.0	1.6	23.4	1.5
1990	397.1	148.0	133.9	1.7	1.3	111.2	1.0
1991	222.0	147.3	40.1	0.9	1.0	32.2	0.5
1992	230.5	195.6	17.7	0.5	0.4	16.1	0.2
Total 1950–92	2,796.8	746.2	1,430.0	104.7	21.3	401.8	89.7
in %	100.0	26.7	51.1	3.7	0.8	14.4	3.2

Note: Between 1950 and 1991, 3036 resettlers came from "other" regions and 52,550 resettlers traveled to Germany via foreign countries.
Source: Bundesverwaltungsamt, Cologne.

of their property (many of them having been farmers in the East) they had to make their living in salaried employment.

Although many social tensions are reported to have built up – the local Germans articulated fears of being marginalized – the refugees were quickly integrated. They participated in the economic takeoff that they had made possible. Not only did they accept partial compensation for the loss of their property (on average 22%; Neuhoff, 1979), but they were also prepared to take jobs below their skill standards and to move to regions where work was offered (Körner, 1976). Working hard was their main chance to improve their social status. For female refugees access to gainful employment was limited by the supply of adequate jobs in the regions where they had to stay (in view of housing capacities) or where they had to move (in view of their partner's job). The experience of the war as a national and individual disaster had generated attitudes of humility that made these German refugees from the East hard workers.

6.3 Guest Workers

As early as 1955, when the unemployment rate was down to 5% and the number of registered unemployed equaled that of job vacancies, the German federal ministry of commerce took the initiative to systematically recruit foreign labor. The political preference for this way of supporting the flexibility of the labor market was openly confirmed and shared by the trades unions. The alternative, namely, to increase the female employment rate, was discarded as too costly and conflicting with the traditional family ideology (Dohse, 1981: 56; Herbert, 1986: 192).

Eight bilateral contracts (Italy 1955, Spain and Greece 1960, Turkey 1961, Morocco 1963, Tunisia 1965, Portugal 1964, Yugoslavia 1968) provided the basis for a rapidly increasing – although not steady – influx of guest workers. *Table 6.3* shows the growing numbers of the respective foreign workers after the dates of the contracts. The table also reflects the mild reduction due to the economic recession in 1967–68, the stronger cuts after the ending of recruitment in 1973, and the effects of financial incentives for foreign workers to return to their home countries which were temporarily introduced in 1984.

The national contracts were implemented by an elaborate bureaucratic procedure for recruitment. No foreigner could simply come to

Table 6.3. Foreign inhabitants and foreign labor in western Germany (including West Berlin) by selected nationalities, 1954–91 (thousands).

Year	Foreign population	Foreign labor total	Employed persons				
			Italians	Spani-ards	Greeks	Turks	Former Yugoslavs
1954	481.9	72.9	6.5	0.4	0.5	—	1.8
1955	484.8	79.6	7.5	0.5	0.6	—	2.1
1956	—	98.8	18.6	0.7	1.0	—	2.3
1957	—	108.2	19.1	1.0	1.8	—	2.8
1958	—	127.1	25.6	1.5	2.8	—	4.8
1959	—	166.8	48.8	2.2	4.1	—	7.3
1960	—	329.4	144.2	16.5	20.8	2.5	8.8
1961	686.1	548.9	224.6	61.8	52.3	—	—
1962	—	711.5	276.8	94.0	80.7	18.6	23.6
1963	—	828.7	287.0	119.6	116.9	33.0	44.4
1964	—	985.6	296.1	151.1	154.8	85.2	53.1
1965	—	1,216.8	372.2	182.8	187.2	132.8	64.1
1966	—	1,313.5	391.3	178.2	194.6	161.0	96.7
1967	1,806.7	991.3	266.8	118.0	140.3	131.3	95.7
1968	1,924.2	1,089.9	304.0	115.9	144.7	152.9	119.1
1969	2,381.1	1,501.4	349.0	143.1	191.2	244.3	265.0
1970	2,976.5	1,949.0	381.8	171.7	242.2	353.9	423.2
1971	3,438.7	2,240.8	408.0	186.6	268.7	453.1	478.3
1972	3,526.6	2,352.4	426.4	184.2	270.1	511.1	474.9
1973	3,966.2	2,595.0	450.0	190.0	250.0	605.0	535.0
1974	4,127.4	2,286.6	331.5	149.7	229.2	606.8	466.7
1975	4,089.6	2,038.8	292.4	124.5	196.2	543.3	415.9
1976	3,948.3	1,920.9	279.1	107.6	173.1	521.0	387.2
1977	3,948.3	1,888.6	281.2	100.3	162.5	517.5	377.2
1978	3,981.1	1,869.3	288.6	92.6	146.8	514.7	369.5
1979	4,143.8	1,933.6	300.4	89.9	140.1	540.4	367.3
1980	4,450.0	2,070.0	309.2	86.5	132.9	591.8	357.4
1981	4,629.7	1,929.7	291.1	81.8	123.8	580.9	340.6
1982	4,666.9	1,809.0	261.0	76.8	116.4	564.6	320.3
1983	4,534.9	1,713.6	238.9	72.3	108.8	540.5	305.9
1984	4,363.6	1,592.6	214.1	67.4	98.0	499.9	288.8
1985	4,378.9	1,583.9	202.4	67.4	102.9	499.3	293.5
1986	4,512.7	1,591.5	193.4	65.9	101.6	513.1	294.8
1987	4,240.5	1,588.9	181.7	64.0	100.9	518.4	292.1
1988	4,489.1	1,624.1	178.0	63.1	98.8	533.8	295.5
1989	4,845.9	1,689.3	178.9	61.6	101.7	561.8	300.9
1990	5,241.8	1,782.6	175.2	61.3	105.5	594.6	313.0
1991	—	1,898.5	171.8	60.7	105.2	632.3	325.3
1992	—	2,036.2	165.0	54.9	102.8	652.1	375.1

Sources: Herbert (1986:188–9, Table 16); Statistisches Bundesamt, *Jahresberichte*; Bundesanstalt für Arbeit (1991).

Germany and look for a job. German employers had to take the initiative using two alternative official channels – both via the German labor market authorities – to hire foreign workers. Because there was no general scarcity but only structural deficits of labor, the recruitment of foreign workers operated quite selectively. Although some firms tried to hire people with specific skills, the most important criteria used by the officials of the German employment services established in the respective countries were: expected productivity, health, and political clearance (Dohse, 1981: 188f).

As a rule, a permit to work and stay in Germany was granted for one year only and was restricted to a specific job and local community. The administration had considerable powers of discretion on whether or not to extend a permit. Because of increased flexibility, time limits were gradually relaxed: the principle of forced rotation after two years' stay (included in the contract with Turkey) was abandoned as early as 1964. In addition, in 1971 foreigners who worked in Germany for more than five years were able to claim special work permits (valid for a further five years). These steps considerably diminished the regulatory power of the guest-worker concept and may be interpreted as a political compromise to take into account the gradual adaptation of the foreign workers' attitudes and aspirations to "indigenous" standards after several years in Germany (Dohse, 1981: 305).

The ending of recruitment abroad – decided in 1973 in view of the growing labor market crisis in Germany – did not lead to an exodus of the guest workers, as the figures in *Table 6.3* indicate. It is not surprising that most of the foreign workers did not "go home" even when financial incentives were offered in 1983. The economic and social prospects in their countries of origin were not too bright. In fact, the ending of recruitment contributed to clarifying the biographical intentions of foreign workers in Germany, many of whom then decided to resettle other family members from their country of origin.

In retrospect, the guest-worker policy turned out to be a mixed blessing. The existence of a docile and cheap work force from abroad kept the German wage levels in some branches fairly low and reduced the necessity to rearrange the structure of wages. Foreign labor allowed the continuation of poor working conditions, and to some extent even a deterioration in conditions, such as in factories with assembly-line work, piece work, shift work, and night work (Dohse, 1981: 226). In other words, the guest-worker policy supported growth but delayed the

Table 6.4. Foreign and German employees according to skill status, 1989 (%).

	Foreigners	Germans
Unskilled workers	21	4
Semiskilled workers	43	12
Skilled workers; supervisors	23	16
Clerks	9	46
Self-employed	4	12
Public servants	—	10

Source: Seifert (1991: Table 1).

modernization of the structure of industries, especially a quicker shift to a service economy. With respect to social dimensions, foreign workers – by filling the lowest strata of the employment spectrum – assisted the indirect upward mobility of their German colleagues. Despite some progress to the benefit of foreigners the segmented labor market was still reflected in the statistics of the late 1980s, as *Table 6.4* demonstrates.

Moreover, the detrimental aspects concerning the development of female participation in employment cannot be overlooked. The recruitment of foreign labor substituted for an increase in gainfully employed German women (as mentioned above), thus helping to preserve existing family structures.

More than 25 years after the introduction of the guest-worker policy, the foreign labor force is now fairly well integrated both economically and socially. Some 50% of the foreign labor force comes from other EU member states (Spain, Italy, Greece, etc.), which means they have the right to stay and work. The situation of the two largest groups, the labor migrants from Turkey (33%) and former Yugoslavia (13%), is worst, even though many of them have stayed in Germany long enough to claim a better protected status in terms of employment, social security, and residence.

6.4 Asylum Seekers

For several years the most heated public debates in Germany concerning migration have focused on asylum seekers. The number of asylum seekers increased considerably in the late 1980s: from 103,000 in 1988 to 438,000 in 1992. The reasons for this development are complex:

- The constitution of the FRG contained a very liberal provision concerning the right to asylum. Germany is attractive because it has one of the most prosperous economies in Europe.
- After the ending of the guest-worker policy in 1973, there has been (until recently) no other "ticket" to enter the German labor market.
- Some centers of recent political crisis are located close to Germany so that the country is more directly affected by the human victims. In 1991, for example, almost 30% of asylum seekers were former Yugoslavs.

Even when the constitutional phrasing of the right to asylum was rather liberal the administrative procedures were highly restrictive, with the result that less than 10% of the applicants were successful. The majority of those whose claims were refused could stay in the country, but for several years (until the legislation was changed in 1991) they were not allowed to take up paid work. This exclusion was introduced with the aim of discouraging so-called economic refugees and of protecting the German labor force. As a consequence, all these people had to rely on social welfare, which placed a heavy burden on the communal budgets that had to provide the resources. Furthermore, this regulation had a negative impact on the attitudes of German locals toward the asylum seekers.

In view of the large numbers of *Aussiedler* and of new guest workers actively recruited from Central and Eastern Europe (see Section 6.5), the heated public discussion on the right to asylum can be interpreted as one of evasion. But the 1992 figure also indicates that there might be a capacity problem. In 1993 mounting public pressure led to an amendment of the German constitution to restrict the chances of successful applications for asylum. In practice, those who enter the country by land are no longer entitled to claim asylum, since they must have crossed at least one neighboring country. All neighboring countries are regarded as "safe countries" since they are signatories to the Geneva Convention. In addition, a so-called "positive list" has been drawn up of all countries where human rights appear to be respected. Thus would-be refugees from either a country on the positive list or another "safe" country are denied access to the formal asylum procedure.

Much less public attention has been focused on another recent change concerning the status of asylum seekers: they may now apply for work permits directly upon arrival. This amendment reflects the experience that blocking access to the official labor market results in the growth of illegal employment. Moreover, the structural mismatches in the labor market were regarded or expected to be serious enough to allow for additional labor with few demands on working conditions.

6.5 New Guest Workers

Another indication that German labor market authorities are looking for additional flexible labor is the "new" guest-worker policy.[2] Starting in the late 1980s and more systematically pursued since 1990, the German Labor Administration has signed contracts with East European countries that open up three channels for limited access of foreign workers to the German labor market. All three are based on the principle of forced rotation, but have different target groups; two of the contracts fix quotas.

- Project-tied employment: This is the legal basis for foreign subcontractors. Maximum numbers per year for (as a rule skilled) workers are set and work permits are given for two years. The German standards concerning wages and social security are obligatory. In October 1992, 70% of the 116,000 foreign workers who entered Germany with this "ticket" were employed in the building sector. About half of the foreign employees who entered under project-tied employment arrangements came from Poland.
- Guest-worker contracts: The aim is to further the vocational and linguistic competences of workers from East European countries and workers from Germany wishing to work in East European countries. The length of stay is limited to one year. The annual quotas set at 500 to 1,000 (depending on the country) have not been used fully, except for Hungary. Not a single German has applied so far. Until October 1992 a total of 4,543 contracts had been signed, 40% in construction and 30% in the metal industry.
- Seasonal workers: Foreign workers can receive German work permits for up to three months at the initiative of a German employer. The working conditions (wages, insurance) must meet local standards and housing facilities must be adequate. In 1992, 212,000 work permits were issued (mainly in agriculture, hotels and restaurants, show business, and the building sector). The fact that 98% of the applications were made for specific individuals indicates that this was mainly a way of legalizing formerly illegal workers.

Altogether, about 330,000 new foreign workers entered the German labor market using these three regulations in 1992. This development went practically unnoticed until recently. The stage on which the new guest-worker policy is set differs substantially from the old one, and not only with regard to the principle of forced rotation. More fundamentally, the whole political and economic landscape has changed. After the collapse of the socialist regimes and in the context of painful economic restructuring processes in Middle and Eastern Europe, considerable migratory movements were anticipated, so that opening up "doors" to the German labor market seems to be a good tactic in a number of respects. *Vis-à-vis* the East European countries it may be interpreted as a sign of good intentions, while at home, it is a kind of symbolic policy pretending that even radical international transformations can be successfully managed by small adjustments.

6.6 Socioeconomic Crisis, Control Strategies, and Xenophobia

Starting in 1990 but sharply increasing since 1991, a wave of aggressive acts of racism has emerged in Germany in both the old and new *Länder*. Politicians and "conventional wisdom" argue that there is a direct correlation between the number of inflowing foreigners and xenophobia. However, there is no direct relationship; empirical research gives evidence that racism can develop even without a single foreigner in the country. Xenophobia is a social dynamic that is generated in times of social and/or political crisis. People are eager to find and accept simple relations of cause and effect that lie beyond their own responsibility. Such stereotyping produces both underdogs and the illusion that the crisis can be easily managed.

Germany is facing enormous political, economic, and social problems. Irrespective of political unification, there are still two societies. Apart from the enormous task of economic restructuring, the processes of social integration are painful – and unexpectedly so. These problems are too delicate to be handled openly, so the tensions are covered and are projected onto "others": foreigners in general and the asylum seekers in particular.

Representatives of all parties have condemned the aggression against foreigners, but the lengthy and acrimonious public debate on how to restrict the constitutional right to asylum has undoubtedly contributed to the xenophobia. The message has been that if it is legitimate to assign an inferior legal status to "foreigners", then more general discrimination may be justified. A nation in economic and social crisis looks for scapegoats.

6.7 Conclusions

Germany has benefited enormously from the influx of labor for almost five decades since the end of World War II. German political authorities have created the institutions and regulations necessary to use the newcomers as a flexible reserve, alleviating or preventing political, economic, and social tensions. This was fairly easy as far as people of different nationality were concerned because Germany could resort to a long tradition with the political concept of "foreigner". During some periods ethnic Germans from East European countries were used as functional equivalents. Giving the different waves of inflowing workers different labels – and never calling them immigrants – is part of the political power play in which Germany is and always has been one of the most potent actors. The declaration to be and to remain a nonimmigrant country indicates that Germany shuts its eyes to the demands of the global transformations. Using the labor resources of other countries at low wages and offering small concessions in return will not work forever, however. Tactics are no longer enough; strategies are needed. Even generous migration policies will be inadequate to cope successfully with the challenges of the future. Attempts to continue with restrictive control strategies or even to sharpen them will hardly be successful but may provoke unintended results, such as the recent rise of xenophobia.

Notes

[1] By definition, German emigrants from the former GDR were called *Übersiedler*, while ethnic Germans from outside Germany (both the FRG and the former GDR) are called *Aussiedler* (resettlers). The *Aussiedler* status, defined by the German constitution on the basis of historical and ethnic considerations, can be claimed by all persons (as well as their descendants and close family members) who lived within the borders of Germany before 1938–45, by those who were German citizens in 1939–45 but lived outside these borders, and by other ethnic Germans living in Eastern Europe, the Balkans and the former Soviet Union.

[2] I wish to thank Andrea Fischer who contributed careful information and comments full of insight to Section 6.5.

Chapter 7

Economic and Social Aspects of Immigration into Switzerland

Thomas Straubhaar and Peter A. Fischer

7.1 Historical Background

Until the end of the nineteenth century Switzerland was fairly poor and underdeveloped, and a country of emigration.[1] But things changed rapidly at the turn of the century, when the process of industrialization and building a basic infrastructure turned out to be highly labor-intensive. The construction of the long railway tunnels through the Alps was not only a challenge to engineers at that time, but also one of the first occasions where workers were recruited abroad.[2]

During World War II, the foreign population in Switzerland fell sharply to reach its lowest point in 1941 with 224,000 foreigners or 5.2% of the population. But after the war, while all surrounding countries suffered serious economic postwar consequences, Switzerland's relatively unaffected economy recovered quickly. Moreover, the country's advanced financial markets, political stability, legislation safeguarding investors, and the Swiss propensity to save ensured an extensive and cheap supply of capital. Switzerland has long been known for its low real interest rates, a feature that is still valid in part today (OECD, 1991a). Switzerland has a highly capital-oriented economy with corresponding high labor productivity and a structural shortage of domestic labor.[3]

The share of foreigners living in Switzerland has risen quickly since 1945. In the early 1960s, the number of foreign nationals living in

Switzerland approached 1 million (equaling 16.7% of the total population in 1965) and fears that that the country would be "flooded" with immigrants started to manifest themselves in strong political pressure. At the end of the 1960s, six public referendums were held on proposals by xenophobic groups to change the Swiss constitution to drastically reduce the number of foreigners living in Switzerland.[4] Although all of the proposals were rejected by an increasing majority of Swiss voters, the political pressure they created exerted a decisive influence on the development of Swiss migration policy.

7.2 Migration to Switzerland: Trends and Features

In 1963 Switzerland started to introduce a restrictive immigration policy, but the number of foreigners continued to increase steadily until it reached a first maximum in 1973, when 1.25 million foreign nationals were living in Switzerland. After the first oil price shock Switzerland, like all other Western countries, was hit by a severe economic crisis. Foreign employment fell by 251,000 (28%) within four years from 894,000 in 1973 to 643,000 in 1977. From 1979 on it started rising again at a moderate pace, increasing in speed during the the economic boom in the late 1980s. Although, as elsewhere, the economic climate has worsened in Switzerland, most recent data on foreign employment available still show an increasing tendency. In August 1991, 1,284,928 foreigners (including so-called seasonal workers) were living in Switzerland, and the number of foreign employees amounted to 989,457 or 27.8% of the labor force. Actually, this share for the first time passed the former peak of 1972, when foreign employment amounted to 27.4% of total employment (and afterward decreased to 21.2% in 1977).

Another feature is the changing composition of foreigners living in Switzerland by type of permit (*Figure 7.1*). In 1965, 19.4% of all foreign nationals were permanent residents and 58.5% held one-year residence permits. In 1979, the ratio was just about reversed: 62.7% were permanent residents, and only 19.6% held one-year permits. Of all others (short permits for special objectives excluded), 9% were seasonal workers, 8.5% commuters living in neighboring countries, and only 0.2% of all foreign nationals or 1,882 were asylum seekers. In 1990, the share of asylum seekers had risen to 2.5% (35,836 persons), that of frontier workers to 12.5%, and the foreign workers' share had remained about constant at 8.5%. The majority of denizens or *de facto* denizens

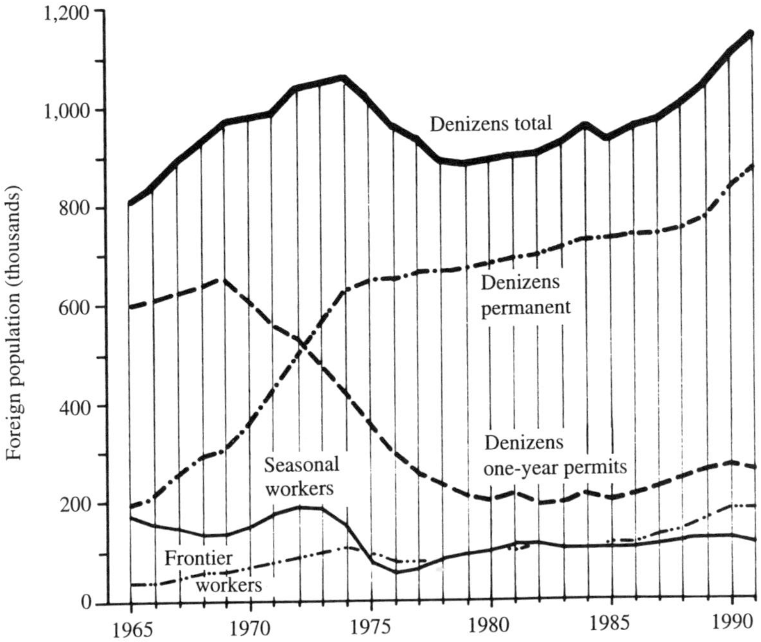

Figure 7.1. Foreigners and foreign labor in Switzerland 1965–91. Sources: Bundesamt für Statistik (1990); Federal Aliens Office; Federal Office for Refugee Questions, Bern; OECD, various publications and personal communication.

still consisted of permanent residents (57.7%), and only 18.8% were one-year permit holders.[5] No data are available on the number of short-term permits that were issued in 1990.

There are various explanations for the change in the structure of foreigners. One hypothesis is that, with the introduction of the first restrictions, the possibility of entering Switzerland after once having left it became increasingly uncertain, so that many preferred to stay and become permanent residents (in general, after five years of uninterrupted residence). The same could be observed with the increasing number of seasonal workers trying to obtain one-year permits. The second hypothesis is that, until recently, Switzerland handled its naturalization policy very restrictively. Thus, the "natural" decrease in the stock of foreigners with permanent residence (denizens) from naturalization was almost negligible (1.1% in 1988). A third hypothesis is that the fall in

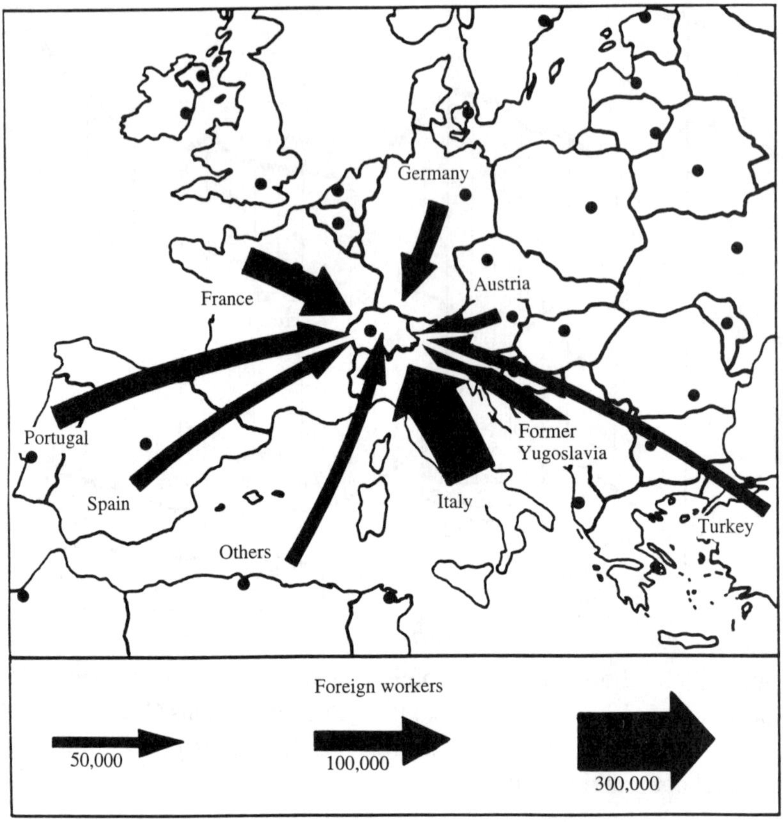

Figure 7.2. Origins of foreign labor in Switzerland, 1991.

foreign employment due to the oil price shock affected mainly one-year permit holders and seasonal workers.

The relative stability of the size of foreign population affected the average age structure, in that it approached the age structure of natives. As a matter of fact, new immigrant workers showed a much more favorable age distribution (i.e., a strong bias toward youth) than foreigners already living in Switzerland, who showed features very similar to those of Swiss nationals. Due to this, the foreign population in Switzerland lost one key feature (the bias toward youth and healthy persons) regarded as one of the most positive effects of migration in traditional literature.

As far as the origin of the foreign population in Switzerland is concerned, a majority of foreign nationals in Switzerland were and still are citizens of the European Union. The distribution by nationality shows

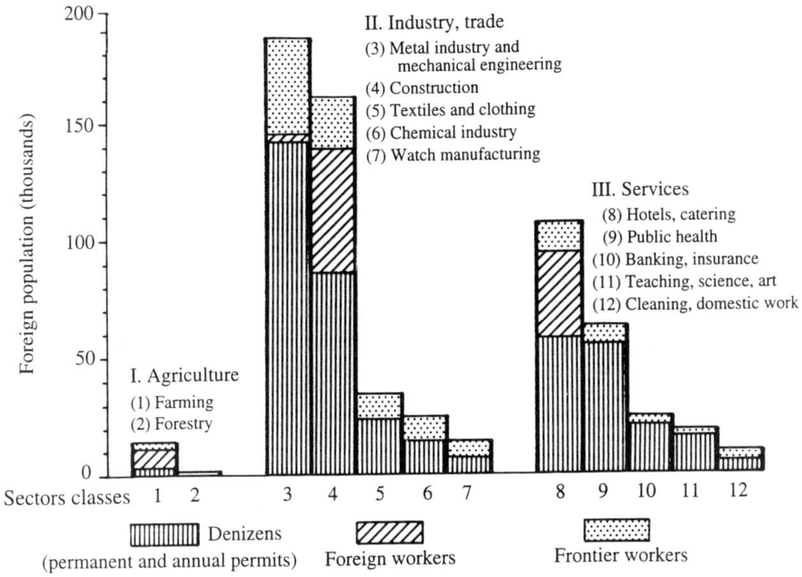

Figure 7.3. Foreign labor force in Switzerland, by sector, 1991. Sources: Swiss Ministry of Labor: Federal Department of Justice and Police, Central Aliens Register, Bern.

the regional patterns clearly (see *Figure 7.2*). Most foreign workers emigrated from neighboring countries, particularly from Italy: in 1980, 42% of all foreign workers were Italians and about four out of five were EU citizens. The corresponding share of EFTA countries was 4.3%, mostly Austrians. Until 1991, the picture changed only slightly. As Italy enjoyed more favorable economic development, new workers for simple jobs were no longer found in Italy, but in the southern European countries such as Portugal, Spain, Turkey, and former Yugoslavia. Nevertheless, in 1991 still 72.6% of all foreigners in Switzerland were EU citizens, the share of EFTA citizens remained constant at 4.3%, while the share of workers from Turkey and former Yugoslavia increased from 13.8% in 1980 to 18.7%. From the previous section we know that immigration from outside (Western) Europe was in principle not accepted, so this is the most important explanation for the low share of non-EU/EFTA citizens.

Some 70% of all employed foreign nationals were males. Differences can be found according to the type of employment (see *Figure 7.3*). While in 1970 some 40% of all working denizens were female

(34.2% in 1991), the corresponding share among seasonal workers was only 10% (18% in 1991). Even more significant are the sex differences according to branches of employment. While in 1991 96% of all foreigners employed in domestic work and 74% in public health were female, 98% of all foreign construction workers were men.

The majority of foreigners in Switzerland still work in poorly qualified jobs. In 1991 the majority of foreign employment was concentrated in the metal industry (19%), construction (16%), the hotel and restaurant business (11%), public health (6%), and textiles and clothing manufacturing (3%). From 1970 to 1991, a shift from industry and trade to the service sector could be observed. In 1970, 63% of foreign employment was in industry and 31% in services, compared with 51% and 47%, respectively, in 1991.

7.3 Swiss Immigration Policy: Design and Development

In Switzerland, immigration was and still is perceived mainly as a tool of labor-market policy, to recruit foreign labor demanded by the Swiss labor market. Foreigners were regarded as guests coming to Switzerland to work for money on a temporary basis only. The basic assumption underlying the Swiss (labor) immigration policy was the rotation principle. Intensive immigration flows were expected to ensure that the foreigners living in Switzerland would be adaptable to changing labor-market demands, thus increasing overall labor-market flexibility.

In the Swiss constitution, the national parliament and government are considered responsible for legislation on immigration, emigration, and residence of foreigners in Switzerland, and the cantons (provinces) for the administrative decision making. The basic law on Swiss immigration ("Bundesgesetz über Aufenthalt und Niederlassung der Ausländer", ANAG), which dates back to 1931, and is still in force today, states the principal duties of foreigners in Switzerland, but leaves the task of specifying the aims and tools of migration policy to the federal government and national administrative bodies. In reality, until the early 1960s, everyone who found a job was allowed to work, but with the expansion of foreign employment in the 1960s, domestic labor organizations and unions started to worry that the situation was getting out of control. In 1963 political pressure led to the introduction of a restrictive policy for the foreign population in Switzerland.[6] The 1963 policy measures focused on individual enterprises and set limits on the share of foreign workers each company could employ. Actually, they mainly produced incentives for foreign workers to change to companies with a previously low share of foreign labor. In spite of several additional attempts to make the company-focused policy even more restrictive, total foreign employment continued to grow. In 1970 the foreign population in Switzerland reached 18.2%, and 26.2% of all employees were foreigners. A proposal by xenophobic groups to change the Swiss constitution in order to bring the foreign population down to 10% of the total population was only narrowly rejected by Swiss voters after the government promised to change its immigration policy again.

In March 1970, the Swiss Federal Council of Ministers decided to change to a centrally administered control system for the foreign population.[7] It was supposed to stabilize the share of foreign population by fixing the number of new permits issued to foreigners entering the country every year. This number reflected the desired volume of foreign population minus foreigners already resident in the country, plus foreigners leaving. Every year, within these defined margins, the central labor authority fixed quotas for new entries to each of Switzerland's 25 cantons and a national quota for special tasks. Now the labor authorities in the districts and in Bern could decide on employers' applications to issue work permits to foreigners. Very often, however, the actual decision making in the districts was handed over to advisory councils, in which representatives of employers' organizations, union syndicates, political parties, and the administration tried to safeguard their respective interests.

The decision to issue a work permit to a foreigner had to follow several additional guidelines. In principle, immigration was restricted to Europeans, although exceptions were made for key North American and Japanese personnel. Permits could be authorized only if the employment of a foreigner corresponded to an evidently urgent labor need, improved the structure of a regional labor market, or suited the overall business policy.

Alongside these more or less explicit tasks of the Swiss foreign labor-market policy there was a general consensus that employment priority should be given to Swiss natives. This restrictive policy, which is still in force, has turned foreign employment policy in Switzerland into an increasingly restricted bargaining process among the administration, employers, and interest groups. Apart from the stabilization task, structural, regional, and political interests were mixed up with business-related targets. As Dhima (1991) has pointed out, exponents of sheltered local businesses were most active and successful in procuring for themselves a cheap labor supply, while international businesses seemed to be reluctant and preferred to move their production abroad.

Once a permit was issued, labor-market policy was very passive. Little attention was paid to the interests of the foreigners themselves, who were supposed to be happy for being allowed to work in Switzerland. Although inaccurate, the common assumption was that all foreigners not married to Swiss nationals would be temporary guests only, so that almost no measures were taken to support integration into the domestic society (there are, for example, government-financed language courses for asylum seekers, but for no other category of foreigners).

For a better understanding of the mechanisms and outcome of the Swiss foreign employment control system, the five kinds of permits are briefly explained below: permits for permanent residence, one-year residence permits, permits for seasonal work, work permits for frontier workers, and short-term permits for special objectives.

Formally, denizens in Switzerland should consist of holders of permanent residence permits only, although a large percentage of persons with one-year residence permits must be regarded as *de facto* denizens. They are distinguished from permanent residence holders through certain restrictions on the freedom to change employers and ownership of real estate. They have to apply for new permits every year, but in general this is merely a formality. Although they are legally considered to be temporary labor migrants, experience shows that many of those with one-year residence permits are in fact just waiting for the right to obtain permanent residence permits after 5–10 years of uninterrupted residence (the difference depending on nationality). Residence permit holders are treated on equal terms with Swiss citizens, except that they do not have the right to vote.

Seasonal permits are issued to workers employed in businesses that are affected by seasonal fluctuations (in restaurants and hotels in the mountains, ski resort maintenance, and so on). Seasonal workers are allowed to stay in the country for a maximum of nine months within any one year, and they have no right to change jobs or to bring spouses or other family members with them. However, due to political pressure, seasonal workers are now entitled to obtain one-year residence permits after working in Switzerland for four consecutive seasons of nine months each.

Frontier workers are persons living outside Switzerland within a geographically defined border area. Their right to work in Switzerland is conditionally linked to daily commuting, i.e., they have to return home every evening. Frontier workers are not subject to the control system, and neither are holders of short-term permits for special objectives.

7.4 Effects of Immigration to Switzerland

In this section we discuss the most important effects of immigration to Switzerland compared with the original intentions of Swiss immigration policy and their social implications.

7.4.1 Effects of immigration compared with original policy intentions

The original intention of Swiss immigration policy was to stabilize the share of foreign population. Secondary goals were to satisfy labor-market needs, to improve business policy, and to induce positive structural effects for the different Swiss regions.

Referring to the first goal (to stabilize the foreign population), the introduction of the restrictions did not have any obvious effect on the development of the number of foreigners living in Switzerland. The policy may have somewhat curbed actual immigration into Switzerland, but if the aim of stabilizing the share of foreign employment in total employment is taken as an absolute criterion, the policy has failed. In fact, this share continued to rise consistently until the first oil price shock, and again from 1977 until today. Indeed, it seems that the development of foreign labor, despite the many employment regulations, was mainly driven by the global labor market performance.

The second and third goals were to satisfy labor market needs and to improve business policy. Having just noted that Swiss foreign employment has been following labor-market trends, our hypothesis is that though politically administered, the intensity of immigration to Switzerland has been determined by factors of pure economic demand. However, the political bargaining system for the distribution of work permits has undoubtedly had some disturbing overall effects.

Probably most important, the administrative restrictions applied in the immigration policy have hampered the efficient allocation of foreign labor in Switzerland. From the point of view of international economics, (free) labor mobility should guarantee an efficient allocation of natural resources. But the more a labor market is controlled, the greater are the possibilities of distorting this allocation. As described earlier, immigration policy in Switzerland concentrated first on the distribution of foreign labor within the country, and not on the efficient allocation of foreign employment.

In a recent study, Dhima (1991) analyzed employment patterns of foreign workers who immigrated to Switzerland in 1981 and stayed until 1989. In brief, he showed that 66% of all long-term immigrants (i.e., those who were still in Switzerland in 1989) had entered the country as seasonal workers, and 47% of all seasonal workers had started a "career" to obtain a permanent residence permit. Because the demand for simple work in the mountain areas was especially efficient in the political bargaining process determining the issue of permits, the majority of seasonal workers had to do unqualified work in agriculture, construction, hotels and restaurants, or public health. But after having obtained a one-year residence permit, they left the mountains and moved into more demanding jobs in industry, banking, insurance companies, the chemical industry, transport, or trade (see *Figure 7.4*).

Of course, to force people to work in jobs that do not suit their qualifications is a poor allocation of labor resources.[8] The inefficient allocation of labor seems in fact to override the economic gains from the reallocation of labor. This is because, on the one hand, workers are not employed according to their potential abilities and, on the other, the cheap supply of labor hampered structural adjustment within certain business sectors and led to a weakening of their competitiveness.

In economic theory, many scholars, referring to Lewis (1954), consider foreign employment to be a kind of "growth machine" for developed economies. They argue that since immigration can provide an abundant supply of labor, it should check wage increases and allow surpluses to be used for capital accumulation, inducing future growth and (in combination with increasing economies of scale) productivity gains. Other theorists (the so-called structural pessimists) find just the opposite to be true. They suppose that cheap labor costs eliminate the most important incentives for rationalization, thus leading to lower productivity

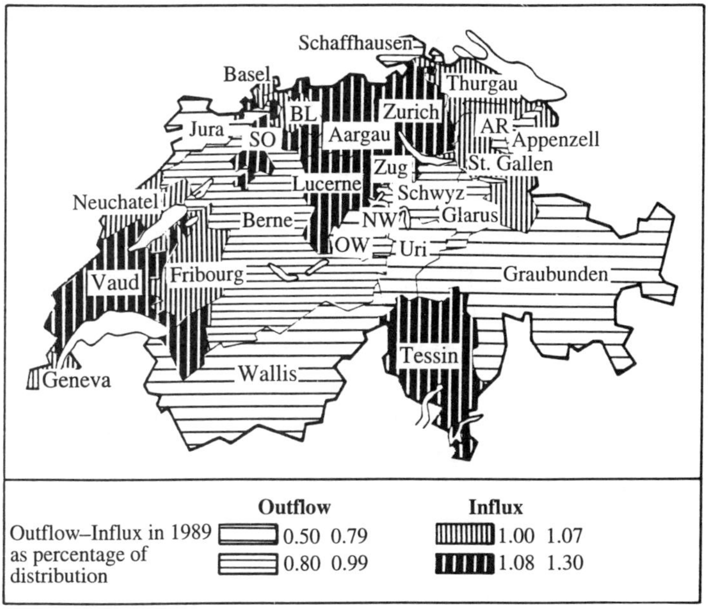

Figure 7.4. Employed denizens: regional migration and tendency to remain between 1981 and 1989. Source: Swiss Central Aliens Office, Bern.

(more comprehensive surveys of theoretical arguments on growth and structural effects of migration may be found in Tuchtfeldt, 1978, and Blattner *et al.*, 1985).

The Swiss experience supports the structural pessimists' hypothesis. In Swiss sectors employing a high percentage of cheap foreign labor we systematically find companies with below average productivity. Schwarz (1988) tried to isolate the macroeconomic effects of foreign employment in Switzerland by means of econometrics and with a simple macroeconomic model. He estimated the contribution of foreign and domestic labor, of capital, and of technological innovations to the average annual economic growth and productivity increase in Switzerland between 1962 and 1986. It is no longer a surprise that the positive and negative economic growth effects of foreign employment have finally roughly neutralized each other in Switzerland, and the real growth of the GDP per capita can mainly be explained by technological innovations and improved use of capital (see Schwarz, 1988: 136–40).

Thus it can be stated that the second goal was also not achieved. The restrictions produced an ineffective allocation that overrode the economic gains. The third and fourth goals also do not seem to have been fulfilled. During the oil price recession (1973–77) total foreign employment fell by 251,000, or 7% of total employment in 1977. The number of denizens remained almost constant and unemployment continued at a very low level (with a maximum of 0.7% in 1976); it seems that Switzerland "exported" its unemployment. Later, however, this mechanism did not work the same way. The reaction of foreign employment to the (less intensive) slump of the 1980s was only very moderate, and from 1990 until the present there has been no such reaction.

The introduction of the restrictive policy increased the risk that a foreigner would lose the opportunity of employment in Switzerland for ever if he emigrated. It created additional noneconomic incentives to stay in the same place and work for the right to obtain a better category of work permit. Thus, the structure of foreign employment by permit category changed, and the flexibility of the labor markets suffered. Following the stabilization criteria of Swiss immigration policy described in Section 7.2, in 1988, the number of work permits available for reissue (excluding the natural decrease in the number of foreign workers through emigration, naturalization, marriage, and other demographic changes, and including the natural increase through the birth of children to foreign nationals, family reunions, and the transformation of seasonal into annual permits) would have been as low as 13,145, or 2.16% of the total foreign community. In fact, 37,880 permits were issued (data from Dhima, 1991: 76). Thus it appears that the effect of Swiss immigration policy was actually to reduce the flexibility of employment policy rather than to increase labor market flexibility.

Up to now, the impact of migration on business cycles in the 1970s has been depicted as mainly positive. However, in an analysis of economic effects of foreign employment, Schwarz (1988: 151–6) finds strong evidence to support the hypothesis that the sharp fall in foreign employment was one major reason for the severity of the recession of the 1970s in Switzerland (see *Figure 7.5*). Compared with other European economies, Switzerland suffered the longest and most pronounced fall in economic growth rates.[9] Schwarz explains this in two ways. First, he argues that the departure of foreigners caused a reduction in domestic consumption that hurt the Swiss economy more than unemployment would have done (for a discussion of the effects of migration

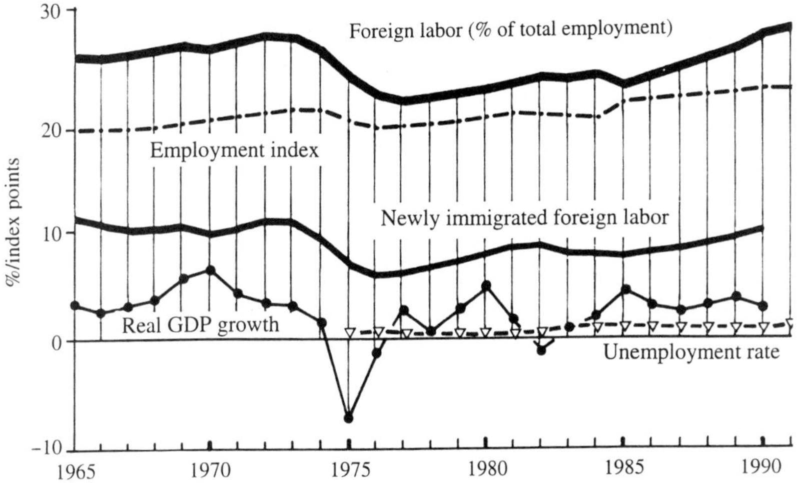

Figure 7.5. Foreign employment and business cycles in Switzerland, 1965–91. Sources: Authors' calculations using data from the Swiss Central Aliens Office, Bern, and OECD.

on domestic demand see Tuchtfeldt, 1978). Second, as discussed in Section 7.3, foreign employment veiled structural adjustment deficits of the Swiss economy that were corrected only when they had already become pronounced.

7.4.2 Social implications

There is little quantitative evidence on the social effects of immigration on Switzerland. Qualitatively, however, it seems clear that the rather large foreign employment rate in Switzerland has had at least three socioeconomic effects.

1. Above all, unqualified immigrants from southern Europe who accepted employment in simple jobs caused a certain stratification of the Swiss labor market. Because "dirty" jobs were done by foreigners, poorly qualified Swiss citizens could improve their labor-market positions during periods of economic growth, but in times of recession they had to compete for work with foreign labor. Consequently, social attitudes toward foreigners depended very much on overall economic performance.[10]
2. Because foreign workers were considered to be short-term guests only, the public welfare system was not at all prepared to deal with

the needs of the increasing numbers of workers who intended (and managed) to stay in Switzerland with their families. As practically no public integration assistance was organized and foreign residents were drawn to the location of certain employers, primary schools suddenly found themselves confronted with large percentages of pupils unable to speak and understand the native languages. If such pupils stayed for two or three years only, things got even worse. Public investment in education had to be made, but this never appeared as foreign labor costs. Swiss parents felt that their children's education was being endangered by the foreign population, and the potential for social tensions grew.

3. The requirement that (above all male) foreign workers had to stay in the country for nine months without their spouses caused considerable psychological stress and family disintegration. Indeed, foreigners' inclination to commit rape and crimes of violence seems to have been significantly higher than that of the native population. In 1986, for example, foreigners represented 16.5% of the total population, and they committed 46.1% of all rapes and 42.1% of all homicides. Rape and crimes of violence were especially common among young male foreigners of low social strata living in urban areas (Kunz, 1989).[11]

Swiss nationals are generally aware of the positive economic effects of foreign employment and normally do not have a negative attitude toward foreigners. But over time, the lives of "colored" foreigners and foreigners with non-European habits or with non-Christian religions became complicated, as they did elsewhere. Although in Switzerland the number of asylum seekers never reached the same level as foreign workers, most emotions and intense political discussion on the presence of foreigners in general arose from those applying for political asylum.

In conclusion, in Switzerland we may note that as economic conditions worsen, the observable tensions caused by foreign employment increase; the foreigners appear "stranger" to the natives; and fewer measures are taken to support the social integration of individuals into society.[12]

7.5 Rethinking Swiss Immigration Policy

In recent years Swiss immigration policy has faced several challenges that have caused changes in the general settings and have induced a process of rethinking that has finally led to a fundamental reorientation of Swiss immigration policy.

7.5.1 New challenges

As in most other highly developed European countries, in Switzerland there has been a steady decline in fertility. Without immigration (net migration balance of zero) the Swiss population is expected to decrease during the next half century by 17% from 6.8 million in 1993 to 5.6 million in 2040. The working-age population (15–60) would decrease from 62% of the total population in 1993 to 54% in 2040 (Straubhaar and Lüthi, 1990). Obviously, such a decrease would create considerable problems for the Swiss economy, as well as for the maintenance of the Swiss social-security system.[13]

With a few underlying simplified assumptions, the population growth and the changing age structure of the population during the next 50 years has been estimated for Switzerland under three different scenarios (Straubhaar and Lüthi, 1990). A restrictive scenario with no migration or an annual net migration of zero was compared with an expansive scenario with a net migration surplus of 50,000 immigrants every year. In between, a liberalization scenario was estimated, in which the sudden abolition of immigration restrictions first causes a backlog immigration surplus of 50,000 per year, and then drops to an equilibrium annual surplus of 20,000 after 10 years. In all three cases there is still a moderate increase in the total population until the year 2000. But while in the restrictive scenario the total population later declines to 5.6 million by 2040, an upward slope reaching 8.7 million was estimated for the expansive scenario. The liberalization scenario brought about an increase in Swiss population by about 500,000 until 2010, followed by negative growth rates after 2020, ending with an overall surplus of 200,000 inhabitants in 2040 as compared with 1993.

This is in no way to say that immigration would solve Switzerland's demographic problems; it might only change the country's dynamic appearance. Nevertheless, thinking about the demographic challenge facing Switzerland has influenced the discussion on immigration issues. Above all, it has stimulated thinking about the previously unreflected problems that a highly restrictive migration policy could generate.

The second challenge is represented by European integration and the political changes in the East European countries. The Swiss economy has for a long time been economically very dependent on other West European countries. In 1989, 78% of its imports originated in EU and EFTA countries, and 63% of exports were directed to this area. For exports from the EU, Switzerland was the second most important trading partner after the USA, and for imports it was third after USA and Japan (Hauser, 1991).[14]

Politically, however, the Swiss perceive their country as a sort of island in stormy European waters. For a long time, the main concepts in Swiss foreign policy have been neutrality and political sovereignty. Meanwhile, the integration of the EU member countries has reached a degree that is making it increasingly difficult and costly for Switzerland to remain outside. At the same time, with the disappearance of the Warsaw Pact, Swiss neutrality is losing its original justification. This change has caused (still ongoing) intensive public discussion and questioning of Swiss political identity and self-perception. It has become clear that Switzerland has to find a new role in a renewed Europe and that this process will involve intensified (political) integration with other European countries; this will require basic changes in Swiss immigration policy.

In Switzerland, the challenge of European integration and the creation of a common European Economic Area (EEA) first caused distinctive fears of mass immigration. In its first official statement on the "EU '92 project", the Swiss government quoted the need to liberalize immigration as one of five major obstacles to Swiss membership of the EU.[15] But a subsequent closer evaluation of the theoretical aspects and experiences with free mobility of labor within the EU or the Nordic Common Labor Market revealed that free migration between highly developed economies such as those of the EU is highly unlikely to cause mass migration, and should improve rather than endanger the functioning of labor markets. Estimates of the migratory consequences of abolishing immigration restrictions for EU citizens predict an increase in the migration potential from European countries to Switzerland of about 100,000 additional immigrants for the decade 1990–2000. But simultaneously they calculate that immigrants from Third World countries will be "crowded out", to little more than 100,000 (Straubhaar, 1991b; Dhima, 1991). If these estimates prove to be accurate, the net migration to Switzerland would decrease slightly from its present level.

The third new challenge is the growing number of asylum seekers. While in 1970 there were only 1,803 asylum seekers and 3,020 in 1980, the demand for asylum in Switzerland rose dramatically during the

1980s, to 41,629 in 1991. Until the 1970s most of the refugees originated in (East) European countries, those in the 1980s came from further away and were mainly members of non-European cultures (in 1990, the principal groups came from Sri Lanka, Turkey, India, Pakistan, and Angola, whereas in 1990 the most important national group comprised former Yugoslavs fleeing the war). Today East European states are regarded as "safe countries", so that the number of asylum seekers from Eastern Europe and Russia has become negligible. In 1991, 120 persons from the former Soviet Union applied for asylum in Switzerland, most of whom were Russian Jews. At present no immigrants from East European countries are accepted for labor market reasons so that Switzerland is essentially closed to East Europeans.

The challenge of the Swiss refugee policy has had two basic consequences: first, decision makers became aware that it might become increasingly difficult to distinguish between refugees fleeing political persecution and those migrating for economic reasons. It was therefore proposed to integrate refugees in a more comprehensive migration policy (BIGA, 1989: 17). Second, it became generally accepted that in order to oppose rising immigration pressure, more attention should be paid to the specific causes of the emigration from other countries. A national immigration (control) policy should in future be accomplished through measures to reduce migration pressure at the international level.

7.5.2 Reorientation of Swiss immigration policy

With its report on a new refugee and foreigner policy of May 1991 the Swiss government proposed a radical change in foreign labor-market policy to a so-called three-circle model (*Bundesblatt*, 1991: 245; OECD, 1991e). This new approach brings about a fundamental reorientation of Swiss immigration policy. The administered bargaining system is to be replaced, by and large, by free mobility of European labor and reliance on market forces in allocating foreign labor in the Swiss labor market. Seasonal work permits are to be phased out and replaced by "normal" residence permits.

In concrete terms, citizens of EU and EFTA countries would belong to a "first circle" of foreign labor recruitment and would enjoy complete freedom to accept jobs in Switzerland. Workers needed for specific labor-market reasons, but coming from countries that are neither

EU nor EFTA members (such as traditional recruitment areas, particularly Turkey, and most likely from East European countries; former Yugoslavia was excluded from the traditional labor recruitment areas in 1991), would also be included in the inner circle. For these workers the administrative formalities would be simplified to help them obtain exceptional rights to work in Switzerland.

All the other applicants from these countries would make up the middle circle of the three-circle model. However, immigration policy toward "second country immigrants" would become more restrictive.

All people from states other than those mentioned above would belong to the third circle. They would not be allowed to enter Switzerland for work or residence, although temporary exceptions could be granted, especially for science, research, teaching mutual education, and development assistance purposes.

The granting of asylum is proposed to remain restricted to political grounds only. To reduce immigration pressure from Eastern Europe, the CIS, and Third World countries, economic, foreign, and development aid policies are called upon to initiate specific action at the international level.

The Swiss government's proposal of May 1991 has so far found considerable political support. It is now generally assumed that more qualified and better adapted foreign labor from Europe will crowd out the less profitable seasonal workers who are employed in Switzerland today.

7.6 Summarizing Suggestions

Although subject to an increasingly restrictive policy, immigration to Switzerland after 1945 was determined mainly by demand. The vast majority of immigrants moved from European countries to Switzerland for labor-market reasons, and the majority attempted to stay more or less permanently. Incentives to "work" for more permanent residence permits hampered labor-market flexibility. The economic benefits of the reallocation of labor in the restrictively administered foreign labor system were neutralized by structural inefficiencies of the political and economic bargaining process that determined the distribution of new work permits.

Briefly, Swiss immigration policy was confined to the restriction of immigrants and the distribution of permits. Distributional aspects generally dominated allocational efficiency. An artificially cheap labor supply for certain sectors gave them an edge over their competitors. While Switzerland continued to suffer from a structural shortage of highly qualified labor, foreigners were (and to some extent still are) allowed to immigrate for comparatively poorly qualified jobs. All in all, the economic benefits of the Swiss labor-market policy remained insignificant.

The Swiss experience supports the argument that between similarly developed economies, liberal market solutions for the reallocation of labor are more effective than administrative bargaining systems for the distribution of foreign workers. In the absence of large differences in wealth that would cause mass migration, the allocational gains of increased labor mobility offset distributional losses. From this point of view, the creation of a common labor market would be the best solution; furthermore, the larger the scope of such a market, the bigger the potential welfare gains are likely to be. Social implications included, the market's demand for foreign labor should therefore be met by liberalization of immigration as far as possible. Thus Switzerland's intention to abolish the foreign worker system and to join a common European labor market is a step in the right direction.

If additional labor immigration is to be allowed from countries that do not belong to the same common labor market, quantitative limits ought to be imposed. In Switzerland, discussion is going on whether to offer such solutions to Turkey, some East European countries, Croatia, or Slovenia. The selection and distribution of foreign labor from such countries should, as far as possible, be left to efficient market mechanisms such as foreign employment taxes or auctions, rather than trying to regulate it by administrative or political processes. The revenue raised through such instruments could, for example, be used to reduce migration potential in countries of origin and to share the benefits of migration more equitably (an interesting proposal for the design of such a system has been made by Majava, 1991).

The rotation principle of the Swiss foreign worker system and the lack of a public policy to support the social integration of foreigners in Switzerland has led to real economic and social costs. Attempts to actively shape structural or regional policies by means of the targeted distribution of foreign labor have also been unsuccessful. Such aims are obviously better pursued using direct fiscal policy measures.

To actively integrate immigrants into Swiss society would have prevented social costs caused by the Swiss adoption of a foreign worker policy that relied on intensive rotation of foreign labor. Swiss experience indicates that the harder times are in economic terms, the more "strange" a foreigner's appearance seems to the natives, the fewer measures are taken to support active social integration of individuals into society, and the higher are the observable tensions caused by foreign employment. Such effects might be an argument in favor of restricting migration within Europe.

Free labor migration is not a realistic alternative for the development of Third World countries nor for the reduction of the existing wide differences in wealth. If at all, large-scale migration problems can only be prevented by means of a consistent common international migration policy of all major industrialized countries. Recent global challenges demonstrate the decisive importance of an agreement of all the leading economies (just as the one on the GATT system) on a General Agreement on Migration Policy (GAMP), the aim of which should be to reduce migration potential in the countries of origin. Possible measures to be considered could be coordinated efforts to reduce income gaps (e.g., by further trade liberalization, capital investment incentives, development cooperation), to create new employment opportunities in less developed economies, to reduce deprivation, as well as to discourage false expectations regarding employment opportunities and living conditions in potential countries of destination. Furthermore, sustainable supranational political action should be taken to force the governments of emigration countries to respect basic human, political, and democratic rights in order to prevent the emigration of political refugees.

Notes

[1] Between 1880 and 1888 about 92,000 Swiss emigrated in search of better living conditions somewhere abroad, while during the same time only 5,000 immigrated to Switzerland (Hagmann, 1991: 238).

[2] Between 1988 and 1900 thousands of Italians helped the Swiss to drive through Gottardo and Simplon. About 127,000 persons immigrated to Switzerland, while only 53,000 left (Hagmann, 1991: 238). In 1914, the foreign population reached a first peak of 600,000, amounting to 15.4% of the total population (Hoffmann-Nowotny and Killias, 1979: 45–6).

[3] If wage levels or GDP per capita (or per member of the labor force) are used as indicators of labor productivity, in Switzerland both have traditionally been among the highest in the world (see OECD, 1991a,b).

[4] Every Swiss citizen has the right to propose a change in the national constitution or in any other law. If such a proposal (or "initiative") is supported by signatures of at

least 150,000 Swiss, it has to be discussed in parliament and must finally be accepted or rejected in a referendum.

[5] Following Hammar (1990), the term "denizens" is used here to describe foreigners permanently resident in a country but without political rights.

[6] Decision of the Federal Council of Ministers of 1 March 1963, on the restriction of admission of foreign labor. For more detailed information on the history of Swiss immigration policy, see Huber (1963), Gnehm (1966), and Haug (1980).

[7] Decision of the Federal Council of Ministers on the restriction of foreign employment, 16 March 1970. Today, the control system is legally based on an annually adjusted ordinance of the Federal Council of Ministers.

[8] By examining the average productivity of branches in which workers were employed before they obtained one-year permits and the productivity of branches to which they moved, an average difference of more than SFr. 5,000 (about US$3,600) per foreign worker and year could be saved if foreign workers were free to choose their jobs directly (Straubhaar, 1991a). In other words, the inefficient allocation of immigrants in 1981 resulted in an annual economic loss of more than SFr. 100 million (US$70 million) that could have been obtained through immigration taxes and used for specific support of mountain areas or businesses with structural problems.

[9] Although the average annual real GDP growth of all OECD countries was 2.7% between 1973 and 1979 (+2.5% on average of EU countries), over the same period the Swiss GDP fell by 0.4% (OECD, 1991f: 48). In fact, Switzerland was the only OECD country with a negative annual GDP growth rate from 1973 to 1979. A similar picture may be derived from the GDP per capita figures. Apart from New Zealand (–0.2%), only Switzerland suffered an average annual decline (–0.1%) in GDP per capita after the oil price shock (1973–79), while in OECD countries the GDP per capita increased by an average of 1.9% (+2.1 in EU countries). Total employment in 1973–79 fell by 0.9% per annum in Switzerland, compared with an annual average growth of 1% in all OECD countries (+0.1 in EU countries; OECD, 1991e: 30).

[10] Between 1970 and 1990, 10 regular referendums were held on proposed laws with xenophobic background, but all of them were rejected. During the same period proposals aiming to improve immigrants' rights were also rejected.

[11] These figures should be interpreted with caution, however, since they also include crimes committed in Switzerland by foreigners not resident in the country. For a more detailed discussion, see Kunz (1989).

[12] Although Switzerland's share of foreigners among the total population is one of the highest in the world, social tensions linked to the presence of foreigners are no higher than in other European countries. We would like to explain this through the hypothesis that the social costs of immigration depend on dynamic changes in the intensity rather than on absolute levels of immigration or of foreigners living in a country. Because the number of foreigners has risen steadily over a long period, the Swiss have become used to it, and it no longer causes any specifically serious tensions. Societies with suddenly increasing numbers of immigrants are much more likely to experience widespread fears of being "flooded" by immigrants and intensive xenophobic reactions, whatever the previous share of foreigners among the total population.

[13] In theory, there are two principal ways to influence population growth. Population policy may aim to change the reproductive behavior of natives, or it could try to influence population growth through migration. A comprehensive analysis of Austrian experiences with migration and population policy are provided by Fassmann and Münz (1990). For Germany, Feichtinger and Steinmann (1992) estimated that some 250,000 immigrants would be needed to keep Germany's population stable. Aiming at an active population policy has proved to be a delicate issue in Switzerland for ethical reasons,

as well as due to a lack of consensus. As far as migration is concerned, the feasibility of a migration policy that would serve demographic tasks is also fairly questionable. Empirical results show that in general immigrants quickly adapt their reproductive behavior to that of the natives. The most important impacts of immigration on the demographic features of a population are therefore closely linked to the biased age structure of immigrants. Provided the immigrant age distribution is "younger" than that of the natives, total population growth increases and the total labor force share of the total population is bound to receive a boost.

[14] Some 25% of inward foreign direct investment flows (FDI), came from EEA (European Economic Area) countries, and 56% of outward flows went to EEA countries (Leskel, 1990). Finally in 1991, 77% of all foreigners living in Switzerland were citizens of EEA countries, in which, in turn, 60% of all Swiss living abroad were resident (Nabholz and Artho, 1992).

[15] Besides the free movement of labor, Switzerland's Federal Council identified four major obstacles to EU membership: neutrality, political sovereignty (above all in foreign policy), Swiss federalism, and (direct) democratic rights such as referendums and initiatives.

Chapter 8

Austria: A Country of Immigration and Emigration

Heinz Fassmann and Rainer Münz

8.1 Self-image and Demographic Reality

There is a yawning gap between Austria's self-image and its demographic reality. Migrants in search of work, asylum seekers, displaced persons, and other immigrants come in tens of thousands. About 15% of the resident population were born outside Austria's present-day borders, 7% are foreigners by nationality, yet this country hardly tends to see itself as an immigration society.

The self-image of Austria as a nonimmigration country has had a number of consequences. Austria lacks a clearly defined immigration policy, public opinion in general favors strict border controls, and the term "immigration" has a negative connotation for many people. For these reasons Austria's basic immigration law (drafted in 1992) is somewhat shamefacedly called "residence law". Labor migrants are still called "guest workers" – a term that implies a limited period of residence. Refugees and asylum seekers are also not very welcome. On the other hand, expatriate Austrians are considered "lost sons and daughters". No one would describe them as economic refugees, although most of them emigrated for similar reasons to those of the Moroccans, Poles, and Turks who come to the countries of Western Europe – in search of higher wages and a better life.

8.2 Austria in Preindustrial Times

Until the mid-nineteenth century the situation in the predominantly German-speaking Alpine provinces of the Habsburg Empire was characterized by three migration movements: the forced expatriation of Protestants and other dissenters for political and religious reasons; the seasonal migration from the Alpine countries to richer agricultural areas caused by over-population and poverty in the Alps; and finally, the immigration of political, artistic, and commercial elites from abroad to Vienna. Prince Eugene of Savoy, Beethoven, and Metternich are prominent examples of this.

8.2.1 The Industrial Revolution

From the mid-nineteenth century, with the beginning of the Industrial Revolution and the building of new transportation systems (railways and steamer ships), migration became a mass phenomenon. Migration to the emerging industrial centers of the Habsburg Empire became just as popular as to the cities of Vienna, Prague, and Budapest (Fassmann and Münz, 1990).

From 1869 the proportion of foreigners in the Austrian part of the Empire increased. In 1910 they comprised about 2% of the population. In this period immigration to Austria from the West decreased, especially from the German Empire. There was, on the other hand, an increase in immigration to Austria from the east of Hungary, the Russian part of Poland, Bosnia–Herzegovina, and Serbia.

At the same time the emigration from Austria to the West began. In 1910 about 623,000 Austrians were living in the German Empire, compared with only about 100,000 German citizens in Austria. Migration between the two parts of the Habsburg Empire was more or less equally balanced: in 1910, 301,000 Austrian citizens were living in Hungary and 270,000 Hungarian citizens in Austria.

8.2.2 The turn of the century

Between 1890 and 1910 emigration from Austria–Hungary increased rapidly, particularly to the USA. Between 1900 and 1910 about the same number of people emigrated from Austria–Hungary to the USA as from Italy, and considerably more than from the German Empire or from Russia. The US census of 1910 documented about 2.3 million citizens who came from the Austrian part of the Empire. For example, by 1914 about 30,000 people had emigrated from what is now Burgenland and what was then western Hungary to the USA (see Horvath, 1988). Fred Austerlitz – better known by his stage name of Fred Astaire – is probably the most prominent son of Austro–Hungarian migrants to the USA from Burgenland at that time.

This emigration was seen by some as a safety valve against poverty and political unrest, but by many others as a national danger that should be reduced by political measures. An emigration law was already drafted in 1914 but the outbreak of World War I stopped all parliamentary procedures.

8.2.3 The interwar period

After the end of World War I emigration from Austria to the USA began again. Before 1914 Austrian emigration to the USA had mostly been from the northeastern (Galicia) and southeastern (e.g., Croatia) parts of Austria–Hungary. Between the wars, 70% of those who emigrated overseas came from the province of Burgenland, which was annexed to Austria in 1921. Between 1921 and 1938 34,200 people left Burgenland for the USA (see Horvath, 1988).

The interwar period was also marked by a smaller stream of return migrants. After the onset of the economic depression in 1929 about 3,500 emigrants from Burgenland returned to Austria with their children. The best-known example is Robert Graf, who was born in New York and later became Minister of Trade and Industry. The end of the interwar period coincided with the beginning of a mass exodus of Jews and other people subjected to political and religious persecution by Nazi Germany, to which Austria was annexed in 1938. In 1938 there were 170,000 Jews in Vienna alone; in 1945 only 150 remained. Many of them died in the holocaust, others managed to find exile abroad.[1]

8.3 Migration from and to Austria: Developments since 1945

8.3.1 Political refugees and economic migrants

Since the mid-1940s Austria has been a country of destination or transit for millions of migrants. Between 1945 and 1950 about 460,000 ethnic

Germans and 140,000 other refugees and displaced persons from Eastern Europe stayed in Austria and were integrated. This first wave was followed in 1956–57 by the mass exodus of Hungarians, 180,000 of whom sought asylum in Austria. In 1968–69 162,000 Czechs and Slovaks left their homeland via Austria, but only 12,000 of them sought asylum. In 1981–82, after the imposition of martial law in Poland, between 120,000 and 150,000 Poles stayed on as "tourists" in Austria, only about 33,000 of them later applied for asylum (see *Table 8.1*).

After some years with fewer applications the number of asylum seekers from Eastern Europe and the Middle East started to grow again. In 1985 only 6,724 applications for asylum were made; in 1988 there were 15,790, in 1991 as many as 27,306, but only 16,238 in 1992. In 1988 Poles (6,670), Hungarians (2,610), and Romanians (2,134) accounted for more than half of all asylum seekers. In 1990 more than half of all applicants came from Romania, and about 10% from Turkey and Iran. In 1991–92 the emphasis shifted to asylum seekers from former Yugoslavia (1991, 6,436; 1992, 7,410), especially from the war-torn areas of Croatia and Bosnia. In 1991 the number of asylum seekers from Romania (7,506) and Turkey (2,252) remained high. About 14,000 victims of the civil war in Croatia were granted temporary residence as *de facto* refugees. While not officially recognized as refugees, they did for a time receive financial support from the federal and provincial governments. It is estimated that a further 30,000 Croats stayed in Austria temporarily, without financial support. In 1992 the main influx was from Bosnia–Herzegovina. Yet, in contrast to 1991, Austrian border officials refused the right of entry or passage to many displaced persons, most of them victims of ethnic cleansing in Bosnia.

In 1992 the reduced number of people applying for asylum in Austria (16,238) is clearly to be seen as a result of more restrictive administrative practices. For this reason two groups of foreigners in Austria seem to be rising: illegal immigrants and *de facto* refugees. In 1993 the 65,000 *de facto* refugees from Bosnia living in Austria were tolerated by the authorities but not recognized as political refugees. However, the main burden of this largest wave of refugees since 1945–46 is being carried by Bosnia, Croatia, and Serbia.

The official asylum statistics do not show the role played by Austria since the 1970s as a launchpad for Jewish emigration from the Soviet Union. From 1973 to 1989 about 250,000 Jewish emigrants from the Soviet Union came to Austria and, with few exceptions, left this country

Table 8.1. Asylum seekers in Austria by country of origin (new admissions per year).

Year	CSFR	Poland	Hungary	Romania	Former Yugoslavia	Turkey	Total number of asylum seekers
1961	52	125	174	19	3,532	—	4,116
1962	53	65	155	13	3,019	—	3,458
1963	89	40	290	5	2,783	1	3,435
1964	434	87	492	15	2,421	2	3,611
1965	552	146	659	21	2,696	—	4,247
1966	636	215	791	45	2,000	—	3,805
1967	886	106	827	53	1,917	—	3,919
1968	4,176	183	812	259	1,742	—	7,362
1969	6,530	206	1,005	575	1,279	2	9,831
1970	1,192	207	1,161	156	151	—	3,085
1971	356	223	1,064	184	87	—	2,075
1972	291	145	968	183	70	—	1,838
1973	123	161	729	213	105	3	1,576
1974	173	202	584	349	156	1	1,712
1975	156	182	471	203	230	1	1,502
1976	194	291	467	203	108	5	1,818
1977	394	538	534	551	81	14	2,566
1978	515	773	525	958	66	49	3,412
1979	1,834	1,095	580	976	49	100	5,627
1980	3,241	2,181	1,043	1,023	45	120	9,259
1981	2,196	29,091	1,225	1,316	40	35	34,557
1982	1,975	1,870	922	737	74	54	6,314
1983	1,651	1,823	961	502	116	39	5,868
1984	1,941	2,466	1,229	501	158	31	7,208
1985	2,333	662	1,642	890	410	56	6,724
1986	2,147	568	2,220	2,329	488	163	8,639
1987	2,705	667	4,689	1,460	402	408	11,406
1988	1,728	6,670	2,610	2,134	477	644	15,790
1989	3,307	2,107	364	7,932	634	3,263	21,882
1990	176	132	46	12,199	768	1,862	22,789
1991	12	19	6	7,506	6,436	2,252	27,306
1992	10	10	0	2,609	7,410	1,251	16,238

Source: *Statistisches Handbuch der Republik Österreich*, BMI.

of transit after a couple of days or weeks. About 65,000 of them chose Israel as their destination, but the majority went to the USA and other countries. Since 1990 Jews from Russia and other CIS countries have emigrated directly to Israel or overseas without passing through Vienna (or Rome). In 1989 Austria was also for a short time the launchpad for migration between East and West Germany. More than 45,000 former GDR citizens crossed the Hungarian border into Burgenland between

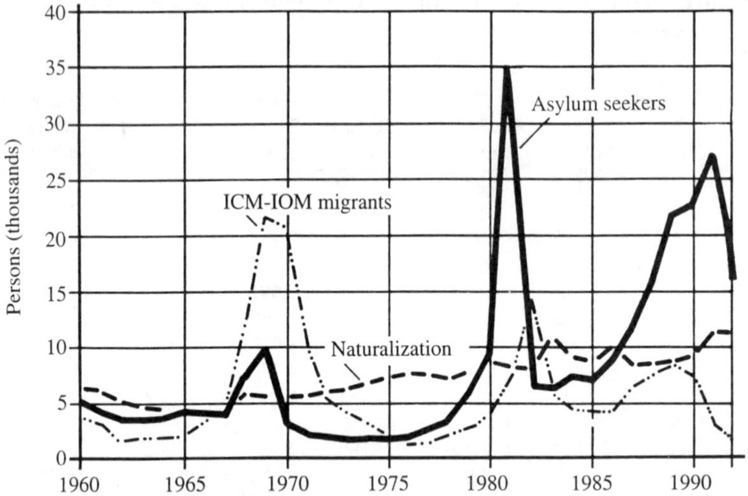

Figure 8.1. Asylum seekers to and transmigrants through Austria.

July and October 1989; at first illegally, but later with the permission of the authorities in Budapest.

Most of the emigrants from Eastern Europe and the former Soviet Union that have come to Austria since the 1950s have gone on to the USA, Canada, South Africa, Australia, and Israel.[2] *Figure 8.1* gives figures on asylum seekers to and transmigrants through Austria. Some returned to their homelands or at least tried to do so. A smaller but visible proportion of the migrants from the East stayed in Austria, became naturalized, and, for the most part, are politically and socially fully integrated.

The cultural heritage of the Habsburg Empire and the ethnic networks that remained from earlier East–West migration obviously helped to integrate some of the new immigrants. A rough estimate suggests that since 1945 more than 2.8 million people have come to Austria as displaced persons, refugees, or transmigrants. Of these:

- Some 550,000 people used Austria only as a transit country (transmigrants).
- Some 1.4 million stayed in Austria for a longer period but emigrated later to another country of destination or returned to their countries of origin.
- Some 700,000 displaced persons, ethnic Germans, and other refugees from Eastern Europe – about 9% of the country's total population –

have settled permanently in Austria. Of these 340,000 have or had a mother tongue other than German.

More recently, although the Austrian authorities have continued to stress that the tradition of granting asylum remains a basic principle of Austrian policy, the social climate and political practices have changed completely. Numerous potential asylum seekers and would-be immigrants are turned away or sent back at the borders or at Vienna airport. In many cases this is done before they have a chance to apply for asylum; others are discouraged from asking for political asylum (e.g., war refugees from Bosnia) or at least are excluded from official support schemes after they have applied. The hidden agenda of such practices is obvious. Austria wants to reverse its traditional image as a country with open doors for East–West migrants – an image that was easy to maintain as long as most of these migrants could move on easily to the USA, Canada, Australia, South Africa, or even Germany. Since 1990, however, none of these countries has provided preferential status for would-be emigrants from Eastern Europe.

Austria's restrictive immigration policy is backed by public opinion. Ethnic stereotypes and negative attitudes *vis-à-vis* foreigners in general and asylum seekers in particular have become more virulent. Both domestic opinion and Western Europe's reluctance to share the burden are the main reasons why in 1992 Austria was able to close its borders to many refugees from Bosnia–Herzegovina without having to deal with strong criticism at home or abroad. The position of the Austrian authorities is that these war refugees and displaced persons would already have been safe on Croatian, Slovenian, or Hungarian soil. While this may be true in principle, it only "solves" the refugee problem at the expense of poorer and more vulnerable states closer to the conflict areas. What would Austria have done in 1956, in 1968, or in 1981–82, if the West had behaved in a similar way while Austria had to deal with a wave of refugees from Hungary, Czechoslovakia, and Poland?

Refugees recognized under the conditions of the Geneva Convention have more or less the same rights in Austria as do Austrian citizens themselves, except for the right to vote. They have the same right of access to the Austrian labor market, and, where necessary, they receive financial support from the federal government.[3] Recognition as a refugee requires an administrative procedure that can last several months, during which time an increasingly smaller number of asylum seekers are provided with accommodation under the direction of the

Minister of the Interior (federal authority care).[4] In mid-1992 about 12,500 asylum seekers and refugees were in the care of the federal authorities in three transit camps and several hundred small hotels and private accommodation. At the same time, some of the 60,000 *de facto* refugees from Bosnia were also receiving financial assistance.

The most important change in the last few years is that not all asylum seekers are supported by the federal authorities for there is no inherent legal claim to this support. Instead, access to federal support depends both on the varying practices of the authorities and on each asylum seeker's self-assertiveness. At the same time an "accelerated procedure" was introduced. If an application for asylum is declared by authorities as being "obviously unfounded" the case is not even processed to determine the material reasons for seeking asylum. This applies to almost all applicants from Eastern Europe and other parts of the world in which the Austrian authorities do not expect any infringement of human rights ("safe country status"). People from these areas are considered to be economic refugees. But this also applies to potential asylum seekers and refugees who do not enter Austria by air with valid papers. Those who disembark at a "safe" airport on their way, or who come to Austria by land are seen by the authorities to have already been in safety; therefore they can under these circumstances no longer show they are in immediate danger of persecution under the terms of the Geneva Convention. Similar restrictions were adopted by Germany in 1993.[5]

Until 1984 asylum seekers had a 50–80% chance of being recognized as political refugees in Austria, yet the figure fell to 13% in 1991 and 10% in 1992. Since the beginning of 1992 a separate Federal Asylum Office decides on all cases. In line with current administrative practices, most applications are rejected in summary proceedings. In the past only 3,000 applications per year were accepted yet in 1993 less than 5,000 people were able to apply for asylum. Many potential asylum seekers move on to another country. Of those whose applications are rejected, however, some stay.[6] Others do not even get in contact with the authorities, and the numbers of illegal immigrants and *de facto* refugees in Austria are growing rapidly.

8.3.2 Foreign labor in Austria and Austrians abroad

In Austria the recruitment of labor migrants began considerably later than in West Germany, Switzerland, or Scandinavia. Austria concluded

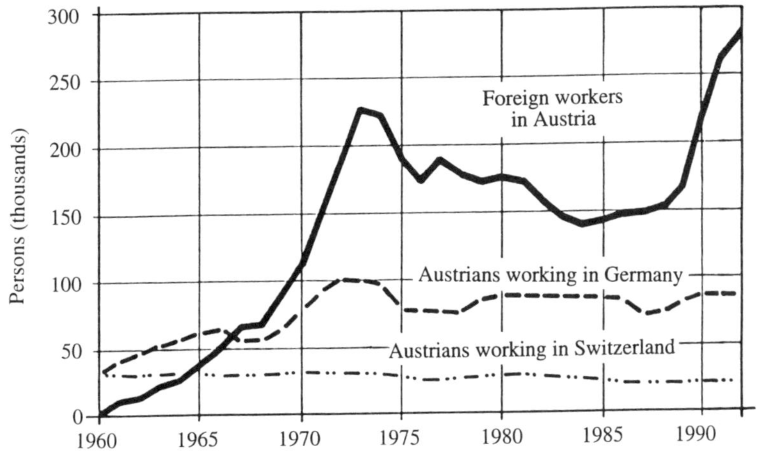

Figure 8.2. Foreign workers in Austria and Austrian workers in Germany and Switzerland.

the first Recruitment Agreement with Spain in 1962, a second with Turkey in 1964, and a third with Yugoslavia in 1966. As a result, so-called guest-worker quotas were negotiated for individual branches by trade unions and employer organizations. Applications for individual work permits only made up a small proportion (about 30%) of the foreign workers. In 1974 the employment of guest workers reached its first peak with 220,000 foreign workers in Austria comprising less than 10% of the labor force at that time (see *Figure 8.2*).

Periods of economic stagnation after 1974 and the arrival of the baby-boom cohorts on the labor market led to significant reductions in the guest-worker quotas in Austria (see *Table 8.2*). In this way, Austria and other West European countries exported their unemployment. In 1984 the number of registered foreign workers in Austria was only 138,710 – a decrease of almost 40% within 10 years – but thereafter the figures again rose appreciably. In December 1992 about 261,000 foreigners were legally employed in Austria, about twice as many as in 1984. A further 34,000 foreigners were unemployed, of whom only a small number (20% in 1990) were still employed as part of branch quotas. One-third of all foreign workers (93,000 in December 1992) were in possession of full work permits that allowed complete mobility in the labor market. In addition to these workers there is also an undoubtedly growing number of East–Central European immigrants who are either

Table 8.2. Foreign labor in Austria by country of origin, 1963–92 (annual averages).

Year	Germany	Italy	Former Yugoslavia	Spain	Turkey	Others	Total	Annual change
1963	5,205	3,549	4,917	984	1,520	5,325	21,500	—
1964	4,463	2,485	9,782	1,176	3,793	4,401	26,100	+4.600
1965	3,860	2,588	19,595	1,120	5,986	4,151	37,300	+11,200
1966	3,355	2,271	34,662	807	6,767	3,638	51,500	+14,200
1967	3,284	1,598	49,436	427	7,632	3,823	66,200	+14,700
1968	3,330	1,296	51,020	287	7,561	4,006	67,500	+1,300
1969	3,620	1,201	65,126	253	11,348	6,152	87,700	+20,200
1970	3,506	995	83,435	232	16,816	6,731	111,715	+24,015
1971	3,546	1,052	115,716	266	21,931	7,705	150,216	+38,501
1972	5,313	1,577	145,267	282	21,356	13,270	187,065	+36,849
1973	5,770	1,710	178,134	291	26,692	14,204	226,801	+39,736
1974	5,890	1,537	169,372	261	29,999	15,268	222,327	–4,474
1975	5,947	1,464	141,199	265	27,026	15,110	191,011	–31,316
1976	10,635	1,655	120,543	225	24,616	13,999	171,673	–19,338
1977	11,806	1,805	131,720	219	27,077	16,236	188,863	+17,190
1978	11,701	1,999	121,050	215	26,209	15,535	176,709	–12,154
1979	11,613	1,940	114,690	211	26,638	15,500	170,592	–6,117
1980	12,071	1,992	115,215	216	28,244	16,974	174,712	+4,120
1981	12,210	2,066	110,820	224	29,069	17,384	171,773	–2,939
1982	11,886	2,139	96,778	210	28,592	16,282	155,988	–15,785
1983	11,380	1,881	89,278	191	27,563	15,054	145,347	–10,641
1984	11,054	—	83,144	—	27,725	16,787	138,710	–6,637
1985	11,179	—	82,015	—	29,101	17,912	140,206	+1,496
1986	11,399	—	83,681	—	31,272	19,610	145,963	+5,757
1987	11,566	—	82,503	—	32,646	20,658	147,373	+1,410
1988	11,984	—	83,108	—	34,205	21,618	150,915	+3,542
1989	12,349	—	90,836	—	39,200	24,997	167,381	+16,466
1990	13,063	—	110,504	—	50,555	43,488	217,610	+50,229
1991	13,687	—	129,144	—	57,541	66,089	266,461	+48,851
1992	13,565	—	136,103	—	55,637	68,579	273,884	+7,423

Sources: Years until 1983 from Biffl (1986: 40); 1984–91 from the Federal Ministry of Labor and Social Affairs and from *Statistische Übersichten* (ÖSTAT/WIFO); since 1984 Italians and Spaniards are listed as "others"; BMAS: Employment of Foreigners 1991. Data for 1992: only Dec. 1992 (BMAS). In 1992 the category "other" comprised 11,086 Poles, 10,715 Czechs and Slovaks, 10,143 Hungarians, and 9,241 Romanians.

illegally employed or working on their own account. The majority of them, however, only have occasional jobs and stay temporarily in Austria.

Since the mid-1970s there have been changes not only in the numbers of foreigners gainfully employed but also in the origins and structure of the new immigrants. Slovenians and Croats were followed by Serbs, Bosnians, and Kosovo-Albanians. Former Yugoslav citizens were followed by Turks and foreign employees of "other" nationalities, most recently particularly by new migrants from East–Central Europe. Male guest workers living on their own have been followed by their wives and other family members, legal immigrants by illegal ones. With the fall of the Iron Curtain, however, the proportion of gainfully employed men among the foreign workers has increased again while the war in Croatia and Bosnia has brought mostly women and children to Austria who are not accepted as political refugees and are therefore denied access to the labor market.

When talking about labor migrants or guest workers, most Austrians think of Turkish or former Yugoslav citizens working in their country. However, Austria was and remains a country of origin of labor migrants. Their postwar emigration began as early as 1950 – well before foreign workers were recruited by Austria. The majority of Austrians abroad live in Germany (183,000 in 1991) and in Switzerland (28,800; OECD/SOPEMI, 1992). In addition, there are (according to the Federal Ministry for Foreign Affairs) some 10,800 Austrians in Australia, 21,300 in Brazil, 20,000 in South Africa, 18,500 in the USA, 10,300 in Canada, 10,000 in Argentina, 10,000 in Italy, 7,000 in Argentina, and 6,500 in the UK (Fassmann and Münz, 1993: 35). According to the 1981 census, a further 50,000 Austrians work abroad either as daily or weekly commuters, mainly to Germany and Switzerland.

On balance, the number of foreign workers in Austria and the number of Austrians working abroad is more or less the same (see *Figure 8.2*), but the structure of the two groups of migrants are quite different. Austrian migrant workers, in Western Europe and overseas, usually occupy positions on the foreign labor markets that are considerably better than those filled by foreign workers in Austria. One can with justification speak of "low in, high out" (LIHO) labor migration. Compared with some 560,000 foreigners (estimate for the fourth quarter 1992) legally resident in Austria, there are some 500,000 Austrians living abroad; it can therefore be assumed that this "throughput" situation is also accompanied by a brain-drain – an outflow of human capital and well-qualified people.

In the late 1980s, alongside the growing stream of asylum seekers, refugees and other immigrants from Eastern Europe, new labor migrants from former Yugoslavia and Turkey also found employment in Austria. Regulations controlling the entry and immigration of foreigners were tightened; the restrictions were unable to stop *de facto* immigration into and through Austria, but they stopped any further increase in the number of gainfully and legally employed foreigners. One must also acknowledge that this restrictive policy might have fostered the growth of illegal conditions of employment and badly paid moonlighting. Some of the immigrants, while not being prevented from immigrating, were and continue to be forced into illegality (see Tabah, 1989; Komitee, 1984).[7]

The position of those foreigners who are legally working in Austria has, on the other hand, improved. After working for a year they get a two-year work permit for one province and with this they can change employers. After five years of uninterrupted employment they can obtain a full work permit ("exemption certificate") which allows them to work anywhere in the country. Such full work permits can be immediately granted to foreign spouses married to Austrians, as well as to the children of foreign workers.[8]

The 1990 amendment to the Law on the Employment of Foreigners laid down quantitative limits. Until further notice, the number of legally employed foreigners was not to exceed 10% of the domestic labor market. In 1993 this "ceiling" was lowered to 8% but the Ministry for Social Affairs can raise it up to 10% when there are special public or economic interests. The actual maximum is now 304,000 either employed or registered as unemployed foreigners.[9]

8.3.3 Legal regulations concerning immigration to Austria

The 1992 Act Concerning the Admission of Foreigners to Austria (Domicile Act) is the basic law regulating migration beyond the granting of asylum and the recruitment of foreign labor. Although an appropriate name was avoided in view of prevailing public opinion, it is in fact a law on immigration that divides potential immigrants into three groups:

- Since 1993 all citizens of the EU and EFTA require neither permission to enter the country nor a work permit.[10]
- For immigrants from the rest of the world the federal government laid down a maximum number of entry permits on an annual basis. These people are subject to a selection procedure. Foreign spouses and children of both Austrian nationals and foreigners living in Austria are given priority when applying for entry permits.[11] Priority is also given to people with specific qualifications for which there is an unmet need on the Austrian labor market.

- In cases of sudden shortages on the Austrian labor market the Federal Minister for Employment and Social Affairs can grant work permits for temporary seasonal employment, beyond the immigration quota.

In principle, applications for immigration to Austria must be made in the country of origin. The granting of permission to immigrate does not only depend on the above-mentioned priorities (family members, special qualifications); would-be immigrants must also provide proof that they have a place to live and means of subsistence. In practice this means that potential immigrants from non-EU/non-EFTA countries must either have a job waiting for them in Austria, or they must be joining heads of family who already live in Austria.

On first immigrating, employed persons are granted residence permits for six months, which can be prolonged for a further six months and then, after a year, for a further two years. After five years foreigners from non-EU/non-EFTA countries may be granted unlimited residence.

When immigrants from outside the EU/EFTA lose their jobs or their accommodation and cannot find new jobs or places to live, they also lose their right of residence. Those directly affected and their dependent family members may in these cases be forced to leave the country. In practice this means that many unprivileged immigrants, although they have paid taxes and social-security contributions, cannot in a case of emergency make use of their social-security rights.

8.4 Migration Policy

8.4.1 The influence of migration on population development

Since the end of World War II the population of Austria has increased from about 6.5 million to about 7.9 million in 1993. Between 1945 and 1992 almost 3.7 million people have come to Austria as displaced persons, refugees, transmigrants, recruited workers, or family dependents. For them Austria has been either their country of destination, a transit country, or just a short stopover. About 1.2 million have stayed permanently in Austria or will probably only return to their country of origin on retirement or in the case of long-term unemployment.[12]

For decades, migration to and from Austria was largely the result of an unplanned process. The political authorities clearly took the initiative only in the case of the regulated interstate recruitment of foreign labor from the mid-1960s and in the reduction of these quotas between 1974 and 1984. But this foreign labor policy was neither conceived as a migration policy nor as a population policy. Only with the 1992 Domicile Act did the state try more closely to control and consciously regulate the number and structure of immigrants with regard to the overall economic and demographic development.

8.4.2 Austria's role in the European migration context

A retrospective analysis reveals some persistent patterns of migration. Since the end of the nineteenth century Austria's position in European migration was and is determined by economic and geopolitical factors. From the perspective of the industrialized West, Austria was – and to a certain extent continues to be – on the periphery. This view is also shared by many Austrians for whom the country's western neighbors, especially Switzerland and Germany, offer attractive labor markets characterized by higher salaries, advanced production structures, and often somewhat more attractive working conditions. Therefore the emigration of Austrians could be interpreted as outflow of human capital.

A similar perspective applies to Austria's eastern neighbors, but the roles are reversed. For them Austria is both a "gateway to the West" and a country of destination for economically and politically motivated migrants. Since 1991, however, Austria has been increasingly trying to stop the influx of new immigrants, asylum seekers, and refugees.

For the foreseeable future it can be assumed that Austria will remain a country of both immigration and emigration (a "throughput" situation). Above all, the fall of the Iron Curtain and the current political and economic upheavals and crises in the eastern part of Europe render improbable a complete stop to the influx from these countries, or the potential influx from the Balkans and the Middle East. Given the increasing freedom of movement in the East and a certain degree of integration between East and West, Austria's control of immigration and emigration will continue to be limited. In 1989 immigrants exceeded emigrants by about 53,000; in 1990 by as many as 123,100; and in 1991 by about 59,000 (see *Table 8.3* and *Figure 8.3*). In 1992–93 another 70,000 displaced people from Bosnia were accepted as *de facto* refugees. From 1989 to 1992 Austria lost a net total of about 21,000 nationals through increased emigration and gained about 292,000 foreigners through increased immigration, almost exclusively from former Yugoslavia, Turkey, and East–Central Europe.

Table 8.3. Population trends in Austria, 1980–92.

Year	Pop. (annual average)	Pop. (end of the year)	Annual change	Balance of births minus deaths	Balance of migration	Naturalizations
Total population						
1980	7,549,433	7,553,326	7,786	–1,570	9,356	—
1983	7,551,842	7,550,967	–4,795	–2,923	–1,872	—
1984	7,552,551	7,555,630	4,663	768	3,895	—
1985	7,557,667	7,560,766	5,136	–2,138	7,274	—
1986	7,565,603	7,569,824	9,058	–107	9,165	—
1987	7,575,732	7,586,416	16,592	1,596	14,996	—
1988	7,596,081	7,602,431	16,015	4,789	11,226	—
1989	7,623,605	7,660,345	57,914	5,352	52,562	—
1990	7,718,248	7,790,957	130,612	7,502	123,110	—
1991	7,825,261	7,860,810	69,853	11,201	53,253	—
1992	7,884,219	7,909,575	48,756	12,140	36,616	—
Austrian citizens						
1980	7,266,739	7,265,125	–3,227	–6,547	–4,856	8,176
1981	7,265,466	7,268,267	3,142	–4,081	–209	7,432
1982	7,271,213	7,275,773	7,506	–1,988	2,335	7,159
1983	7,276,826	7,281,834	6,061	–7,011	3,172	9,900
1984	7,283,789	7,286,121	4,287	–2,148	–1,357	7,792
1985	7,285,947	7,288,428	2,307	–4,900	–104	7,311
1986	7,289,940	7,291,857	3,429	–2,912	–1,719	8,060
1987	7,292,724	7,294,026	2,169	–1,499	–2,950	6,618
1988	7,297,366	7,299,540	5,514	1,299	–3,100	7,315
1989	7,300,973	7,302,992	3,452	1,247	–5,100	7,305
1990	7,304,856	7,308,812	5,820	2,439	–5,600	8,981
1991	7,313,067	7,318,566	9,754	4,017	–6,267	11,137
1992	7,322,464	7,328,042	9,476	2,320	–4,500	11,656
Foreigners in Austria						
1980	282,694	288,201	11,013	4,977	14,212	–8,176
1981	299,163	319,106	30,905	5,330	33,007	–7,432
1982	302,872	279,989	–39,117	5,489	–37,447	–7,159
1983	275,016	269,133	–10,856	4,088	–5,044	–9,900
1984	268,762	269,509	376	2,916	5,252	–7,792
1985	271,720	272,338	2,829	2,762	7,378	–7,311
1986	275,663	277,967	5,629	2,805	10,884	–8,060
1987	283,008	292,390	14,423	3,095	17,946	–6,618
1988	298,715	302,891	10,501	3,490	14,326	–7,315
1989	322,632	357,353	54,462	4,105	57,662	–7,305
1990	413,392	482,145	124,792	5,063	128,710	–8,981
1991	512,194	542,253	6,010	7,184	59,520	–11,137
1992	561,755	581,533	39,280	9,820	41,116	–11,656

Source: Estimates of the Austrian Central Statistical Office (ÖSTAT).

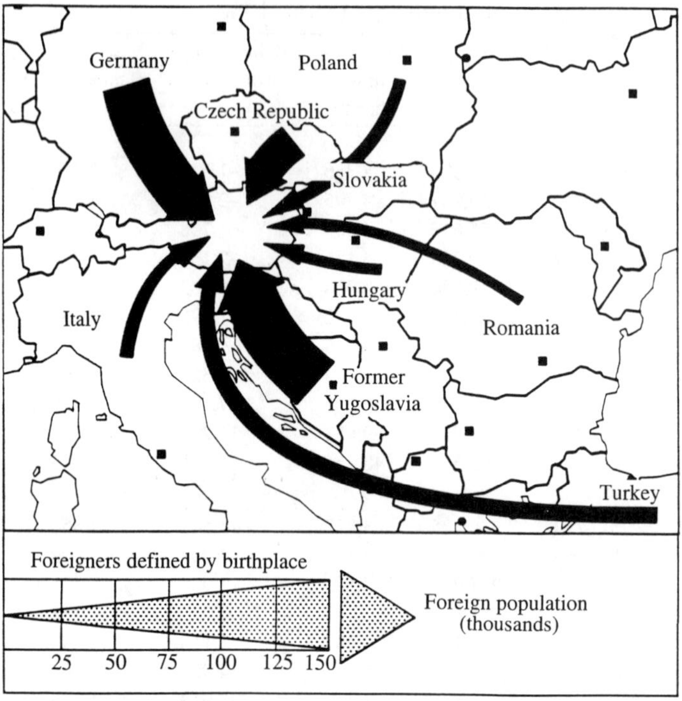

Figure 8.3. Immigration to Austria, 1988, based on a survey of representative random sample of Austrian households carried out in 1988. In interpreting the figure, care should be taken not to confound Austria's foreign-born population with foreigners living in Austria. Many immigrants to Austria, especially those who came before 1965, have become Austrians through naturalization.

8.4.3 Police state or migration policy?

Because of its economic attractiveness and its geographical position, Austria must actively come to terms with its role as a *de facto* immigration country. What could a national policy achieve with regard to international migration in light of the limited room for maneuver? First, a more realistic self-image and a comprehensive policy are needed. Priority should be given to a shift from a mostly reactive and defensive immigration policy to a forward-looking one; this is necessary for demographic, economic and social reasons. Low birth rates and the emigration of highly mobile university graduates and a highly qualified

Table 8.4. Naturalization of foreigners living in Austria.

Year	Total number naturalized	Germans No.	Germans %	Former Yugoslavs No.	Former Yugoslavs %
1980	8,176	2,077	25.4	1,823	22.3
1981	7,432	1,842	24.8	1,496	20.1
1982	7,159	1,799	25.1	1,185	16.6
1983	9,900	2,552	25.8	2,224	22.5
1984	7,792	2,293	29.4	1,411	18.1
1985	7,311	1,769	24.2	1,437	19.7
1986	8,060	1,497	18.6	1,439	17.9
1987	6,618	889	13.4	1,391	21.0
1988	7,315	793	10.8	1,723	23.6
1989	7,305	512	7.0	2,293	31.4
1990	8,981	485	5.4	2,639	29.4
1991	11,137	441	4.0	3,217	28.9
1992	11,656	398	3.4	4,329	37.1

Source: ÖSTAT.

work force to Western Europe are likely to continue. Therefore migration policy should both secure the constant immigration of particular categories of foreign labor to Austria and their long-term integration. It should be made easier for these immigrants to become Austrian citizens. At present the right to apply for Austrian citizenship only arises after ten years of residence in Austria. Since 1980 only 2–3% of all foreigners have made use of this option each year (*Table 8.4*).

The 1992 Act Concerning the Admission of Foreigners to Austria regulating immigration to Austria from outside the EU/EFTA can be seen as a first (albeit inadequate) step toward a rational immigration policy. Between 1989 and 1992, however, the policy on foreigners had, to some extent, other aims. The unspoken desire for a new "Iron Curtain" was and remains dominant. In 1989 visas were introduced for Bulgaria; since 1990 Turks and Romanians again require entry visas for Austria. Since 1992 this also applies to Serbs, Montenegrins, and Bosnians with "Yugoslav" passports. For a short time in 1990–91 even Poles needed visas. Existing legislation on passports, border controls, and asylum procedures has also been amended. Since April 1990 foreigners may be prevented from disembarking from a plane, casually returned over the border, or detained in custody pending deportation. It is now also legally possible to deport foreigners before they can apply for asylum or after their applications have been rejected. The deportations can even take place when the person concerned has appealed against deportation or against rejection of an application for asylum. Since September 1990

Austrian troops have been stationed on the "green" Austro–Hungarian border at the request of the Minister of the Interior. In the future this job will be done by armed border guard units.

Officially, the above measures are intended to fight uncontrolled immigration and to protect the Austrian labor market. But they are in line with mainstream domestic public opinion. Austria's policy also reflects the attitude of the EU, Switzerland, and Scandinavia to East–Central Europe, the Balkans, and the countries of the former Soviet Union. The West is increasingly trying to close its borders to immigrants from these countries now that citizens have passports and greater freedom to travel. In line with this view, even Turkey is no longer part of the West.

8.4.4 Why an immigration policy?

In the long run, Western countries like Austria will have to rely on immigration. In the case of Austria, demographic forecasts show that after the year 2000 an annual immigration of 25,000 people would balance the birth deficit, halt the population decline, and reduce the pace of the aging process.

The main arguments in favor of a stabilization of the population are related to both fiscal and social policy. The financing of health and pensions insurance could be more broadly based, for example, and most social and educational services are easier and less expensive to deliver within a larger and stable population. The pressure for substantial system reforms, major cost-cutting programs, and reallocations of funds would be smaller with a stationary population than with a rapidly aging and shrinking one.

8.5 Future Prospects

For the moment the main obstacles to immigration are growing unemployment, serious housing shortages, and increasingly hostile public opinion. On the whole, rational arguments are inadequate in the face of hostility to and fear of foreigners, yet historical experience has shown that during the last 50 years Austria has been able to absorb and integrate large numbers of immigrants. On average, annual net immigration to Austria amounted to 27,000 people. There is also evidence that the economic yield and fiscal contributions of immigrants were substantially greater than the social benefits and public expenditure they received.

In the past immigration thus turned out to be a "good bargain" for a receiving country like Austria. One should also bear in mind that immigration cannot be held responsible for most defects of a Western society but, by and large, simply makes them more obvious or aggravates them. Unemployment, petty crime, moonlighting, the housing shortage, right-wing extremism, and hatred of foreigners would also exist without immigrants. It goes without saying that the existence of such problems hinders the integration of immigrants while adversely affecting their conditions of life.

This diagnosis does not advise against immigration but for a rational and comprehensive immigration policy that includes an annual upper limit on the number of immigrants. It must go further than a mere neglecting tolerance of asylum seekers, refugees, and labor immigrants; a planned migration policy must also influence public opinion, try to gain acceptance, and purposefully employ public funds for integration measures.

For these measures to be effective, countries like Austria require a legal and institutional framework regulating immigration. The Act Concerning the Admission of Foreigners to Austria (in force since 1993) is a first step in this direction. Austria has become the first European country to follow the US or Canadian examples, to attempt to control spatial mobility with a genuine immigration law. The conflict that remains is also known from the US experience. In the coming decades those who are ready and willing to come to Austria will outnumber by far those who will be eligible.

Notes

[1] According to information from the Documentation Archive of the Austrian Resistance Movement, about 125,000 Austrian Jews managed to emigrate after 1938 and about 45,000 died in concentration camps.

[2] Some East European immigrants and refugees applied directly to the authorities of one of the traditional immigration countries, others found a country of destination through the International Organization for Migration (IOM, previously the ICM).

[3] The 1992 Domicile Act also empowers the federal government in an emergency to consider whole population groups as endangered and to grant them temporary residence in Austria, even where the strict criteria of the Geneva Convention (the danger of individual persecution) do not (yet) apply. These groups of people can be supported by public funds.

[4] This status can, however, be altered over time. In the summer of 1989 about 5,000 Poles and Hungarians were "discharged" from federal care in view of the changed political conditions in their countries of origin, and were thus reduced to mere *de facto* refugees. Moreover, at the present time, there is in general no accommodation

(in federal care) for asylum seekers from Romania, Bulgaria, and Turkey (with the exception of some of the Kurdish asylum seekers) and for those entering Austria without valid papers.

[5] All Austria's neighboring countries, including the Czech Republic, Slovakia, Hungary, and Slovenia, are now signatories to the Geneva Convention on Refugees. Hungary, however, only recognizes European refugees (Ratification of the Geneva Convention with European proviso).

[6] According to the special Police Law on foreigners, persons not recognized as refugees cannot automatically be sent back to their country of origin if there is still a danger of political persecution following their return, even if no such immediate danger existed before they left (*non-refoulement*). In practice, however, such distinctions are not always made.

[7] In 1991 an estimated 90,000 foreigners were illegally working in Vienna alone; one-third of them from Turkey, another third from Poland, and the rest mostly from Romania, Bulgaria, former Yugoslavia, the Czech Republic, Slovakia, and Hungary.

[8] On condition that these children (second-generation immigrants) have either spent more than 50% of their lives here or have had at least half of their schooling and completed compulsory education here.

[9] In line with an established formula, permission to take up employment and work permits for the nine provinces can be granted for up to 90% of this maximum quota.

[10] Similar status is enjoyed by: foreign employees of international organizations based in Vienna (e.g., UN, UNIDO, IAEA); "foreigners sent by their firms" (mostly specialist and managerial staff of multinational or foreign companies); employees of foreign media (newspaper, radio, TV, and news agency correspondents); foreign artists (as long as their incomes are derived from their artistic work); and recognized refugees.

[11] The right to bring in one's family only exists if the family head has been a legal resident in Austria for over two years. Spouses joining their partners who are resident in Austria must have been married to them for at least a year. Both minimum periods may be shortened in special cases.

[12] This number includes those in employment and their dependents; refugees, asylum seekers, and tolerated *de facto* refugees; and not gainfully employed foreign spouses of Austrian nationals.

Part III

Migration to and from East–Central Europe

Chapter 9

Emigration from Poland after 1945

Piotr Korcelli

9.1 Introduction

The factors and nature of emigration from Poland have evolved over time. In the mid-nineteenth century the country (at that time partitioned among Russia, Prussia, and Austria) underwent rapid demographic growth, matched only partly and locally by the demand for labor in industry and related economic activities. As a consequence, the human pressure on agricultural land became acute, causing increasing land fragmentation and widespread rural poverty. This in turn led to the emigration of some 3.5 million people by 1914 and an additional 1.5 million during the interwar period (1919–39). The USA was the destination of more than one-third of all emigrants; other important destinations included Germany (mainly the Ruhr area), France, Canada, Brazil, and Australia. Also many thousands of Poles were subject to deportations to Siberia and other parts of the Russian Empire throughout the nineteenth century, in particular following the national uprising of 1863–64.

During World War II there were further mass deportations of the Polish population to both Germany and the Soviet Union. In the years immediately following the war, the large-scale boundary shifts caused massive movements of both Germans and Poles, involving several million people. At the same time, the majority of members of Polish armed forces in the West chose not to return to postwar Poland.

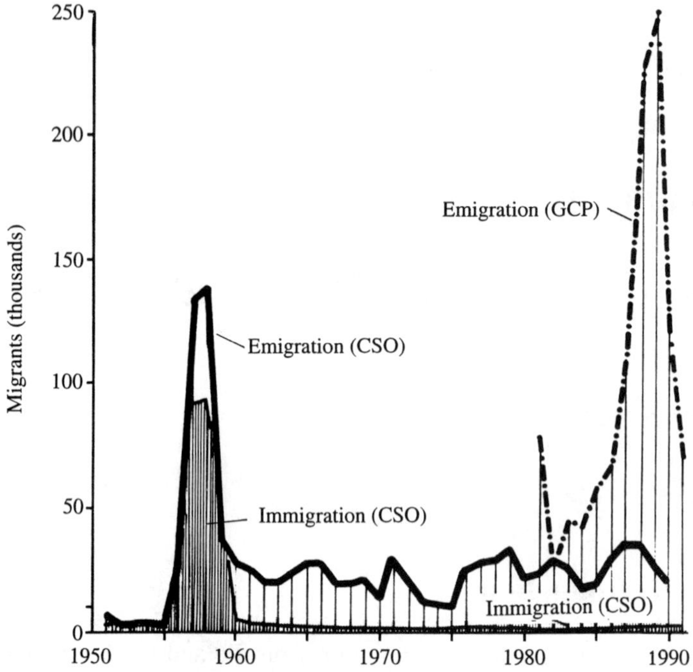

Figure 9.1. Emigration from and immigration to Poland, 1951–91. Source: Central Statistical Office (1991).

During the Cold War in the early 1950s international migration (as well as travel across the borders) from and to Poland was almost impossible. A period of political liberalization that began in Poland in 1956 allowed for the out-migration of some of the remaining ethnic German population as well as for the repatriation of a few hundred thousand ethnic Poles from the Soviet Union. However, these policies were soon discontinued, which is reflected in a sharp decrease in the volume of international migration in the late 1950s. During the 1960s emigration from Poland to the USA, Germany, Israel, Sweden, and other countries amounted to between 20,000 and 30,000 annually. In 1968 a considerable share of Poland's remaining Jewish population left the country. During the early 1970s emigration reached another low level of 10,000–15,000 per year on average (see *Figure 9.1* and *Table 9.1*).

A larger-scale emigration to Germany, officially labeled as a family reunion program, was resumed in the mid-1970s. The outset of the political, social, and economic crisis which became evident in the late

Table 9.1. Foreign migration to and from Poland (thousands).

Year	Emigration (CSO data)	Immigration (CSO data)	Emigration (GCP data)
1946–1950	1499.9	2543.6	
1951	7.8	3.4	
1952	1.6	3.7	
1953	2.8	2.0	
1954	3.8	2.8	
1955	1.9	4.7	
1956	21.8	27.6	
1957	133.4	91.8	
1958	139.3	92.8	
1959	37.0	43.2	
1960	28.0	5.7	
1961	26.5	3.6	
1962	20.2	3.3	
1963	20.0	2.5	
1964	24.2	2.3	
1965	28.6	2.2	
1966	28.8	2.2	
1967	19.9	2.1	
1968	19.4	2.2	
1969	22.1	2.0	
1970	14.1	1.9	
1971	30.2	1.7	
1972	19.1	1.8	
1973	13.0	1.4	
1974	11.8	1.4	
1975	9.6	1.8	
1976	26.7	1.8	
1977	28.9	1.6	
1978	29.5	1.5	
1979	34.2	1.7	
1980	22.7	1.5	
1981	23.8	1.4	79.1
1982	32.1	0.9	27.3
1983	26.2	1.2	45.5
1984	17.4	1.6	41.4
1985	20.5	1.6	55.8
1986	29.0	1.9	67.4
1987	36.4	1.8	108.3
1988	36.3	2.1	288.0
1989	26.6	2.2	(c. 250.0)
1990	18.4	2.6	(c. 120.0)
1991	21.0	5.0	(c. 70.0)

Source: Central Statistical Office (1991); GCP (1989).

1970s, prompted a sudden rise in the population outflow to Western Europe, the USA, and Canada.

The available data suggest that about 1 million people left Poland for Western countries between 1980 and 1990. This represented the largest component – about one-half – of the total East–West migration in Europe during the 1980s. Since 1990 the volume of emigration from Poland has been declining, although it remains relatively high. The political factors responsible for the bulk of population outflow during the Communist period have ceased to exist, but the economic push and pull factors are still generating a substantial migration potential among the Polish population.

9.2 Data on International Migration

Migration statistics, which normally represent the weakest part of demographic statistics in general, also tend to be piecemeal and in the case of international population movements are often unreliable. This applies to Poland, mostly with regard to emigration, which has been considerably underreported since 1945.

The basic source of data on international migration is the current population register, which reports on permanent domicile registration in Poland by immigrants and on domicile cancellations by emigrants. These data are published annually by the Central Statistical Office (1991) and enter the official population accounts. They are also used as a basis for various population projections.

Such data, however, are incomplete and do not reflect the real magnitude of emigration from Poland and from comparable East–Central and East European countries. Between the late 1940s and the late 1980s emigration decisions by individuals were subject to approval by the relevant government agencies (the Ministry of Internal Affairs). The procedures of issuing passports, especially those with "exit visas", were quite complicated and took a long time. Practically, the only reason for emigration that was regarded as valid by the officials was for family reunion, but even then there was no guarantee that passports would be issued by the authorities. Public opinion was molded to create a strongly negative image of an emigrant (this image, of course, did not apply to prewar emigration from capitalist Poland), but such efforts had little effect in terms of real societal values and aspirations. Emigration to a Western country became a widely accepted goal.

Under conditions of strong restrictions on "formal" emigration, "informal", undocumented emigration became a logical alternative. The dominant mechanism of the latter type of migration was travel abroad for allegedly different purposes. In practice, reasons such as tourism and family visits were entered in the appropriate passport applications both by short-term visitors and by "would-be emigrants". Along with the gradual liberalization of passport policies after 1956, and especially since the 1970s (except for the period of martial law, 1982–83), the number of undocumented emigrants grew steadily. Once in a Western country, many of them were entitled to claim asylum. The West accepted them until 1989–90 as refugees from the Communist countries.

Such departures, which were defined as illegal at the place of origin, were either not fully reported (for example, the domicile changed to "address unknown") or they entered the population register only after some delay, often at the time of the next census. The category of "migration to foreign countries", appearing in the official population statistics, was undernumerated in the 1970s, and then totally irrelevant during the 1980s, when several hundred thousand Polish citizens emigrated "unofficially" to the West.

The partial character of the international migration statistics may account for some of the observed discrepancies between the time-series data derived from the current population register and the results of periodic population censuses. The census results led to downward adjustments of the size of the total population of Poland. In the case of the 1970 census this difference amounted to about 280,000, in the 1978 census to 82,000, and in the 1988 census to 85,000 persons. Hypothetically, the census coverage can be incomplete resulting in the undernumeration of the *de facto* population, so that one could conclude that in Poland the census coverage improved between 1970 and 1988. However, data from the current population registers referring to net international migration (see *Table 9.1*) suggest that the migration outflow was 2–6 times smaller than the actual size of net emigration. Therefore, a more likely interpretation is that differences between the data from the current population register and those from the population census can at least in part be attributed to undocumented emigration during the intercensal periods (see *Table 9.2*).

This is a plausible hypothesis for the years 1961–70, and to some extent for the 1971–78 period as well. A somewhat different interpretation is needed with regard to the last intercensal period of 1978–88.

Table 9.2. Basic population accounts for Poland, 1968–90 (thousands).

Year	Total popula-tion (1)	Change (2)	Births (3)	Deaths (4)	Net int. migr. (5)	3−4+5 (6)
1968	32,426	263	524	244	–17	263
1969	32,671	245	531	263	–20	248
1970	32,658	–13	546	267	–12	267
1971	32,909	251	562	284	–29	249
1972	33,202	293	576	265	–17	294
1973	33,512	310	599	277	–12	310
1974	33,846	334	621	277	–10	334
1975	34,185	339	644	297	– 8	339
1976	34,528	343	670	304	–25	341
1977	34,850	322	603	313	–27	263
1978	35,081	231	666	325	–28	313
1979	35,414	333	688	323	–33	332
1980	35,735	321	693	350	–21	322
1981	36,062	327	679	329	–22	328
1982	36,399	337	702	335	–31	336
1983	36,745	346	721	349	–25	347
1984	37,063	318	699	365	–16	318
1985	37,341	278	678	382	–19	277
1986	37,572	231	635	376	–27	232
1987	37,764	192	606	378	–35	193
1988	37,862	98	588	371	–34	183
1989	37,963	101	563	381	–24	158
1990	38,119	156	546	388	–16	142

Source: Central Statistical Office (1991).

The 1988 census intended to cover those individuals who were staying "temporarily" abroad for at least two months on the day of the census (December 6). The figure was 508,000. According to Okolski (1991a), this was at least 250,000 below the actual number, which suggests a population overcount in the previous census. This seems to have been a consequence of a specific character of emigration as observed during the late 1980s. The peak of the last emigration wave in fact occurred during the census year, when a considerable proportion of migrants preferred to retain formal resident status in Poland just in case they wanted or were forced to return. Such a status might, for example, allow them, or their family members, to maintain access to subsidized housing at the place of origin. Hence, we may have witnessed an overreporting, rather than a more conventional underreporting with regard to the resident population in the 1988 census. The real test will come with the next population census, which will probably be held in 1998.

Alternative information on migration was provided by the passport data bank, established at the Ministry of Internal Affairs in 1980. It comprised a computerized population registration system introduced in the late 1970s as a means of total police control. The data bank, which was discontinued at the end of 1989, recorded all exits and re-entries of Polish citizens from and to Poland. Initial estimates of the size and composition of emigration from Poland during 1981–87 derived from that source, were published early in 1988, and were subsequently extended and elaborated by the Governmental Commission on Population (GCP, 1989).

Data on emigration from Poland are also available from reports on immigration by appropriate government agencies in the receiving countries. These are usually reliable sources, but the data are often piecemeal and mutually incompatible due to different definitions used and the time intervals covered. Also, these data may not account for incidents of *de facto* re-migration to the country of origin or of forward migration to third countries.

9.3 Recent Trends in Migration

During the 1980s approximately 1 million people emigrated from Poland. The accelerating deterioration of economic conditions and living standards (following the relative prosperity of the 1970s), combined with the loosening of restrictions on foreign travel, and the emerging symptoms of political chaos, led to strong pro-emigration attitudes by large segments of the society. The population outflow abroad was particularly large in 1981, when the showdown between the Solidarity-led social and political movement and the Communist party apparatus became imminent. Subsequently, emigration fell considerably in 1982 as a consequence of the imposition of travel restrictions under martial law, and rose dramatically during the late 1980s, when signs of a deep economic crisis and political crisis coincided with the implementation of "passports for everyone" policies, carried out by the last "reformist" Communist government.

Available data indicate that about 1.7 million journeys were undertaken by Polish citizens to Western countries during the peak emigration year of 1988. These included 26,000 "permanent migrations" and 1.66 million "temporary moves" for such (self-declared) purposes as tourism, family-related visits, participation in sport events, and scientific and business-related activities. Out of the 1.66 million exits some 280,000, i.e., one in eight, were one-way. This means in December 1988 the persons involved still remained abroad and the journey had already lasted more than one month longer than originally intended (according to the passport application). Out of these 280,000 persons, 202,000 had not returned to Poland by the end of November 1989. Together with the 26,000 "official emigrants", these made up the total of 228,000 emigrants in the year 1988.

Since emigration registration at the Polish borders was abolished in 1989, there is no direct information that would allow this figure to be adjusted by deducting those migrants who returned within the following year. An extrapolation of the proportion of returnees (those who moved back between 6 December 1988 and 23 November 1989) among the earlier emigrants (those who left Poland in 1981–87) yields an estimate of some 25%. Thus, the effective ("permanent") emigration from Poland in 1988 might be scaled down to some 180,000. However, in *Table 9.1* the 228,000 figure has been retained since it represents the only number documented in the GCP report of 1989.

Where did these emigrants go? The GCP refers to countries of first destination, while data published by the Central Statistical Office (1989) list the final destination countries (again, as declared in the passport applications by the prospective migrants). According to the latter source, West Germany accounted for 64.0% and the USA for 12.3% of the "official" emigration from Poland to Western countries during 1981–88. The GCP published slightly different shares. According to this source some 48.7% of all official emigrants went to West Germany and 14.0% to the USA. The report attributed 13.6% of all temporary migration during 1981–88 to Austria, Greece, and Italy. But these countries served mainly as transit countries for Polish emigration to North America, Australia, and South Africa.

Based on these accounts, one can estimate the size of emigration from Poland to West Germany (including West Berlin) to be within the range 335,000–360,000, i.e., 51–55% of the total emigration of 653,000 during 1981–88. Emigration to the USA can be estimated at 110,000–125,000 (17–20% of the total) and to Canada 60,000–80,000 (9–12%). Other important destinations were Australia, South Africa, France, Sweden, Italy, and Austria (see Korcelli, 1991).

According to official West German sources (see Mackensen, 1991) the total net emigration from Poland to West Germany during the 35-year period 1954–88 amounted to 790,500, including 468,900 ethnic Germans (*Aussiedler*) and 321,600 ethnic Poles. According to other data, the total number of ethnic German resettlers (*Aussiedler*) from Poland was 853,300 during 1968–89; of these, 328,500 had arrived by 1982, 134,300 during 1983–87, 140,000 in 1988, and 250,000 in 1989 (Mackensen, 1991: 74). The report by the Council of Europe (1991) quotes a total emigration figure from Poland to Germany of 608,300 in 1987–90 (see Rudolph, Chapter 6, this volume).

These data suggest that for 1954–80 the figures listed in the German sources are roughly comparable with those published by the Polish Central Statistical Office (1989); in the case of 1981–88 the same holds true with respect to the data of the GCP (1989). Independent of the different sources, the crest of the emigration wave occurred in 1989 rather than 1988, with a high intensity of outflow continuing in 1990.

However, since the *Aussiedler* do not enter the official German statistics as immigrants until they receive resident status (permanent domicile) in Germany, there is a delay of a year or so before they appear in the immigration data (Mackensen, 1991: 73–4). Therefore, the figure of 250,000 arrivals from Poland in 1989 is probably considerably inflated, while a large part reflects moves that had already taken place in 1988–87. This suggests some undercounting for those years in the data of the GCP.

The rapid increase in emigration from Poland during the late 1980s clearly reflected a coincidence of the mounting internal political and economic crisis with new passport regulations that allowed individual travel and emigration without bureaucratic procedure. With the inevitable demise of the Communist rule in Poland clearly in sight by mid-1988, a number of prospective emigrants chose to take advantage of the possibility, still open at that time, of claiming refugee status in a Western country. The above of course does not apply to persons eligible for the *Aussiedler* status, which is defined by the German constitution on the basis of historical and ethnic considerations. This status can be claimed by all persons (and their descendants and close family members) who lived within the borders of Germany before 1938–45, by those who were German citizens in 1939–45 but lived outside these borders, and by other ethnic Germans living in Eastern Europe, the

Balkans, and the former Soviet Union. Within the territories taken over by Poland in 1945 (West Prussia, Silesia, and the southern part of East Prussia excluding the free city of Gdansk), the number of remaining autochthonous population was 1 million (compared with the total of 8.5 million inhabitants of these territories before the war). They were interpreted as being of Polish origin by the Polish authorities, but at least partly as ethnic Germans by the West German government. In fact, such different evaluations apply to earlier periods as well. In 1925, according to official German statistics, the number of ethnic Poles living within the territories annexed to Poland after World War II was calculated at 683,000 (including 543,000 in the western part of Upper Silesia and the Opole region), while Polish researchers (Romer and others) put their number at 1.2 million (see Kosinski, 1963: 24–5).

In 1970, after the first phase of the so-called family reunification program, the German Red Cross estimated that 290,000 ethnic Germans were still living within Polish borders (according to Korbel, quoted in Okolski, 1991b: 14). This figure contrasts with the approximately three times as many migrants who have moved to Germany from Poland as *Aussiedler* since 1970, as well as with the most recent estimates of the size of the ethnic German minority in Poland, i.e., about 440,000.

9.4 Selected Characteristics of Migrants

Migrants are typically a selected category with respect to age, education, and economic ambitions. In Poland, a high proportion of children (the age group 0–17 years) were among those emigrants who left "illegally", i.e., who left the country for a temporary period, but remained permanently (or at least much longer than originally stated) abroad (see *Figures 9.2* and *9.3*). Apparently, it was more difficult for families with small and school-age children to obtain official exit visas than was the case for older persons. One can also notice a much higher proportion of women than of men among the young adults who left "temporarily".

The considerable share of children and young adults among emigrants of the late 1980s has caused adverse changes in the age composition of the resident population of Poland. According to the GCP (1989), the total number of persons of working age (18–64 years of age) fell by 257,000 between 1986 and 1988.

The migrants of the 1980s were better educated than the population from which they originated. Among those (18 years of age and above)

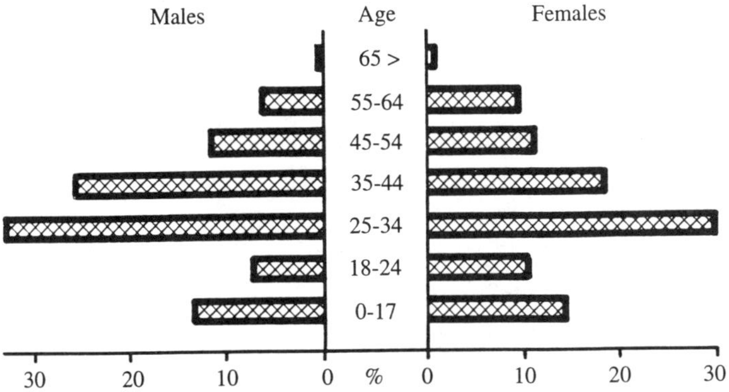

Figure 9.2. Age composition of official "permanent" emigrants, 1988. Source: Census (1988).

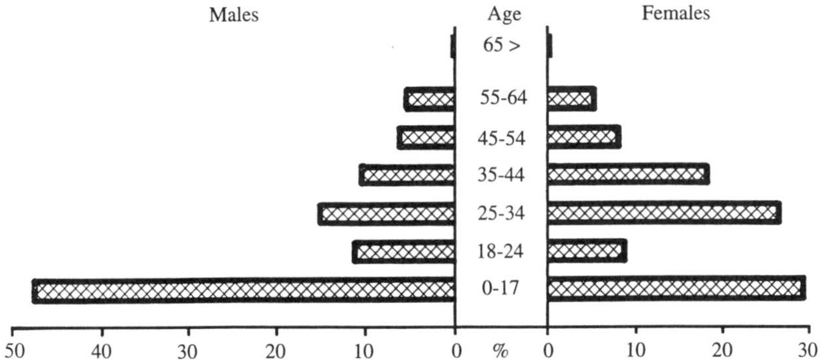

Figure 9.3. Age composition of illegal "temporary" emigrants, 1988. Source: Census (1988).

who emigrated or left for extended periods, college and university graduates accounted for 13.3%, and those who had completed secondary school for 46.4%, compared with 6.5% and 31.3%, respectively, in the total population of Poland in 1989. Among those who emigrated between 1981 and 1988 were 19,800 engineers, 8,800 scientists and academics, 5,500 medical doctors, and 6,000 nurses. Some 15,000 students interrupted their studies in Poland to go abroad, where the majority of them took jobs below their skill level, often in the informal sector. These are typical features of the brain-drain phenomenon, which is unlikely to disappear in the near future.

Figure 9.4. Regions of origin of emigrants, 1981–88 (as percentages of total population in 1984). Source: Calculated on the basis of statistics from GCP (1989).

Figure 9.4 shows the regions of origin of migrants during the period 1981–88. One distinct characteristic of this spatial pattern is the high emigration rate from the Opole (Oppeln) district, which contains the main clusters of the remaining ethnic German minority. To a lesser degree, the same applies to the western part of the Upper Silesian conurbation (Katowice district). Another feature is an overrepresentation of the large urban regions among major migration origins. Aside from the Katowice region, the regions of Warsaw, Gdansk, Cracow, and Wroclaw accounted for higher proportions of migrants than the national mean. The map does not reflect the observed gradual shift of migration origins from the western to the central and eastern regions of Poland.

Until the late 1980s, the contemporary emigration from Poland was not a popular topic of scientific research, largely for political reasons, but also due to the lack of reliable statistical information on international migration. Therefore, few such studies are available so far, but an interesting case study of emigration from the Warmia–Mazury region, in the southern part of former German East Prussia, has been described by Sakson (1986). The local, autochthonous population of the region, estimated at 350,000–500,000 in the interwar period, lived mostly in the rural areas. They constituted a typical peripheral agrarian society that adopted traditional values and behavior patterns, and spoke a local dialect of Polish at home and German in public. After the war, with the resettlement and forced and voluntary migration during 1945–48, this group shrank to 113,000 in 1948. Conflicts with settlers from central and eastern Poland, combined with discrimination by local officials, resulted in a collective desire to emigrate. The first wave occurred in 1956–58, when some 37,000 left for West Germany, but also for the former German Democratic Republic. At the end of the first "family reunion" program in 1958, the autochthonous population of the region was estimated at only 75,000. Emigration, although on a smaller scale, continued after 1958. Between 1975 and 1983 a second wave of emigration involved some 36,000 persons, and since then most of the remaining population of Warmia–Mazury have also emigrated to West Germany.

Unlike in Warmia–Mazury, where the local communities were tightly knit and emigration typically involved whole families, the Upper Silesian region has been characterized by some degree of intermarriage among members of the so-called autochthonous population in the former German territory, the population of the neighboring region, as well as migrants from other regions (Rykiel, 1989) that became part of Poland after World War I. Inter-group contacts have been stimulated by local migration (related to housing projects), the patterns of work in industry, and the educational system. As a result, emigration from Upper Silesia, which began during the late 1960s, but reached high levels from the late 1970s on, has included wider and wider circles, in social, ethnic, and territorial terms. This has been an example of the phenomenon of "non-Euclidean demography" (Brubaker, 1991), where emigration from a given region, or country, results in a growth, rather than a contraction, of the population eligible for emigration on the basis of existing family and other social ties.

9.5 Future Migration Trends

The new political and economic order in Poland has some consequences for international migration. Emigration for true or alleged political reasons is no longer in question. Economic determinants have also changed, although there are some new forces (such as unemployment) which may stimulate both permanent and temporary emigration. The brain-drain is certain to continue, particularly among the groups with the highest educational qualifications and skill levels, such as scientists and medical doctors, but also nurses. The push factors will be increased by the rapidly increasing numbers of new young entrants to the labor market starting from the mid-1990s, a trend that reflects the large size of the cohort born during the period of high birth rates in the late 1970s and early 1980s.

Nevertheless, the peak of emigration from Poland, which represented the largest component of East–West migration in Europe during the 1980s, has already passed. Other origins in Eastern Europe and the former Soviet Union will take its place. Recent survey results suggest that only 2–4% of Polish citizens would like to emigrate, compared with the 70% of secondary school students who were in favor of emigrating permanently or temporarily from Poland in the late 1980s. Even today, a sizable proportion of all respondents consider a several-year long stay in a foreign country as the best choice to be made by a young Pole.

Although permanent migration from Poland has decreased considerably, the number of Polish citizens living abroad has probably grown since 1990, with the introduction of visa-free travel agreements between Poland and most European, as well as many non-European, countries. The relevant figures are very difficult to estimate, but it is known that many thousands of Poles have been working in the informal sectors of the economy in Austria, Germany, the USA, Italy, and Greece. With regard to the USA, Poles have been very active and successful participants in the US immigration lottery, accounting for about one-half of all "winning tickets" in both 1991 and 1992. Taking these recent developments and factors into account one can forecast that a sizable emigration from Poland will continue during the 1990s, perhaps at half the level as observed during the 1980s (see Korcelli, 1991); this would imply an outflow of 400,000–500,000 people between 1993 and 2000, excluding irregular migrants. In any case, permanent emigration will account for a minor fraction of all Poles having direct contacts in Western Europe and North America. The category of legal contract employees, which now number some 350,000 (most of them working in Germany), will probably expand further by the late 1990s.

The majority of those who left Poland since the 1980s were ethnic Germans and others entitled to claim German citizenship, most of whom will never return. A smaller fraction of the emigrants, who consider themselves ethnic Poles, left at a young age during the 1970s or the

1980s. Some of them have become entrepreneurs and are now interested in investing capital and knowledge in their home country. Others became successful researchers and scientists. Virtually all major universities in North America, and many in Western Europe, have Polish emigrants among their faculty members. A third group is represented by hundreds of Polish ex-students, who cling to poorly paid jobs in the construction or restaurant sectors in cities such as New York. Since they have to rely on the local press for the evaluation of the current political and economic situation in Poland, they are not fully aware of alternative opportunities back home, and are unwilling to be regarded as failures by returning to their families and friends without bringing with them sizable amounts in savings; they live rather hopeless lives waiting for their big chance to come.

In the past few years there has been a substantial increase in immigration to Poland, although the level remains rather low (5,000 in 1991, according to official statistics). At the same time, Poland has become a major destination for temporary emigrants from the Commonwealth of Independent States (CIS) and Romania. The number of "trading tourists" from the CIS has been estimated at 350,000, about 50,000–70,000 of whom have been working in the informal sector of the economy (in construction, services, and agriculture), a large proportion of them in Warsaw and its environs. Further immigration to Poland will be determined not only by remigrants but also by an estimated 2–3 million ethnic Poles and people of Polish descent living in Lithuania, Belarus, and Ukraine. They represent a considerable immigration potential, particularly if their living conditions deteriorate in economic or political terms.

In Poland, the status of Poles living in these neighboring countries to the east and those deported to Central Asia during or shortly after the war, is regarded as an important issue. It is thought that these people and their descendants should be granted restitution of their Polish citizenship, and hence the right to settle in Poland. However, concrete policies and legal action in this respect have been delayed, overshadowed by other, more pressing political and economic problems.

Chapter 10

Hungary and International Migration

Zoltán Dövényi and Gabriella Vukovich

10.1 Introduction

Until very recently Hungary was an emigration rather than an immigration country. Four distinct periods can be identified in modern Hungarian emigration history. The first started with the onset of mass migration in the mid-nineteenth century and lasted until the end of World War I. It was marked by relatively heavy out-migration, particularly to the USA.

During the second period, 1920–48, migration was influenced by more diverse push factors than before, but the flows at the beginning of the period were greatly reduced by immigration restrictions in the most favored country of destination, the USA. The years after the end of World War II were marked by the troubled history of postwar Central Europe.

During the third period of the Cold War and the Iron Curtain, which lasted until 1988–89, emigration was minimal, except during the few months when the borders were open in 1956. Immigration during this period was even less significant than emigration. Elections that brought an end to Communist rule were held in 1989, but the turning point in migration history came in 1988.

Hungary has now entered a fourth phase in its migration history, and has become an immigration country. This process started when Hungary began to accept refugees in 1988, and signed the Geneva Convention in March 1989. Since then the issue of refugees and immigrants has become more complex. At first, the overwhelming majority of refugees were ethnic Hungarians from Romania, but now the national and ethnic composition of immigrants has become more diverse. Most recently, the war in former Yugoslavia has led to an influx of large numbers of refugees fleeing the fighting; both the refugees themselves and the host country expect their stay to be temporary. Different attitudes and policies are needed to accommodate conventional refugees and other immigrants such as labor migrants, whose settlement is expected to be long term or, possibly, permanent.

A further new feature brought about by the democratic change in Hungary is the fact that in the West emigrants from Hungary no longer qualify as refugees. Should a Hungarian citizen wish to move to another country temporarily or permanently, he or she has to go through regular immigration procedures of the country of destination without preferential treatment.

10.2 Migration Flows before World War I

Migration in Central and Eastern Europe became a mass phenomenon in the mid-nineteenth century. Technical developments in transportation enabled the movement of large masses of people. Communications also improved, and people received news of remote areas rather quickly. During the late nineteenth century migration became an important means of relieving social and political tensions, as well as shortages of human capital in one region or abundances in another.

The characteristic direction of geographic mobility in Central and Eastern Europe was toward the more developed West. *Table 10.1* gives an illustration of this through the evidence of the stock of foreign population in Austria and in Hungary. Overseas emigration from Hungary started with political and/or religious refugees fleeing to the USA, but they were not very numerous. Migration from the Austro–Hungarian Empire to the USA became more important only during the last quarter of the nineteenth century, but, once the mass movement started, the flow grew rapidly. In the first decade of the present century the Austro–Hungarian Empire was the most important pool of trans-Atlantic migration. Emigrants from the politically dominant ethnic groups of the Empire, Germans and Hungarians, were underrepresented compared to their share in the total population: 19% of the migrants were Poles,

Table 10.1. Austrians and Hungarians as foreigners in the respective other part of the Austro–Hungarian Empire, 1900 and 1910 (thousands).

	Hungarians in Austria	Austrians in Hungary
1900	270.8	207.6
1910	301.1	227.6

Source: Austro–Hungarian Census, CSO.

16% Serbs, Croats, and Slovenians, 15% Slovaks, but only 15% Hungarians and 12% German-speaking migrants; two-thirds of the German-speaking migrants came from the Hungarian part of the Empire (John, 1991). On the whole, migratory movements were marked by the out-migration of ethnic minorities, mainly from the eastern and southern peripheries of the Empire. In the western provinces internal migration was more characteristic than international migration (Fassmann, 1991). In general, internal and international migration were complementary rather than simultaneously observed patterns of behavior in the various regions of the Empire.

During the nineteenth and the first half of the twentieth centuries neither Hungary nor Austria were immigration countries; on balance, both countries released more migrants than they received. Moreover, the majority of immigrants to the Austrian part of the Empire came from Hungary (e.g., in 1910 more than half of all immigrants), and immigrants to Hungary came mainly from Austria (almost 85% in 1910; Fassmann, 1991).

Immigration to the USA from Central Europe accelerated after 1882. The new immigrants, although mainly of peasant origin, arrived at the time when the conquest of the American West was already more or less completed, and despite their agricultural backgrounds most of them settled in industrial and mining centers.

While economic push factors were the dominant reasons for emigration from Hungary, the importance of other social, political, and cultural factors is shown by the ethnic composition of migrants, i.e., ethnic minorities were more likely to migrate than Hungarians. There is evidence that entire ethnic village communities emigrated to the USA. However, until World War I, a significant proportion of migrants moved with the intention of temporarily staying there and returning after a while to their homelands with their savings.[1] Migrants to Canada, whether they went directly or via the USA, were more likely to settle permanently, as they were allotted land and could start farming; this was a strong incentive for the settlers who were mainly of peasant origin.

World War I was a turning point in the migration of Hungarians in that it barred emigration and return migration for a number of years, thus keeping large numbers of originally temporary migrants permanently in the USA. The motivation of migrants after World War I and throughout the successive interwar period was completely different from the predominantly economic push-and-pull factors that marked the flows of the nineteenth and early twentieth centuries.

10.3 Migration Patterns between 1920 and 1945

After World War I migration from Europe to the USA slowed down. The lowest figures were registered during the 1930s, when an annual average of 139,000 persons migrated from Europe. The reduced migration flow was due to two major factors: the restriction of labor migration and the economic depression. Restrictions on immigration to the USA were imposed in 1921 by the Quota Act, which limited the annual number of authorized immigrants from each ethnic group to 3% of their number resident in the USA as registered in 1910. Later, in 1924, the Immigration Restriction Act introduced further limitations by changing the basis of calculation to the 1890 population census.

These quotas did not affect the migration flows from Western Europe as severely as those from Eastern Europe, as migration from West European countries had already slowed down considerably by the time the limits were enacted. Movements from Central and East European countries, including Hungary, were restricted more by the willingness to accept migrants than by the desires of people to move.

On the other hand, with the dissolution of the Austro–Hungarian Empire and owing to the new boundaries established by the Trianon treaty, the territory of Hungary had been reduced to one-third and the population to less than half of its original size. The majority of non-Hungarian ethnic groups lived in areas that were annexed to the neighboring countries. But the new borders also created large Hungarian-speaking minorities in these countries. Subsequently the out-migration of non-Hungarians from these new nation-states slowed down, whereas the out-migration of Hungarians who became ethnic minorities in the neighboring countries began to increase. According to estimates at the time, about 70,000 ethnic Hungarians emigrated to the USA between 1922 and 1927, 40,000 from Hungary and 30,000 from neighboring countries.[2]

A further new feature of the 1920s was the change in the principal destinations. Due to the restrictive measures implemented in the USA, migration to Canada, to South America, and to Australia gained importance. For example, between 1924 and 1930 some 30,000 Hungarians settled in Canada, the majority of whom were of peasant, agrarian origin from the underdeveloped northeastern region of Hungary. The Canadian and South American labor markets favored agricultural labor, as opposed to the needs of US industry.

The socioeconomic composition of migrants is difficult to reconstruct from the scarce information available, but it is evident that migrants from rural areas were dominant until the 1930s, and although the proportion of migrants from urban areas grew steadily, their number only exceeded that of rural migrants during the 1930s. The traditional regions of origin remained the underdeveloped northern and eastern regions of Hungary.

After World War I the factors of emigration were more complex than in the prewar period. In addition to labor migration, political refugees and forced emigration also emerged, and growing numbers of intellectuals, professionals, and other middle-class strata emigrated during the 1920s and 1930s.

Before World War I few migrants were members of the middle classes compared with the migrants from other nations, possibly because their total numbers in Hungary were very small, and they could achieve their aims within the Austro–Hungarian Empire. After the Trianon treaty, between 1920 and 1924, some 350,000 ethnic Hungarians moved to the new, smaller territory of the country from the areas that had been annexed to the neighboring countries (see *Figure 10.1*)

The majority of these migrants had previously been public administrators and from other middle strata of society; thus the sizes of these socio-occupational groups increased considerably within the new boundaries of the country. Consequently, their higher initial concentration and later, shortly before and during World War II, the political and ideological climate initiated increased emigration of intellectuals and other middle strata, many of whom were of Jewish background (Puskás, 1981). However, the number who emigrated in this period was statistically far less important than in former emigration waves.

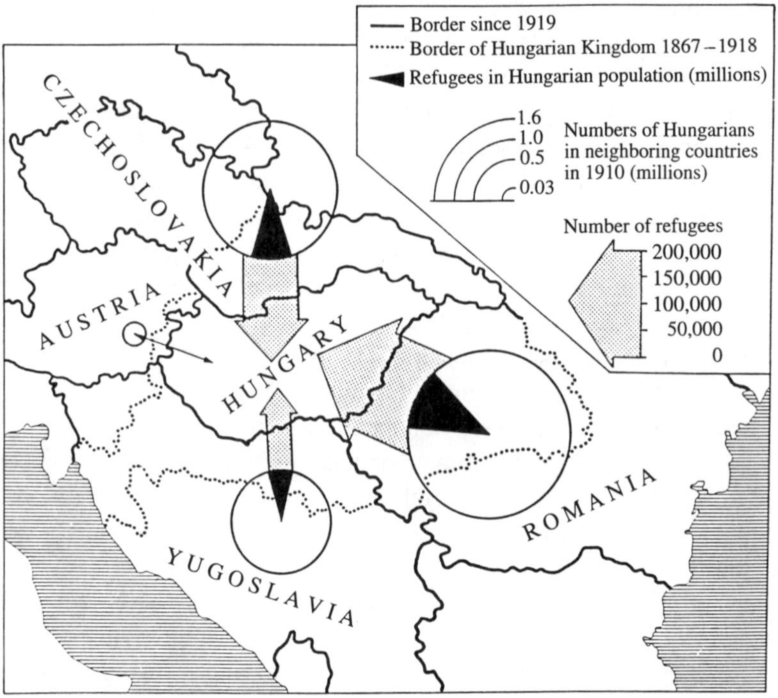

Figure 10.1. Migrations of ethnic Hungarians to the new, smaller Hungary after World War I. Data compiled by Zoltán Dövényi.

10.4 Migration between 1945 and 1988

The end of World War II brought about massive migrations in Europe. These displacements were both caused by the fighting during the war and the political changes thereafter, in particular by the forced population exchanges and expatriations finally decided by the Allies in 1945 at the Potsdam conference. As ethnic minorities played an important role in these movements, Hungary was forcibly affected considerably by this migration wave (see *Figure 10.2*).

In 1945–46 almost as many ethnic Hungarians immigrated to Hungary from the neighboring countries as after World War I: 125,000 from Romania, 120,500 from Czechoslovakia, 45,500 from Yugoslavia, and 25,000 from the Soviet Union. At the same time sizable population groups were forced or chose to leave Hungary. The largest forcibly displaced group was that of the ethnic Germans who were declared

Figure 10.2. Forced migrations: influx and outflows, 1945–48. Data compiled by Zoltán Dövényi.

collectively responsible for war crimes. About 20,000 had already chosen to follow the withdrawing German army, and another 185,000 were forced to leave Hungary. Under the population exchange agreement between Czechoslovakia and Hungary, some 73,000 ethnic Slovaks moved to Slovakia. Compared with these flows, only a small group of political refugees left Hungary when the Communist party gained power in the late 1940s.

Data on international migration during the Cold War after 1948 are even more difficult to obtain than those relating to previous periods. According to some estimates, in addition to the deported or exchanged populations, about 196,000 persons emigrated from Hungary to Western

Europe and to more remote destinations between 1945 and 1955, mostly between 1945 and 1948 (Randé, 1987).

International travel was practically abolished after 1948. The Communist regime regarded the desire to live outside the country as a manifestation of anti-Communist views. On the other hand, those who were authorized to cross the border were not trusted to be willing to return; consequently individuals or families who were granted passports and exit visas normally had to leave "hostages" behind to ensure their return. Those who did manage to cross the border illegally, or who crossed legally but did not return, were tried as criminals, sentenced to prison terms (partly in their absence), and their property confiscated. The defectors had to face permanent or at least very long-term emigration since, until recently, they could not even visit Hungary as tourists. Moreover, their relatives were subjected to harassment, questioning, and suspicion. Under such circumstances, whether to leave for "the West" was an attractive but difficult decision to make.

Nevertheless, there was still some illegal emigration, although reliable and consistent statistical sources on international migration flows during the period 1948–88 are still scarce. Also, each year between 1,000 and 2,000 legal emigrants applied for and were granted "emigration passports". A considerable proportion of both legal and illegal emigrants were of ethnic German origin who could settle in the Federal Republic of Germany.

The 1956 revolution opened the Hungarian borders for a few months during the Soviet military intervention, which made mass emigration possible. In 1957, a report entitled "Main characteristics of persons who have left the country illegally" was prepared by the Central Statistical Office (CSO), but was strictly confidential, and remained in the archives of the CSO until 1991. According to this report, Austrian and Yugoslav sources reported that 193,900 persons emigrated between 23 October 1956 and 30 April 1957, representing 1.5% of the population of Hungary.[3] Most of the migrants were from urban rather than rural areas: the city of Budapest alone lost 4.2% of its population. The other main flow of migrants came from Hungary's provinces, probably because of the proximity of the border with Austria. These provinces lost much higher proportions of their population than the central and eastern parts of the country (see *Figure 10.3*).

In 1956–57 two-thirds of all Hungarian emigrants (66%) were men, one-third (34%) women, and the majority of all emigrants were young,

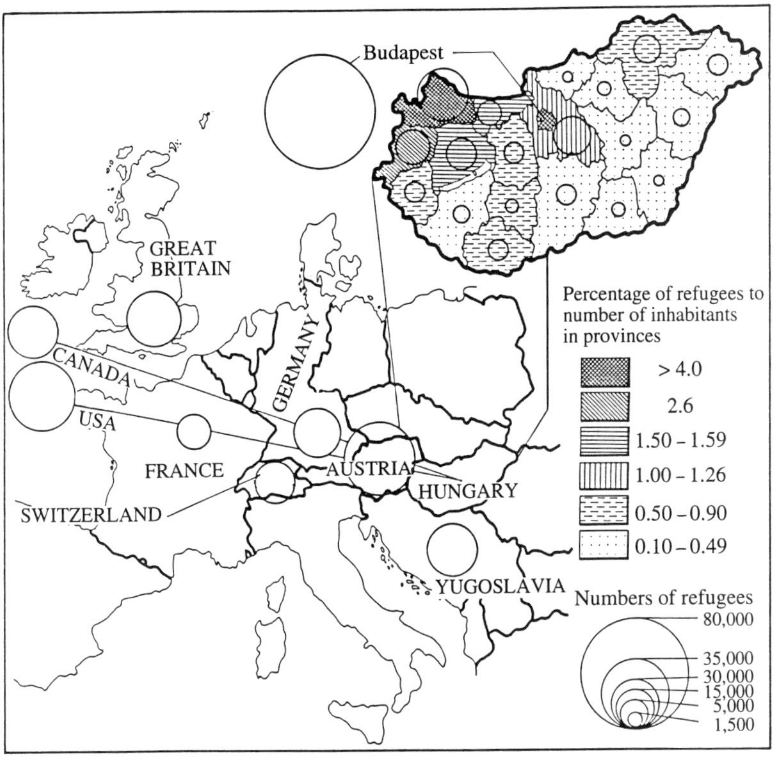

Figure 10.3. Destinations of Hungarian refugees after the 1956 revolution. Inset: origins of refugees and proportion of population of provinces. Source: Statisztikai Szemle, 1990/12; data compiled by Zoltán Dövényi.

aged 15–24 years (40%) or 25–39 years (30%). The emigration rates were highest among engineers (10.6% of all engineers left the country), other professionals with technical skills (6.8% of all technical professionals left), and medical doctors (4.9% of all medical doctors emigrated). Of all skilled manual workers in the country 4.2% (35,500 persons) emigrated. The rates were much lower among other professional groups. These figures indicate the severe loss of human capital from Hungary, particularly young, flexible, and highly skilled individuals.

Apart from the recently released CSO report on emigration during the 1956 revolution, Hungarian statistics on international migration are scarce and partly unreliable. Migration statistics, with the exception of tourism statistics, were processed in the Ministry of the Interior. Until

1988, a form had to be filled out in duplicate by anyone who crossed the border; one copy had to be handed to the border control on departure, and the other when returning to Hungary. The form requested details of the country of destination, intended length of stay, and purpose of the visit, as well as personal details. The Ministry of the Interior was able to keep track of any person who did not hand in the form upon return, and could verify whether such a person had stayed abroad illegally. The forms were also used as the basis of all travel and migration statistics.

The information thus gathered by the Ministry of the Interior on illegal emigration was, however, classified confidential and even the CSO was denied access to it. The official emigration figures covered those who had applied for and were granted permission to emigrate legally and to settle in another country, which amounted to 1,700–2,000 emigrants per year between 1958 and the mid-1970s. According to published border statistics, an average of 1,900 emigrants left Hungary per year between 1958 and 1972, and by the mid-1970s it had decreased to an annual average of 1,200. According to the same source, immigration between 1960 and 1972 amounted to an average of 950 per year, and between 1975 and 1987 it increased to an annual average of 1,600. Until the early 1970s the migration balance was negative, with a net loss of some 1,000 persons per year. The 1970s showed a change in the flows, as the balance turned positive, with an annual gain of 200–1,200.

Other sources which were made available by the various departments of the Ministry of the Interior or the Office of the National Population Register only cover short reporting periods, and in each case the communication was unofficial. Some of the tables that were made available did not even mention the source or the agency that compiled the figures, and in many cases the reported figures on emigration and immigration were somewhat contradictory. Only the data and therefore the migration balance which could be calculated from the data provided by the Ministry of the Interior for the period 1970–80 were close to the above-mentioned figures, which were complied from the border statistics.

Another set of data was provided by the passport and alien administration relating to the period 1979–88. During this period, the average annual number of immigrants was 22,300 which is 10–15 times higher than the number reported by the border statistics. The average number of emigrants during the same period was, according to the passport and alien administration, 4,400 per year for the period in which the border statistics time series and the passport administration time series overlap, i.e., between 1979 and 1987 when the passport administration reported 3–4 times higher numbers of emigrants. Of all emigrants an average annual number of 2,800 were reported to have crossed the border or stayed abroad illegally and 1,500 legally. It seems strange that the highest number of illegal emigrants is reported for the year 1987, close to the end of the socialist regime, when all travel restrictions were abolished. Another peak, 4,600 illegal emigrants, is reported for 1980, but the lowest illegal emigration figure was reported for 1984, when 2,100 persons left or stayed abroad illegally.

A third source was an unofficial table covering the period 1980–85 containing data provided by the Office of the National Population Register. They did not report all immigrants, but only those who were categorized as return migrants. The annual number fluctuated between 40 and 170, except for 1982, when 3,148 return migrants were reported by the register. The emigration figures compiled by the Office of the National Population Register were again different from any of the previous sources. The number of legal emigrants was lower than the number registered by the passport authority, with an average of 1,300 per year. The numbers of illegal emigrants they reported were lower in some years but higher in others than the passport authority communicated. Nevertheless, the average was the same: 2,800 per year.

The last year for which international migration statistics were collected was 1987, when the system of observation, the statistical bulletin collected at the border, was abolished.

It would be difficult to draw conclusions of how many emigrants or immigrants may have actually left or entered the country, but on the whole it seems that migration was insignificant during the period 1948–88, with the exception of a short period in 1956–57 linked to the revolution and Soviet military intervention. This seems to indicate a certain spatial immobility of the Hungarian society, even at times when living circumstances were definitely not very attractive (push factor), whereas there has always been an exaggerated image of the West (pull factor). In addition, until 1989 almost all Hungarian emigrants could count on being granted refugee status or being otherwise admitted to a West European country, since fleeing from a socialist country in itself usually justified some kind of preferential treatment.

It seems, therefore, that additional factors should be introduced to explain the relatively small emigration flows prior to 1988–89. The prosecution that illegal emigration entailed did not affect the emigrants personally since they were already out of reach, but the fact that they were tried and sentenced under penal law also meant that they could not return even for short visits for indefinite periods. Personal relationships of any kind with relatives and friends therefore became difficult or impossible to maintain. Also, unless their moves were very carefully planned and successfully executed, the illegal emigrants lost any property or assets they had accumulated. These, besides the usual considerations that influence decisions whether to move to another country, may have played a role as arguments against emigration.

The fact that until the early 1980s immigration to Hungary was negligible is also relatively easy to understand, since the political, economic, and social system was not particularly attractive, the country was not known for welcoming refugees, the language is difficult, etc. The most important groups of immigrants were Greek refugees at the end of the 1940s and refugees from Chile after 1973. At that time Hungary had not yet signed the Geneva Convention, there were no legal provisions for accommodating refugees, so that their entry to Hungary and their status were regulated by special government decrees.

It is not clear what definitions of immigration were used by the various sources mentioned above; some of the sources may include temporary labor migration, whereas others may not. Movements between East European countries were easier than between Eastern and Western Europe, but still restricted. Labor migration within the region was not characteristic and never significant, and was usually arranged under bilateral agreements between governments, under technical cooperation projects in construction, within the frames of contracts between enterprises and under individual work permits.

The first bilateral agreement was signed in 1967 between the governments of the GDR and Hungary and was in force, with amendments, until the end of 1983. Between 1974 and 1983 some 1,000 GDR citizens worked in Hungary. Under another bilateral agreement with Cuba, which was in force between 1985 and 1987, an average of 2,000–3,000 Cubans came to Hungary for work and training annually. A further agreement was signed with Czechoslovakia and provided labor exchange for 1,000 persons from each side of the border, according to the needs of enterprises. The employment of Polish workers was regulated by foreign trade agreements. In 1985 there were approximately 8,000 Polish workers in Hungary (Hárs, 1992).

10.5 New Migration Patterns since 1988

Since 1988 Hungary's role in international migration has changed significantly. In the last months of the Communist regime there were radical changes in international relations that had an immediate impact on migration patterns. Refugees from Romania were admitted in large numbers, citizens of the GDR took temporary refuge and were eventually allowed to cross the Hungarian–Austrian border, and political refugees and increasing numbers of other immigrants from African and Asian countries also started to appear. Many of them do not intend to settle in Hungary, but want to move to Western Europe.

In the late 1980s all remaining travel restrictions for Hungarian citizens were abolished. Now they can cross the border without limitations on the side of the Hungarian authorities, and they no longer need visas to enter other European countries for short-term visits. From the Hungarian side there are also no administrative limits to labor migration to other countries. Despite this liberalization, however, there is no sign of any dramatic increase in emigration from Hungary. The system of statistical observation of international migration is only just being organized, and as yet there are no data that can be evaluated. Indirect evidence of immigration to European and some non-European countries as reported by the receiving countries shows, however, that although the total number of immigrants from Hungary increased from 11,400 in 1987, to 16,300 in 1988, and 19,100 in 1989, it decreased again to 16,612 in 1990 (see *Table 10.2*). On the whole, the numbers are not very high. Either the domestic push factors are not forceful enough or the entry restrictions in the potential countries of destination are too strict.

Despite the lack of Hungarian data, evidence for the migration flow can be found in the immigration statistics of other countries, although such data should be interpreted with caution for two main reasons. First, the definitions used by the various receiving countries are not uniform, so that persons who move to different countries with the same intentions as to length of stay and purpose of going there may be counted as migrants by one and not be counted as such by the other country. Second, but more important, is that the aggregate figures do not specify the nationality of the immigrants arriving from a given country. Emigrants from Hungary may not necessarily be Hungarian citizens; for instance,

Table 10.2. Immigrants from Hungary, as reported by receiving countries, 1987–90.

Country	1987	1988	1989	1990
Canada	717	1,201	1,003	806
CSFR	39	55	44	45
Denmark	33	39	69	80
Finland	49	40	—	129
France	53	66	124	97
Germany	8,938	12,966	15,372	12,523
Iceland	5	7	—	5
Netherlands	129	206	321	346
Norway	—	—	36	40
Poland	14	30	10	12
Romania	—	—	—	162
Sweden	390	507	713	567
Switzerland	298	351	413	403
CIS	—	—	17	4
UK	—	—	—	300
USA	641	701	844	946
Former Yugoslavia	1	—	2	—
Australia	100	130	110	140
New Zealand	11	15	8	7
Total	11,418	16,314	19,086	16,612

Source: Matrices compiled by the UN Economic Commission for Europe (UN/ECE, 1991).

many Romanian migrants move first to Hungary from Romania and only later try to move on to Germany. The numbers of emigrants from Hungary and the total of Hungarian immigrants to various countries are thus necessarily dissimilar, although in the absence of Hungarian migration statistics there is no way of verifying the differences. It is important to note, on the other hand, that the bulk of the increase in the number of Hungarian immigrants to other countries was absorbed by Germany (82% of the increase in 1987–88, and 87% of the increase in 1988–89). Therefore the heterogeneity of the definitions adopted by the various countries do not apply in their case.

Very little information is available on the actual numbers of immigrants, migrant workers, or other entrants to Hungary. Each category of immigrants is handled by a different authority, and, although each authority is supposed to keep an administrative register, the categories, classifications, and definitions they use are not homogeneous and do not contain adequate information for statistical or demographic analysis. In 1991, however, the CSO began the harmonization of the various registration and reporting systems.

Not only is information on immigrants meager, but, even if immigrants are properly registered, they do not necessarily inform the Hungarian authorities when they leave the country. Consequently, even if it were possible to capture the migration flows, the stock of the foreign-born population still could not be estimated with any accuracy as long as deregistration is not compulsory.

According to all estimates Hungary can now be considered an immigration country. It would be difficult to establish exactly when this new period started, but the first large immigrant flow from Transylvania arrived during the last weeks of 1987. Until the middle of 1991 the inflow consisted mainly of refugees from Romania. More than 13,000 refugees were registered by the Hungarian authorities in 1988, more than 17,000 in 1989, and more than 18,000 in 1990. The fluctuations between months show that the flows were largely affected by the political events and turbulence within Romania.

According to a reliable assessment published by the Office of Refugees (Tóth, 1991), in 1991 there were 3,000 refugees, 20,000 asylum seekers, 80,000 other foreigners who had settled as immigrants, and 20,000 labor migrants and seasonal workers living in Hungary.[4] Tóth (1991) estimated that the number of illegal immigrants was twice as high as the number of legal immigrants. Illegal migrants are not included in any register; therefore there is no direct way of establishing their actual numbers.

Almost as soon as the massive inflow of refugees and immigrants from Romania slackened, the war in Yugoslavia initiated a new wave of refugees to Hungary. In November 1992, according to UNHCR estimates, some 90,000 former Yugoslavians had been registered as refugees or had not been registered but took refuge with friends or relatives. The fluctuations over time of refugees arriving in Hungary were influenced by the political events in Central and Eastern Europe (see *Figures 10.4* and *10.5*).

A comparison of the refugees and immigrants arriving from former Yugoslavia and from Romania shows that the latter group was mainly composed of ethnic Hungarians, whereas in 1991–93 only about 25% of refugees from Yugoslavia were ethnic Hungarians; the majority of those from Yugoslavia are women and children, whereas the refugees and other migrants from Romania were mainly young men, particularly at the beginning of the flow.

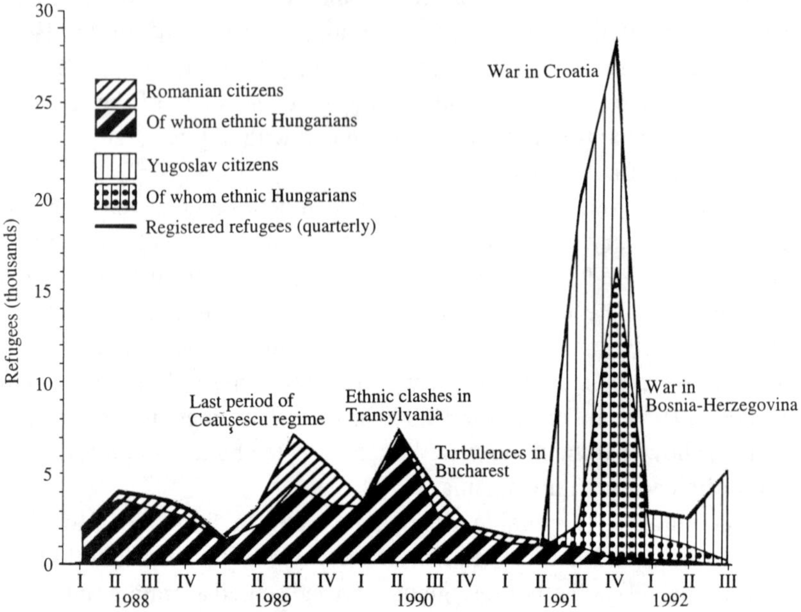

Figure 10.4. Changes in registered refugees in Hungary, 1988–92. Data compiled by Zoltán Dövényi.

Who are the labor migrants working in Hungary?[5] The number of work permits issued to foreigners by the end of September 1991 was 36,623, of which 26,364 had been issued by the end of June of the same year. The proportion of Romanian citizens among foreign workers varied from 70 to 80%, and the majority of the immigrants from Romania were ethnic Hungarians. Polish workers represented around 10%, but their total number and proportion within the foreign workers decreased from 3,600 at the end of June to 3,100 at the end of September 1991. The significant rise in the number of work permits issued during the second half of 1991 was probably due to the increase in Chinese immigrants to Hungary.

Besides the foreign workers who are resident in the country, there is a large number of foreigners who arrive as asylum seekers or refugees, and also appear in the labor market but need not apply for work permits. The geographical distribution of labor migrants is highly uneven within the country, but they are concentrated in Budapest and large industrial centers. The distribution of other immigrants and refugees, on the other hand, is rather different. Budapest is the favored destination of all

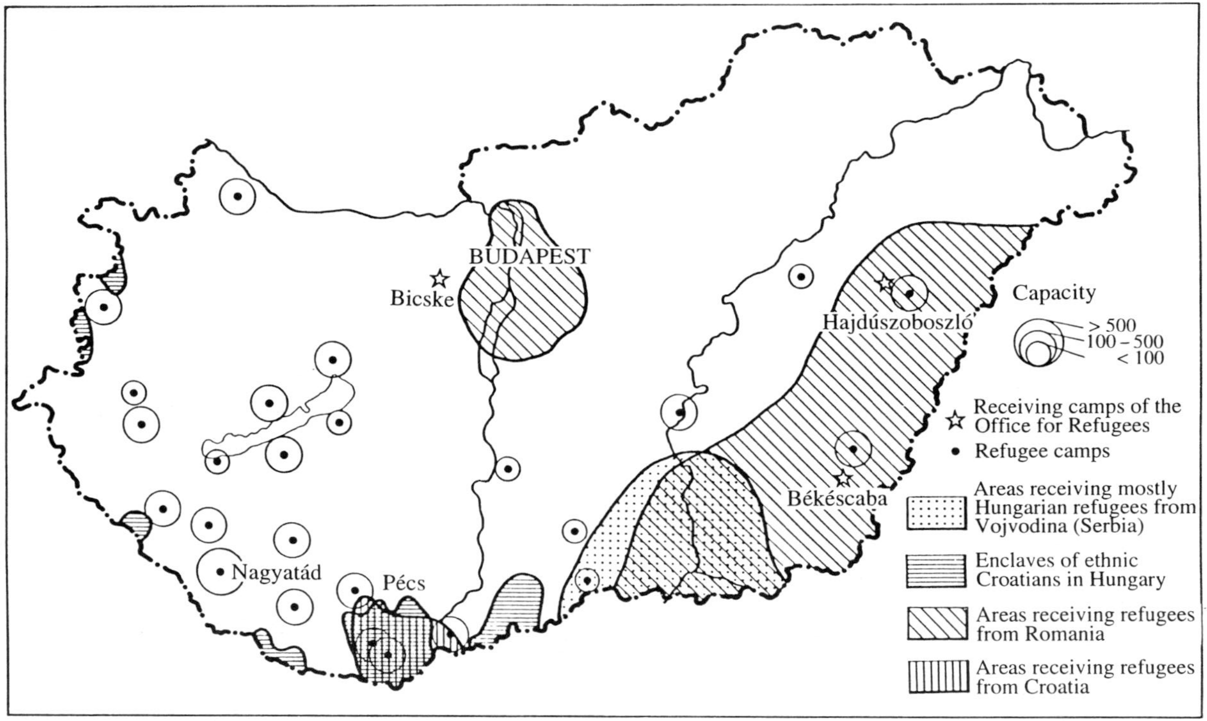

Figure 10.5. Spatial distribution of refugees from Romania and from former Yugoslavia, early 1992. Data compiled by Zoltán Dövényi.

immigrants, but although a large proportion is scattered all over the country, there is an evident concentration in the eastern and southern border region, easily explained by the significant number of immigrants from Romania, Croatia, and Bosnia who prefer to stay in the vicinity of their former home countries.

The socio-professional backgrounds of immigrants cannot be accurately established, since the classifications adopted by the various reporting authorities are hardly comparable. It seems to be clear, however, that the majority of those gainfully and legally employed have jobs as manual workers in the construction sector (37% of all foreign workers) or in industrial production (36%). Only very few foreigners are to be found in the agricultural sector (2%).

The public acceptance of labor migrants is not unanimous. Unemployment in Hungary is increasing rapidly, and by mid-1992 had reached more than 9%. Security of employment was an unquestioned principle and regular practice in the former political and economic system. Workers and employees unused to the phenomenon now face the threat of unemployment, a fate to which society and individuals have not yet adjusted. The fact that even under such circumstances tens of thousands of migrant workers have been able to find jobs might have inspired a certain amount of hostility among the native Hungarians. But some aggressive reactions and violence could also be attributed to the rise of Hungarian nationalism. In any case it is doubtful whether the unemployed themselves, or those threatened by unemployment, understand that their uncertain situation is rooted in structural and economic factors rather than caused by the immigrants.

10.6 Outlook

Handling the phenomenon and the implications of immigration is a new challenge for Hungary. During the transition period Hungary is currently living through, a number of social tensions have arisen that may not be favorable to immigration. Refugees obviously have to be accepted within certain limits, and labor immigrants or other persons who wish to settle in the country should also be welcome, but the attitudes of many Hungarians may nevertheless be less than welcoming because of the rising unemployment. Also, there is a fear that in the future large population groups may want to leave Russia, the Ukraine, and other CIS countries, and that Hungary may be the desired destination for too many of them, but this is not very likely. A large proportion of those who want to travel to the West will probably only pass through Hungary. In this respect Hungary is not a unique case. The issue of migration has come into the limelight in most countries, and multilateral efforts to handle the problem and to curb international migration are already under way. The migration policies that are called for will certainly be influenced by international relations, and the emergence of the Central and Eastern European countries on the European political scene may give due consideration to their existence and concerns.

Notes

[1] There are literary anecdotes of Slovakian villages in Hungary where people spoke English among themselves in the normal course of life, because the whole village was populated by return migrants from overseas.

[2] Trans-Atlantic migration from Hungary again diminished in the 1930s. In 1935, for instance, only 130 new Hungarian immigrants were registered in the USA. The number of return migrants to Hungary exceeded the number of immigrants to the USA throughout the 1930s (Puskás, 1981).

[3] Hungarian statistics on the emigrants of 1956 were based on the deregistration form introduced by the Ministry of the Interior in the first months of 1957 and established for each person who had left the country. The form was supplemented by a statistical bulletin, which was then processed by the CSO. Some 151,700 statistical bulletins reached the CSO, 42,000 less than the estimates based on other (Yugoslav and Austrian) sources. The official figures probably underestimate the size of the emigrant population.

[4] These data relate to the period prior to the large flow of refugees from former Yugoslavia.

[5] The following overview of foreigners in Hungary only covers persons staying legally, based primarily on the register of work permits issued by the National Labor Force Center and cited in a study prepared by Hárs (1992).

Chapter 11

Labor Migration from Former Yugoslavia

Janez Malačić

11.1 Introduction

Former Yugoslavia consisted of six large Slavic nationalities and many other national minorities. Each large Slavic nationality (Slovenians, Croats, Serbs, Muslims, Montenegrins, and Macedonians) had its own republic within the federal state. In Serbia, there were two autonomous provinces: Kosovo, which was inhabited predominantly by ethnic Albanians, and Vojvodina, with a large ethnic Hungarian minority. The constitution of 1974 gave to Kosovo and Vojvodina federal status, which was only slightly less important than the status of the republics. In the second half of the 1980s Serbia abolished the high degree of the autonomy of its provinces and started the constitutional changes that finally led to the dissolution of the Yugoslav federation.

The wars in Croatia (1991–92) and Bosnia–Herzegovina (1992–93) and the repression of ethnic minorities in Vojvodina, Serbia, and Kosovo led to the largest wave of migration in Europe since 1945–46. Between 1991 and 1993 some 5 million citizens of former Yugoslavia became refugees or displaced persons. Of them only 700,000 have come to Western Europe: 355,000 to Germany, 80,000 to Switzerland, 74,000 to Sweden, and 70,000 to Austria. In most cases they are not recognized as political refugees, but are tolerated as *de facto* refugees. Most Western countries have now closed their borders to the victims of war and ethnic cleansing in this part of the Balkans, so that 4.3 million refugees and displaced persons remain in the successor states of former Yugoslavia. In mid-1993 there were 690,000 refugees in the parts of Croatia under control of the authorities in Zagreb, 110,000 in parts of Croatia controlled by Serbian militias, 565,000 in Serbia, 82,000 in Montenegro, 45,000 in Slovenia, 27,000 in Macedonia, and 2.74 million in Bosnia–Herzegovina (data from UNHCR; Morokvasić, 1993; UN/ECE *Rapid Bulletin* 3/1993).

On 15 January 1992 Yugoslavia ceased to exist, but the effects of labor migration from this area are still visible, determining the distribution of foreigners in Western Europe. This chapter is not only of historical interest, although the analysis is limited to international migration from and to Yugoslavia prior to 1991.

For former Yugoslavia, two principal sets of data for international labor migration have been used. The first set was the last two population censuses taken in 1971 and 1981, which gave a relatively complete cross-sectional picture of the process. The second set, the National Employment Service's annual statistics on legal migration, was incomplete, because it did not cover spontaneous and unofficial migrations. Both sources, combined with other international data sources, have been used in this chapter, although the main focus has been on the census data.

Yugoslav census statistics covered those international economic migrants who maintained connections with their former home country and who planned to return.[1] The census definition of a temporary economic emigrant was very broad; the main criterion was Yugoslav nationality, even in cases of dual citizenship. The National Employment Service's definition of migrant population was narrower, covering only those migrants who had found employment abroad through the cooperation between the Yugoslav National Employment Service and foreign employers. According to the estimates of Yugoslav researchers, however, only about 50% of the economic emigrants found jobs abroad through the Employment Service.

11.2 Post–World War II Migration from Former Yugoslavia

Traditionally, the regions that constituted former Yugoslavia, played a significant role in overseas and intra-European migration. Until 1939 the determinants of Yugoslav migrations had been predominantly economic, but this pattern was interrupted by World War II. At the end of the war, huge numbers of political emigrants left former Yugoslavia. Collaborators left with the occupying forces, and several hundred thousand Yugoslavs of ethnic German, Italian, and Hungarian origin were expelled. At the same time the Tito government organized remigration and repatriation of Yugoslav emigrants all over the world. The action was not very successful, given the degree of destruction, poverty, and underdevelopment of the country. During the late 1940s and the early 1950s borders were closed and there were very few emigrants, most of whom tried to apply for political asylum in Western Europe. During the 1950s, the politically motivated emigrants were increasingly replaced by labor migrants, as the liberalization led to a considerable increase in international migration from former Yugoslavia. Between the census years 1953 and 1961 Yugoslavia's net migration balance amounted to –277,675 (Centar za demografska istraživanja, 1971: 47). In this period the majority of emigrants who left the country permanently were members of the Turkish minority living in the southeastern parts of the country. Most ethnic Turks emigrated to Turkey; Macedonia, for example, lost 165,000 people (i.e., approximately 10% of its population).

Toward the late 1950s and early 1960s international migration changed its patterns and direction. Labor migration, partly temporary, became dominant.

11.3 Developments since 1960

Yugoslav labor migration to Western Europe and overseas can be divided into four periods. During the first period, until 1964, the overall number of migrants was not large. The second period, 1964–73, was characterized by an emigration boom. During the third period, 1974–79, the extensive layoffs of Yugoslav workers abroad brought a halt to emigration. In the last period, 1980–90, return migration was evident. At the same time, the deep economic, social, and political crisis in Yugoslavia slowed down the process of return migrations and prepared for a new wave of emigration.

Up to 1964 Yugoslav international labor migration was spontaneous and unofficial; no statistical information is available. Spontaneous emigration started from the northwest of the country and from traditional emigration regions. At the end of the period an estimated total of 100,000 economic emigrants were living outside the country.

Between 1964 and 1973 emigration from former Yugoslavia was caused by internal and external factors. The main internal factors were connected with changes in the economic system and economic policy. The government officially accepted the necessity for economic emigration as the consequence of the transition from an extensive to an intensive economy. For some years after 1965 the numbers employed in the "socialist sector" of the economy steadily declined from 3.66 million in 1965 to 3.56 million in 1967 (SGJ, 1970: 87).

At the same time, the postwar baby-boom generation started to enter the labor market. The annual inflow of young workers doubled during the 1960s. The main external reason for Yugoslav emigration at that time was the growing demand for foreign labor in Western Europe, the higher wages and salaries, and the relatively short distance between Germany, Switzerland, Austria, and other recruitment areas. Since 1964 the National Employment Service of former Yugoslavia was involved in this emigration process in cooperation with foreign employers. In the period 1964–90, the government signed a series of bilateral agreements with West European governments to regulate the migration processes.

The estimated numbers of Yugoslav migrant workers in European countries in 1964–90 are shown in *Table 11.1.* In 1973 the number of emigrants peaked, with 850,000 citizens living abroad. Their number grew particularly in the years 1964–65 and 1968–71. The 671,908 economic emigrants from former Yugoslavia calculated from the 1971 census is probably too low; Baučić (1973) calculates that there was an underestimation of 15%.

In the third period (1974–79) the number of emigrants fell by 140,000 in just one year (1973–74). During the whole period employment of Yugoslavs in Western Europe decreased. *Table 11.1* shows that there were considerable return migrants and relatively few new emigrants. Return migration during this period was a direct consequence of the economic crises in Western Europe caused by the first and second oil price shocks. For Yugoslavia this period was characterized by the return of large numbers of migrants, and at the same time the receiving countries of Europe started to change their immigration policies and introduced increasingly restrictive measures.

The fourth period, 1980–90, was characterized by reduced return migration. A considerable number of Yugoslav immigrant workers and

Table 11.1. Yugoslav migrant workers in Europe, 1964–90, absolute numbers and indices.

Year	Number	Indices 1964 = 100	Annual change (previous year = 100%)	Number of emigrants (census data)
1964	100,000	100.0	—	
1965	140,000	140.0	140.0	
1966	220,000	220.0	157.1	
1967	260,000	260.0	118.2	
1968	330,000	330.0	126.9	
1969	420,000	420.0	127.3	
1970	540,000	540.0	128.6	671,908
1971	660,000	660.0	122.2	
1972	740,000	740.0	112.1	
1973	850,000	850.0	114.9	
1974	710,000	710.0	83.5	
1975	670,000	670.0	94.9	
1976	590,000	590.0	88.0	
1977	578,000	578.0	98.0	
1978	570,000	570.0	98.6	
1979	564,000	564.0	98.9	
1980	558,000	558.0	98.9	625,069
1981	554,000	554.0	99.3	
1982	540,000	540.0	97.5	
1983	525,000	525.0	97.2	
1984	510,000	510.0	97.1	
1985	500,000	500.0	98.0	
1986	505,000	505.0	101.0	
1987	515,000	515.0	102.0	
1988	525,000	525.0	101.9	
1989	540,000	540.0	102.9	
1990	550,000	550.0	101.9	

Sources: For 1964–76, estimates of Tanić (Tanić, 1979: 177); for 1981, census data; and for 1977–80 and 1982–90 authors' estimates, based on the statistics on return migrations. State as per mid-year.

their families stayed on in the receiving countries, and the process of the transformation of temporary into permanent immigration has continued. At the end of the 1960s it was estimated that one in eight temporary emigrants would become permanent (Komarica, 1970), while revised estimates made in the early 1980s, suggested that no less than 50% of the migrant workers would stay on permanently in the receiving countries (Mulina *et al.*, 1981).

The 1980s were also characterized by a deep economic, social, and political crisis in former Yugoslavia. High unemployment, stagflation, and the foreign debt crisis hardly encouraged economic emigrants to return. Without Western Europe's restrictive immigration policies there would have been even more new emigrants from former Yugoslavia. The transformation of temporary into permanent migrants can be seen in the 1981 census data. A new category of emigrants, the family members of labor migrants, had started to play an important role, indicating the growing number of family reunifications. According to the 1981 census 625,069 migrant workers and 249,899 family members were living outside former Yugoslavia, among them 553,656 migrant workers and 197,964 family members in Western Europe (*Saopštenje*, 1983).

11.4 The Selectivity of Temporary Economic Emigration

Voluntary migration is selective (Sauvy, 1969: 43). In general, there is "natural" selection in the case of emigration and "artificial" selection in the case of immigration. The second one is caused by the criteria set by the immigration policies of the receiving countries. For this analysis we can distinguish between two types of migration selectivity. The first denotes the differences between characteristics of the migrants and of the nonmigrant population from which they originate. The second denotes the differences between the characteristics of migrants and nonmigrants at the place of destination.

Among Yugoslav postwar population censuses only those of 1971 and 1981 contain data on economic migrants, on the basis of which indices of selectivity can be determined and analyzed.[2] However, the data of the two censuses are not fully comparable.[3] *Table 11.2* shows indices of selectivity of economic migration from former Yugoslavia for 1971 and 1981, given by republics and autonomous provinces, age, sex, education, occupation, and ethnic group.[4] The index can be understood as a percentage that denotes the magnitude of the (positive or negative) difference between the shares of a particular group or category under investigation in the migrant and the nonmigrant population.

In former Yugoslavia economic emigration started from the northwestern regions; later, the recruitment area expanded toward the southeast. With some exceptions, indices of selectivity by republics and autonomous provinces illustrate this development. The emigration was the most intensive from Croatia and Bosnia–Herzegovina, and least intensive from Montenegro and Kosovo. Similar conclusions can be derived from the indices of selectivity by ethnic group. There are only three ethnic groups with positive indices of selectivity: Croats, Romanians, and Hungarians.

The differences between 1971 and 1981 show the process of aging of the Yugoslav emigrants and the absence of new emigration waves until the late 1980s.[5] Education and occupation selectivity are positive for those with 4–7 years of primary education and three years of secondary education and for those working in agriculture, manufacturing, and services. The lower educational level of emigrants is the consequence of the low educational level in former Yugoslavia. The high selectivity among those with three years of secondary education had particularly negative effects on the country, in that mainly traders and skilled workers from the mining, manufacturing, agricultural, transport, and service sectors found employment abroad. In the more developed parts of the country, skilled emigrant workers were often replaced by unskilled workers and immigrants from less developed regions.

11.5 Return Migration

Return migration to former Yugoslavia began after the first oil price shock of 1973, when many West European countries stopped recruiting migrant workers and started to encourage return migration. According to Mikulić (1987: 51), some 625,000 Yugoslavs returned between 1970 and 1981, another 110,000 returned between 1981 and 1985. But the population census of 1981 shows only 282,873 return migrants for the period 1965–81 (*Saopštenje*, 1983). These data seem to indicate that the number of return migrants dropped at the end of the 1970s.

Yugoslav population census data on return migration for the year 1981 allow analysis of who came back.[6] In 1981 the indices of migration differentials were positive in Slovenia, Croatia, and Bosnia–Herzegovina (see *Table 11.3*). The shares of return migrants to these republics were higher than their respective shares in the total population of former Yugoslavia. Obviously, this was also a result of the intensity of previous emigration. In any case the data show that the process of return migration was more intensive in the northwest of the country. Male migrants and economically active persons were overrepresented in the returning population. The magnitude of sex differentials is indirectly related to the process of family reunification.

Table 11.2. Migrant and nonmigrant populations in former Yugoslavia with respect to republics and autonomous provinces, age, education, occupation, and nationality. Indices of migration selectivity in the years 1971 and 1981.

	1971 Migrants	Nonmigrants	Index of selectivity	1981 Migrants	Nonmigrants	Index of selectivity
Republics and autonomous provinces						
Slovenia	48,086	1,679,051	−15.4	41,826	1,838,381	−21.2
Croatia	224,722	4,201,499	58.0	151,619	4,391,139	19.1
Serbia proper	114,581	5,135,784	−34.1	152,932	5,491,043	3.9
Vojvodina	60,545	1,891,988	−5.4	48,078	1,969,181	−15.4
Bosnia–Herzegovina	137,351	3,608,760	12.3	133,902	3,941,316	16.0
Montenegro	7,829	521,775	−55.0	9,781	565,467	−38.5
Macedonia	54,433	1,592,875	1.0	57,964	1,808,214	10.7
Kosovo	24,361	1,219,332	−41.0	28,965	1,544,976	−36.1
Age group						
0–19	54,276	7,430,923	−78.3	8,824	7,324,018	−95.8
20–24	165,151	1,589,176	207.5	42,061	1,818,274	−20.2
25–34	250,342	2,563,681	189.1	252,383	3,336,850	162.3
35–49	173,271	4,137,667	24.0	240,600	4,058,811	104.8
50–64	19,719	2,431,585	−76.2	55,811	3,154,510	−39.0
65+	3,296	1,611,606	−93.8	4,405	2,030,073	−92.6
Education						
Less than 3 years of primary school	68,174	4,022,954	−59.3	49,546	2,874,769	−55.1
4–7 years of primary school	310,063	6,836,128	9.5	221,707	4,323,519	34.0
Primary school	133,112	2,414,677	32.9	185,098	3,918,333	23.3
3 years of secondary school	113,318	1,403,941	93.0	131,521	4,191,772	−18.6

Grammar school	7,793	325,804	−40.0			
Other secondary schools	20,400	706,113	−30.2			
University	10,167	463,414	−46.6	15,578	928,340	−56.1
Occupation (selected)						
Farmers, agricultural and related workers	304,131	3,516,096	155.9	196,472	2,321,509	190.7
Miners and manufact. workers	188,239	2,034,394	174.5	132,642	2,815,242	61.8
Sales workers	7,684	274,126	−21.4	37,090	969,221	31.1
Service workers	18,365	349,330	50.0			
Clerical workers	9,145	522,739	−48.0	7,833	882,858	−68.3
Administrative managerial workers	579	91,539	−80.0	334	153,411	−85.7
Professional, technical and related workers	20,902	646,640	−6.0	24,820	897,261	−4.8
Ethnic groups (selected)						
Montenegrins	5,260	503,585	−68.0	5,589	573,434	−66.7
Croats	261,721	4,265,061	80.9	169,998	4,258,007	37.4
Macedonians	38,298	1,156,486	−1.7	36,466	1,303,263	−3.3
Slovenians	46,856	1,631,176	−16.6	35,409	1,718,145	−28.7
Serbs	191,342	7,951,904	−28.7	203,101	7,937,351	−11.7
Muslims	40,565	1,689,367	−29.4	41,260	1,958,697	−27.5
Albanians	34,748	1,274,775	−18.7	44,692	1,685,672	−9.0
Hungarians	19,552	457,822	26.0	11,653	415,213	0.0
Romanians	5,285	53,285	166.7	5,782	49,172	350.0
Turks	3,618	124,302	−16.7	2,549	98,642	0.0
Total	671,908	19,851,064		625,067	21,549,747	

Source: Yugoslav population censuses (1971 and 1981).

Table 11.3. Indices of migration selectivity in the case of Yugoslav return migration with respect to republics and autonomous provinces, sex, and activity in the year 1981.

Characteristics of migrant and nonmigrant populations	Migrants	Nonmigrants	Index of differential
Republics and autonomous provinces			
Slovenia	26,190	1,850,038	9.4
Croatia	97,338	4,449,850	68.6
Serbia proper	54,329	5,541,532	−24.7
Vojvodina	9,472	1,986,694	−15.4
Bosnia–Herzegovina	67,005	3,990,354	29.5
Montenegro	2,464	574,529	−65.4
Macedonia	20,784	1,851,172	−13.1
Kosovo	5,291	1,555,445	−73.6
Sex			
Males	210,068	5,906,448	22.6
Females	72,805	3,681,424	−33.1
Activity			
Active population	231,202	8,733,604	101.7
Agricultural	49,246	2,321,509	61.1
Nonagricultural	176,852	6,412,095	109.7
Persons with income from other sources (e.g., pensioners)	13,851	1,856,320	−43.0
Dependents	28,730	10,491,511	−79.1

Source: Yugoslav population census (1981).

11.6 Destinations of International Economic Migrants

In general, emigration from former Yugoslavia was directed toward several highly developed and industrialized countries of Western Europe (see *Table 11.4*). In 1971 and 1981 the majority of the Yugoslav labor migrants worked in Germany and in Austria, but during this period their share fell from 83.8% to 76.2%. Of the two Mediterranean countries listed in *Table 11.4*, France and Italy, France was the most favored destination for Yugoslav workers. It ranked third among the countries of immigration of Yugoslav workers in 1971, and ranked fourth ten years later. However, it is impossible to place the whole country in the Mediterranean region. As is well known, the majority of Yugoslav immigrants in France found employment outside the Mediterranean regions. In the case of Italy the situation was quite different. Traditionally, Italy itself had a high rate of emigration, but somewhere in the 1970s it became a country with high immigration. In spite of such a situation migrants from Yugoslavia have never been a numerous group of

Table 11.4. Number and percentage of Yugoslav workers and employees in selected European countries according to Yugoslav census statistics (1971 and 1981).

Country of immigration	1971 Number	1971 %	1981 Number	1981 %	Index 1971=100
FRG	411,503	69.7	324,324	58.6	78.8
Austria	82,957	14.1	97,618	17.6	117.7
France	36,982	6.3	32,903	5.9	89.0
Switzerland	21,201	3.6	59,624	10.8	281.2
Sweden	16,359	2.8	16,829	3.0	102.9
Benelux	7,358	1.2	7,913	1.4	107.6
Italy	—	—	5,956	1.1	—
Europe (total)	590,428	100	553,656	100	93.8

Sources: *Saopštenje* (1983, No. 131).

temporary workers in Italy.[7] In 1981 their number was still low. On the other hand, unofficial estimates from the literature give a range of 20,000–40,000 of Yugoslav temporary workers in Italy at the end of the 1970s (Heršak, 1983: 132), the majority of whom found work in the northeastern regions of Italy near the border. This estimate is probably more reliable, because it takes into account both legal and illegal employment of Yugoslav workers in Italy.

11.7 Development and Efficiency of Migration Policy

Four stages of Yugoslav migration policy can be distinguished. Until 1964 there was no migration policy at all, and spontaneous and unofficial migrations dominated. From 1964 to the early 1970s, migration was seen as temporary, and both Yugoslavia and the receiving countries expected the "rotation" model to work. At that time labor migration was encouraged by the Yugoslav National Employment Service in cooperation with foreign employers. The Yugoslav government had concluded bilateral agreements with the receiving countries in order to regulate employment and to protect the legal and social status of Yugoslav workers abroad.

During the third stage, in the early and mid-1970s Yugoslavia's migration policy was reviewed. From the early 1970s the discussions focused on the need for greater social engagement for the return and organized reintegration of migrant workers. In the last stage, from the end of the 1970s, this policy was implemented at federal, regional, and communal levels.

The official position of former Yugoslavia was that there was no need for permanent emigration from the country, so that the temporary character of the ongoing migrations was stressed and portrayed as a transitional phenomenon linked to a certain stage of Yugoslavia's socioeconomic development. Migration was also seen as an opportunity for the unemployed and inadequately employed population, allowing them to contribute to their own future economic advancement in former Yugoslavia through temporary employment in foreign countries (Baletić and Baučić, 1979: 85).

The aims and targets of Yugoslav migration policy were, of course, derived from its economic and geopolitical situation. The main targets were to speed up economic development through transfers of hard currency, to ensure the return of as many emigrants as possible, especially of skilled workers and experts, and the creation of a social climate in which the migrants would later invest their savings in domestic production.

The results of this policy were disappointing. The major obstacles were inadequate investment programs for remigrants, underdeveloped consulting services, a lack of political support at the local and communal levels, an inadequate legal system with contradictory laws, restrictive customs regulations, too frequent changes in the legal system, and legal and political restrictions for the private sector of the economy, including agriculture.

At the end of the 1970s it was predicted that by the mid-1980s "unemployment and insufficient employment of the surplus agrarian population will cease to be a motive for emigration" (Baletić and Baučić, 1979: 91). On the contrary, the deep economic crisis of the 1980s, an inefficient return migration policy, and the political disintegration of Yugoslavia created new reasons for emigration. The restrictive immigration policies of the receiving countries were the only obstacles to the realization of this new emigration potential. At the same time, return migrants contributed little to the creation of new jobs in the country but caused additional pressure on the labor market by competing with the domestic unemployed population for the few jobs that were available. This situation continued until 1991–92, when the violent dissolution of the country and the wars in Croatia and Bosnia caused Europe's largest wave of migration and ethnic cleansing since 1945–46.

Notes

[1] Yugoslav official statistics used the expression "persons who temporarily work abroad". In the period 1970–90 such an expression became problematic because of the transformation of migrants from temporary to permanent ones.

[2] The index of selectivity compares characteristics of migrants with those of the entire population.

[3] For comparison with the 1971 census, only migrant workers are included in the indices of migration selectivity for 1981. Migrant workers' family members living abroad are subtracted from the nonmigrant population of former Yugoslavia in 1981, but are not taken into account in the emigrant population for that year.

[4] In former Yugoslavia, Slovenia, Croatia, Serbia proper (without provinces), and Vojvodina constituted the more developed part of the country; Bosnia–Herzegovina, Montenegro, and Macedonia belonged to the less developed part; and Kosovo was the least developed part of the country.

[5] Indices of selectivity with respect to sex are calculated on the basis of the active nonmigrant population. Such a procedure leads to more reliable results in the case of females.

[6] For return migration the index of selectivity is calculated almost in the same way as for emigration. The only difference is in the migrant population. However, census data are less reliable and thus less useful in the case of return migration. The main reason for the lower quality of the data in the case of remigrants is caused by changes in the characteristics of migrants during their absence.

[7] In the 1971 census migrant workers were classified according to the country of destination. Italy was grouped with other European countries, so that no separate data are given for Italy for 1971 in *Table 11.4*. Ten years later Italy was shown separately.

Chapter 12

Emigration from and Immigration to Bulgaria

Daniela Bobeva

12.1 Historical Overview

Until the end of the World War II the unstable boundaries of Bulgaria were the basic factor explaining migration, especially in the border regions. After five centuries within the boundaries of the Ottoman Empire, the Bulgarian state was restored in 1878 and its borders underwent numerous alterations afterward. The most intensive migration processes (both emigration and immigration) took place immediately after the restoration of Bulgaria. Under the provisions of the San Stephano Peace Treaty (1878) all territories inhabited at least partly by Bulgarians (Macedonia, Eastern Thrace, and Dobrudja) were included in the Bulgarian state. A year later, as a result of the Berlin Congress (1879), the area of Bulgaria was reduced considerably and mass immigration from these territories began. For several decades these territories became a permanent source of immigration to Bulgaria; for example, after the St. Elija Uprising in Macedonia (1903), 30,000 immigrants settled in Bulgaria.

Before World War I the immigration flows were greater than those of ethnic emigration (e.g., ethnic Turks) which stemmed from the consolidation of the Bulgarian nation-state and the stabilization of its boundaries. In 1878 over 1.5 million Bulgarians were living outside the

Table 12.1. Ethnic structure of the Bulgarian population (% of total population.

	Bulgarians	Turks	Gypsies	Pomaks[c]	Others	Total
1900	77.1	14.2	2.4		6.3	100.0
1905	79.8	12.4	1.7		6.1	100.0
1910	81.1	10.8	2.8		5.3	100.0
1920	83.3	10.7	2.0		4.0	100.0
1926	83.2	10.5	2.5		3.8	100.0
1946	86.4	9.6	2.4		1.6	100.0
1956	85.5	8.6	2.6		3.3	100.0
1965[a]	87.9	9.5	1.8		0.8	100.0
1991[b]	82.6	7.0	5.9	2.9	1.6	100.0
1992	85.5	9.7	3.5		1.5	100.0

[a]After 1965 the publication of statistics on the ethnic structure of Bulgaria's population was interrupted.
[b]1991 data are preliminary due to the lack of censuses since 1985.
[c]Until 1965 and in 1992, the Pomaks (i.e., ethnic Bulgarian Muslims) were counted as either Bulgarians or Turks.

borders of the country, in Middle Asia, southeastern Thrace, Epirus, and Moldova.

During both world wars Bulgaria was allied with Germany and therefore on the losing side, and so had to give up some parts of its territory in 1918 and again in 1944–45. In the interwar period, and especially during the crisis of 1929–33, migratory movements were strongly influenced by economic factors. At that time mass migration to the USA reached a peak, leading to a build-up of a Bulgarian minority of about 70,000 in the USA (Petrov and Nikolov, 1988: 178).

In modern history the principal migratory flows from Bulgaria have always been those of ethnic Turks to Turkey. In the period 1878–1913, after the liberation of the country from the Ottoman Empire, some 250,000 Turks left Bulgaria, but a considerable number remained to form the Turkish minority. Despite the high natural growth rate of this population, its share fell from 14.2% in 1900 to 7% in 1991 as a result of mass emigration (see *Table 12.1*).

After World War II and the establishment of the Communist regime, one result of the socialist model was that no political and intellectual emigration was registered, since the closing of state borders stopped almost all migration flows. Official data for this period are not available, but there is evidence from biographical literature that at least some intellectuals and political opponents of the regime managed to leave. For the great majority, however, any travel or emigration to the West became impossible. The regime also began an ideological battle against emigration and criminalized would-be migrants. Emigrants were called "persons-never-to-return"; some of them were even killed. The same regime also oppressed the national minorities through forced "Bulgarization", including compulsory changes of first and family names. On several occasions such developments led to mass emigration of Gypsies and ethnic Turks. Political oppression and ethnic discrimination also contributed to the formation of a huge emigration potential which exploded in the first years after the end of Communist party rule.

In 1988 under pressure of *perestroika* and the new political climate in Europe, the access to passports and exit visas for Bulgarian citizens was liberalized. The opening of the borders "set the spirit free from the bottle" and led to an unforeseen increase in international migration from this part of the Balkans.

12.2 Emigration to Turkey

Since the early twentieth century Bulgaria's Turkish minority has been highly affected by mass emigration to Turkey (*Figure 12.1*). Some political efforts were made to regulate the process, which can be interpreted as both a result of Bulgarian nation-building and as part of a decolonization process. For instance, the Bulgarian–Turkish Emigration Agreement signed in 1935 was followed by mass emigration in 1936–38 when an average of 12,000 Turks left the country for ever each year. In 1912–13 the Bulgarian Pomaks became targets of forced conversion to Christianity.[1] In 1938 the government started attempts to force the Turks to change their names to Bulgarian ones.

After 1944 when Communist party rule was established, waves of emigration from Bulgaria to Turkey took place following each emigration agreement that was signed between the two countries. Between 1950 and 1953 some 250,000 ethnic Turks were allowed to leave, compared with just 25 in 1954–68. Under the provisions of the 1968 Agreement 95,210 Turks were granted the right to emigrate to Turkey, of whom only 14.1% were reluctant to emigrate and remained in Bulgaria (unpublished data from the Ministry of the Interior). The Turkish government negotiated an annual emigration of 10,500 ethnic Turks but did not stand by its obligations; in 1975, for example, only 338 Turks were accepted, and another some 14,250 were denied permission to resettle in Turkey.

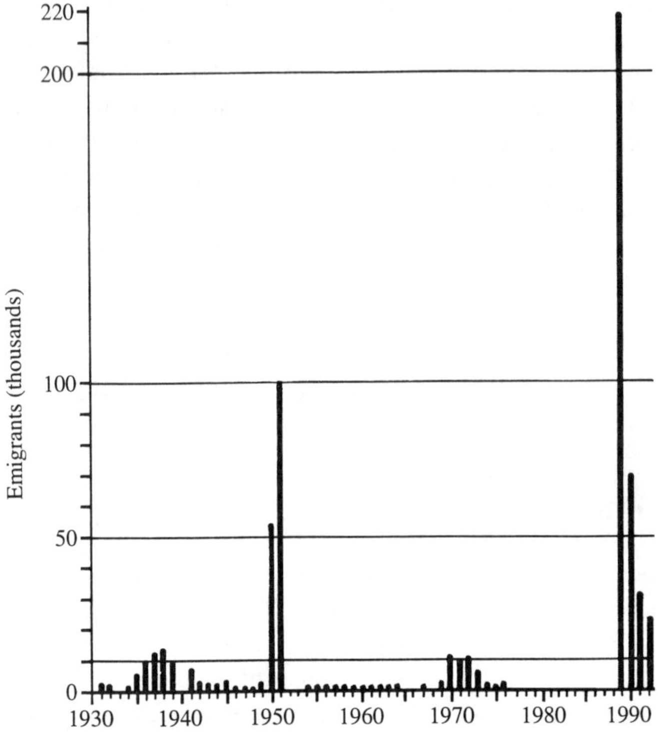

Figure 12.1. Bulgarian emigrants to Turkey, 1935–92. The data are only for legal emigrants according to the bilateral agreements with Turkey. These are persons who left the country in order to live permanently in Turkey. Source: Data from the Ministry of Interior.

The attempts of the Communist government to assimilate the minorities by enforced change of names and by depriving them of their rights caused ethnic conflicts and a wave of emigration of Turks and Pomaks to Turkey in 1988–89. The wave was motivated by political and ethnic factors, and it stopped with the return of the right to use original names and the restoration of the citizen rights of Turks and Pomaks within the country – the reintroduction of the Turkish language in schools, freedom of religion, traditions, etc.

Besides its ethnic background this wave was caused by both the attractiveness of Turkey – a country of relative economic prosperity and higher demand for a qualified labor force – and the unstable political situation and the expected economic crisis in Bulgaria. One of the main

Table 12.2. Emigrants by sex.

	Number			Percent		
	1989	1990[a]	1991	1989	1990[a]	1991
Males	106,432	68,759	19,112	48.8	78.2	47.5
Females	111,568	19,136	21,152	51.2	21.8	52.5
Total	218,000	87,895	40,264	100.0	100.0	100.0

[a]Since 1990 the National Statistical Institute has accepted the UN methodology for defining the status of emigrants. These are persons who have resided continuously in the country for more than one year, or who are departing to take up residence abroad for more than one year. The number of all emigrants in 1992 was 65,000.

pull factors was the willingness of the Turkish government and citizens to receive these immigrants. Integration programs were introduced, financed by various international institutions. In 1989, for instance, the US government granted $9.5 million for the Bulgarian Immigrants' Education and Employment Program; the Council of Europe Settlement Fund provided a loan of $250 million for the construction of 21,488 dwellings for the Bulgarian immigrants; for the same purpose, the Turkish government allocated $15 million and liberalized the regulations for acquiring Turkish citizenship.

According to data from the National Statistical Institute, 218,000 Bulgarian citizens emigrated to Turkey in 1988–89 (*Table 12.2*).[2] In 1990 and 1991 the outflow to Turkey subsided (*Figure 12.2*). A slight rise in the number of emigrants was registered in 1992 when emigration to Turkey again rose to 60% of the total. But there was also return migration from Turkey. For the whole period 1988–92 a good estimate of the net emigration to Turkey (both legal and illegal) would be 280,000, which partly coincides with data on legal immigration from Turkish sources (Gokder, 1992).[3]

According to these sources, a total of 247,959 Bulgarian Turks received Turkish citizenship from mid-1989 to mid-1992, of whom 32.4% were adult males, 32.0% adult females, and 35.6% children. By 1992 some 73,400 of these immigrants had already found employment. According to the same sources, around 160,000 illegal emigrants from Bulgaria also arrived in Turkey with tourist visas. The Bulgarian data on the balance of those leaving for Turkey and those returning to Bulgaria do not correspond to these numbers. If the Turkish estimates are accurate, the last wave of emigration from Bulgaria to Turkey would have comprised more than 400,000 people. However, a considerable

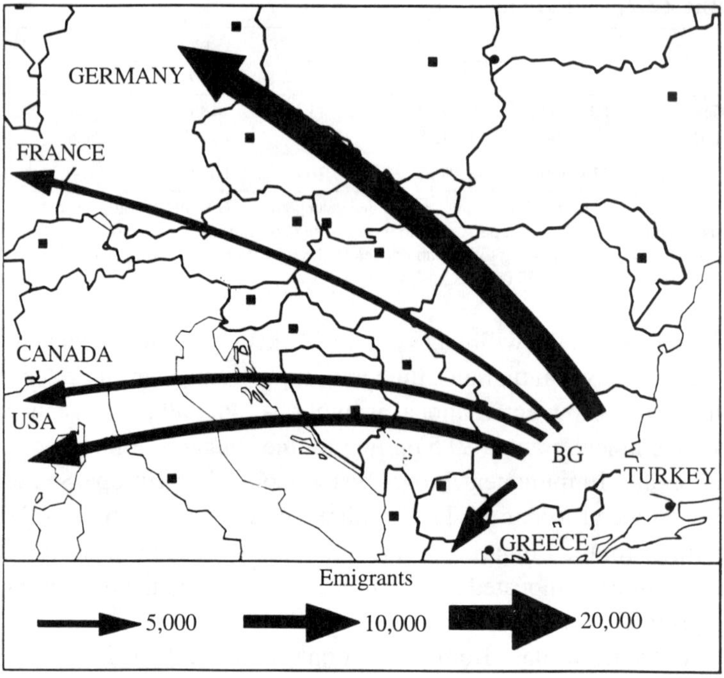

Figure 12.2. Emigration from Bulgaria by destination, 1990. Source: National Statistical Institute.

number of ethnic Turks also returned to Bulgaria, thus reducing the negative migration balance.

Due to recent political reforms Bulgaria has become the only Balkan country with a fairly high participation of ethnic minorities, especially Turks, in the government. As a result of the 1991 elections the Movement for Rights and Freedoms (MRF), representing the Turkish minority, became the third leading political force in the country after the Union of Democratic Forces and the Socialist party (former Communists). Besides, 58 municipalities elected ethnic Turks as mayors, and the government was elected with the mandate of MRF. These political achievements of the Turkish-speaking minority have helped to reduce the ethnic tensions in Bulgaria, and they have also reduced the number of emigrants.

In 1992 a second wave of emigration to Turkey was discussed in the media and in political debates. It was very difficult to identify the size of this wave, which gave way to political speculation. Turkey introduced strict immigration regulations, and as a consequence the number of illegal migrants with tourist visas rose sharply. An indicator of the magnitude of the emigration outflow to Turkey in 1992 is the balance between the number of Bulgarian citizens that left for and those returning from Turkey. By the end of September 1992, 29,119 of those who left Bulgaria did not return, compared with 25,139 in the same period of the previous year.

Today, the reasons for the emigration of ethnic Turks to Turkey are predominantly economic, particularly the growing unemployment (14% of the active population at the end of 1992). The future prospects are for a continued steady outflow. Evidence for the economic motivation for this outflow can be found in the fact that most of the emigrants come from depressed southern regions populated mainly by ethnic Turks. The demographic effects are already visible. The mass emigration to Turkey in 1988–92 caused a significant decrease in the population of southern Bulgaria and some municipalities were even rendered desolate. In contrast, the number of ethnic migrants from northeastern Bulgaria was much lower in 1991–92 than in 1988–90.

The demographic composition of the ethnic migrants shows almost equal numbers of males and females (*Table 12.2*), and their age distribution does not differ significantly from that of the whole population (*Table 12.3*). Both facts seem to indicate that most of these migrants intend to settle permanently in Turkey. A substantial number of them (9,000, according to the Turkish statistics) are university graduates. This brain-drain from the Turkish minority group in Bulgaria is likely to have a negative impact on the development of this group in the new democratic situation. The deficits of engineers, teachers, and economists in the regions populated by Bulgarian Turks will become additional obstacles to the economic restructuring of these underdeveloped regions.

In some southern regions, such as the Rhodopes region, the level of unemployment among the active population exceeds 40%. Economic restructuring would require huge investments in infrastructure and production which cannot be afforded by the state, since it already has an external debt of $12.5 billion and an internal debt of BGLv9 billion (end of 1992). The activated trade and investment process from Turkey to regions inhabited by Bulgarian Turks is one means of overcoming the crisis. The economic restructuring of these regions is being assisted by the several projects of the EU's PHARE program (the Project for Regional Restructuring and Development in the Rhodopes Region, to

Table 12.3. Emigrants by age.

	Number			Percent		
Age groups	1989	1990	1991	1989	1990	1991
0–4	10,612	—	467	4.9	—	1.2
5–9	14,044	—	1,426	6.4	—	3.5
10–14	12,800	1,111	2,350	5.9	1.3	5.8
15–19	14,372	5,576	2,805	6.6	6.3	7.0
20–24	21,293	11,847	3,217	9.8	13.5	8.0
25–29	28,234	12,877	4,927	13.0	14.7	12.2
30–34	28,569	14,480	5,632	13.1	16.5	14.0
35–39	22,433	14,051	5,162	10.3	16.0	12.8
40–44	12,926	11,478	4,618	5.9	13.1	11.5
45–49	10,759	8,442	3,255	4.9	9.6	8.1
50–54	9,815	4,618	2,221	4.5	5.2	5.5
55–59	10,071	2,310	1,796	4.6	2.6	4.5
60 and over	22,072	1,105	2,388	10.1	1.2	5.9

Source: National Statistical Institute.

which ECU 7.5 million have been allocated) and some EU direct investment projects. But the process of restructuring is expected to be quite long. Both the fall in living standards and the growing unemployment will maintain the emigration at a non-negligible level for some time to come.

12.3 Waves of Emigration

The opening of Bulgaria's borders allowed a huge increase in foreign travel. In 1989 some 921,987 Bulgarians traveled abroad; in 1990 the number rose to 2.4 million, representing one in every four Bulgarians. This intensity of foreign travel remained stable in 1991 and 1992 as well. In general this can be interpreted as a positive development, for intensive cultural, economic, and political exchange are essential parts of the transformation process. Travel for tourism is dominant (1992: 55%), followed by paid visits to foreign countries (1992: 38%). Business trips dropped both in absolute numbers and in relative terms from 7.6% in 1990 to 5.6% in 1992.

To a certain extent the large number of trips abroad can be seen as a mechanism for channeling future migration, since the travel routes often coincide with the main migratory flows. In 1990 Western Europe became the main destination rather than Turkey. That was the time of the second wave of emigration after the initiation of the reforms, although it differed substantially from the first "ethnic" wave in terms of motivation, intensity, and demographic and professional composition of the migrants. The emigration wave of 1990 was caused by two major factors: first, by the disappointment of a great part of the population, especially young people, with the results of the 1990 elections when the ex-Communist party won a solid majority of seats in parliament; and, second, by the fact that people began to fear the lack of fuel, cold winters, and possible starvation. Thus the West became increasingly attractive (Dimova *et al.*, 1990). The second wave differed considerably from the first: 92% of these emigrants were of working age (*Table 12.3*), more than 75% were males (*Table 12.2*), and a large proportion were well educated. More than half of the emigrants in 1990 had received secondary education, and more than 10% were university graduates (*Table 12.4*). Therefore we can say that some brain-drain took place. Among the highly qualified workers the largest share (10%) were technical specialists, followed by economic and agriculture specialists (6%) and engineers (5%). High on the list of these emigrants' motives were the desires to develop and practice their professional knowledge, as well as to escape from the growing threat of unemployment resulting from the closure of many scientific and research institutions.

In contrast to the first wave (1988–89) of emigrants, many of those of the second wave chose to go to highly developed West European countries and to the USA; only 6.3% headed for Turkey. Germany attracted the largest proportion (20%) of Bulgarian emigrants of this second wave, most of whom were seeking political asylum, not because of a new era of political repression in Bulgaria, but rather because they saw no other way of establishing themselves legally in Germany. A bilateral agreement between German and Bulgarian governments was signed in November 1992 for the return and reintegration of these migrants. The project envisages the foundation of three professional training centers for unemployed return migrants. Such programs are seen as an effective way to deal with the problem of reintegration of the returning migrants.

During the period under review, the seasonal migration to neighboring countries, especially Greece and Turkey, has also become more important. Unpublished data from the Ministry of the Interior suggest that in 1990 some 33,000 Bulgarian citizens migrated to Greece as seasonal workers, most of whom took up jobs in the agricultural sector. Because seasonal labor migration takes place under the form of tourism it is difficult to estimate the real size of this flow, but can be regulated

Table 12.4. Emigrants by education, 1990–91.

	Number		Percent	
	1990	1991	1990	1991
Unfinished elementary	176	—	0.2	—
Elementary/ Basic (8 years)	21,006	16,025	23.9	39.8
Secondary	20,919	7,127	23.8	17.7
Vocational training	31,818	4,751	36.2	11.8
College	3,955	7,368	4.5	18.3
University	10,021	4,993	11.4	12.4
Total	87,895	40,264	100.0	100.0

Source: National Statistical Institute.

under bilateral agreements; one such agreement between Greece and Bulgaria is currently under negotiation.

Comparing 1990 and 1991, the numbers of male and female emigrants were about the same, with a slight increase in the number of emigrants below working age (about 15%). The intensive emigration of highly qualified workers continued; of the total emigrants in 1991, some 12% were university graduates and 18% had received college education (*Table 12.4*).

In 1991 and 1992 the emigration wave was smaller than that in 1989: some 40,264 in 1991 (*Table 12.2*) and 38,000 in 1992. Total emigration from Bulgaria is decreasing, but not so the desire of would-be migrants to move westward. The main reasons for the smaller number of emigrants are the mounting barriers set up by Western Europe. For instance, Bulgaria's association with the EU is based on an agreement signed in March 1993, in which the Bulgarian government committed itself to measures to control and reduce the East–West mobility of its citizens.

Emigration during the first four years of economic and political reforms after the fall of the Communist regime (1989–92) led to a net loss of population of about 400,000, according to preliminary data from the December 1992 census.[4] If 1988 is included, the total loss could be estimated at 600,000 people. So far, this mass emigration has not had a positive effect on Bulgaria because a substantial part of the emigrants did (and will) not return at all and those who return have not acquired experience, skills, or financial means during their stay abroad. This means that in most cases short-term migration cannot ensure anyone's future in Bulgaria and therefore will not contribute to the acceleration and the successful implementation of the reforms.

At the same time, however, emigration has led to the establishment of substantial groups of Bulgarians in some West European countries such as Germany. The consistent policies of European governments to restrict immigration and to stimulate the return of immigrants to their countries of origin creates a new problem: how to deal with the returnees. The problem is being complicated by the fact that upon return these people are confronted with higher levels of unemployment, a further decline in material output, and even tougher competition in the labor and the other markets than at the time of their departure.

12.4 Immigration Inflows

The fall of the Iron Curtain intensified not only emigration, but also the inflow of people into Bulgaria. Despite the poor state of its economy, Bulgaria is becoming more and more attractive to immigrants. Evidence can be found in the official statistics on arrivals of foreigners in Bulgaria. The number of foreigners visiting Bulgaria is growing, and in 1991 reached a peak level of 7 million, mostly tourists and businessmen. In 1992, 6.12 million foreigners entered the country, about 28% of whom were Turks, 27% Romanians, 6% Greeks, and 6% from the CIS countries. Compared with arrivals during 1991, the number of visitors from the former socialist countries in Central Europe has fallen: from Poland by 80%, from Hungary by 20%, and from the Czech Republic and Slovakia by 30%. Visitors from the USA, Germany, and other Western countries increased, largely due to the intensification of business contacts.

The number of transit travelers is also increasing: from 4.42 million in 1990 to 4.33 million in 1991, and 4.8 million in 1992. Such transit has also become the basic mechanism for illegal immigration both to Bulgaria and to Western Europe (often using Bulgaria as a starting point), particularly for citizens of Morocco, Nigeria, and other African countries. During and after the Gulf War various other Arab countries also tried to use this migratory channel. On several occasions the police and the Ministry of the Interior discovered criminal organizations dealing with the transfer of people from Africa and the Middle East to Western Europe. But Bulgaria is also becoming a transit country for migrants from several CIS countries, Turkey, and some Arab states to Europe; only a few tend to remain in Bulgaria.

Information on the number and status of immigrants in Bulgaria is very limited and so far has not been published. The Law on Foreign Residence in Bulgaria recognizes two categories of foreigner: permanent and temporary residents. By the end of September 1992 some 28,000 permanent foreign residents were registered in Bulgaria (data from the Ministry of the Interior): 20,000 from the former Soviet Union (CIS countries, Georgia, and the Baltic republics), 1,000 citizens from former Yugoslavia, 800 Poles, 800 Czechs, 450 Germans, and 4,950 others. Of the temporary residents, about 13,000 were considered to be illegal, among them 4,000 from Syria, 2,000 from Iran, around 2,000 from Sri Lanka, Bangladesh, and Pakistan, 1,000 from Bosnia, etc.[5]

One reason for the considerable illegal immigration is the liberal regulations for entry into the country. Bulgaria has not imposed any visa requirements for citizens of almost all "sending" countries. A voucher for a hotel or other accommodation providing for an overnight stay is sufficient to enter the country and to stay as a tourist. In the early 1990s the Ministry of the Interior increased its attempts to control the illegal resident foreigners, and several citizens of Nigeria, Mozambique, Ghana, Morocco, and Sri Lanka were expelled. In 1992–93 an immigration wave of people from Romania, the former Soviet Union, and former Yugoslavia reached Bulgaria, which has no visa regulations with these countries.

As in Western Europe, there is also fear in Bulgaria that a wave of immigration from the former Soviet Union might result from the introduction of a new Law on the Freedom of Travel in Russia and several other CIS countries. In early 1993 Bulgaria therefore introduced some restrictions designed to limit the immigration and transit migration of Russians to Europe across Bulgaria.

Labor immigration is emerging as a new problem in Bulgaria. At the end of 1992 the unemployment rate reached 14% of the active population, and the labor market has become extremely sensitive to any additional labor-force supply. At present (1993), the Law on Foreign Residence in Bulgaria (Article 9) does not restrict the access of foreign persons to the domestic labor market irrespective of the kind of stay in Bulgaria. The access of foreigners to the Bulgarian labor market is also facilitated by the Law on Economic Activity of Foreign Persons and on Protection of Foreign Investment. According to Articles 2 and 3 of this law, foreigners are allowed to employ Bulgarian and foreign workers, and the latter have the same rights and obligations as Bulgarian citizens.

Despite the liberal laws regarding foreign labor, the growing numbers entering the country at a time of high unemployment have encouraged the authorities to try to restrict the employment of foreigners. Since mid-1991 special work permits have been issued by the Ministry of Labor and Social Welfare: only 58 permits were issued between June and December 1991, and 380 between January 1992 and March 1993. This means that the majority of foreigners in Bulgaria are working without permission, largely because there is no clear distinction between the cases of issuing working visas and the cases of issuing business visit permits. For the latter, the procedure is simplified, there are no restrictions, and the term of the permits is three months; it may be renewable thereafter. The lack of clear legal distinction and administrative supervision on behalf of the state institutions facilitates mass immigration of foreign labor, especially from Turkey and Russia. Ironically, the mass emigration of Bulgarian citizens to Turkey is being accompanied by mass labor immigration in the opposite direction.

The occupational structure of foreign workers is as follows: some 75% are employed in trade and services sector, 6% in construction, and 7% in entertainment. Foreign workers are employed mainly in small and medium-sized enterprises, such as bakeries, handicrafts, and trading companies. Immigrant labor is also legally employed by intermediary companies (as of the end of March 1993 there were more than 112), operating mostly with CIS countries and recently also with Chinese citizens.

Labor migration to Bulgaria is not a completely new phenomenon. Under the Communist regime foreign labor was recruited – on the basis of bilateral agreements – from Vietnam, Nicaragua, and some other countries. This recruitment took place to cover a deficit of manual workers produced by overemployment. These foreign workers became "useless" at the beginning of 1990 when it was found that there was no deficit of manual workers, and hidden unemployment in other segments of production. The population developed a rather negative attitude toward the Vietnamese in the country, and domestic public opinion pressed for their removal. Before the terms of the bilateral agreements expired all Vietnamese and Nicaraguan workers were expelled at the expense of the Bulgarian state. This case reveals that the Bulgarian people are neither prepared nor inclined to tolerate foreign workers. This means that if the inflow of foreign workers is not limited it may cause internal social tensions, the consequences of which are unpredictable.

12.5 Refugees and Asylum Seekers

Due to its economic and social problems Bulgaria has not yet become an attractive destination for asylum seekers and refugees. In 1993 only 120 persons from Croatia possessing legal refugee status were residing in the country, mostly mothers and small children accommodated by the Ministry of Labor and Social Welfare. They were not allowed to work, and the expenses for their stay were covered by an emergency fund of the state budget. At the end of 1992 another 40 persons were seeking asylum in Bulgaria. As long as the procedure was not legally regulated, refugee status was acquired through decisions made by the Bureau of the UNHCR in Sofia. In the future the Bureau for Refugees at the Ministry of the Interior established in 1993 will be responsible for decisions on whether to grant refugee status.

A draft Law on Refugees in Bulgaria worked out by the People's Rights Commission of the National Assembly defines the term "refugee" in accordance with the conditions of the Geneva Convention ratified by Bulgaria in 1991. The procedure is also defined: it should take no longer than 90 days and the expenses for the refugee's stay during that period are to be covered by the state. The draft provides for preferential status for refugees over other foreigners staying in the country. Parts of this draft are included in the draft for amendment and completion of the Law on Foreign Residence in Bulgaria. Thus the refugee's status may be regulated within the Law on Foreign Residence in Bulgaria as well. A first refugee camp was being built in 1993.

12.6 Emigration and Immigration Policy

Bulgaria has difficulties in formulating and implementing a comprehensive migration policy, some of which have to do with the fact that migration flows have changed markedly since the beginning of political and economic reforms. Under Communist party rule emigration was almost impossible and had a negative label. At the same time Bulgarian society had no experience with immigration.

Today emigration is still not accepted as a normal social phenomenon. In a public opinion survey only 35.5% expressed a positive attitude, 35.8% negative, and 28.7% expressed no attitude at all (Bezlov, 1991). In these interviews more people over age 60 (43.3%) rejected emigration than younger cohorts. Positive views were expressed by

48.5% of university graduates and 52% of all people below age 25. A large majority of both unemployed and scientists questioned were in favor of emigration. Between 1989 and 1992, Bulgaria's migration policy included:

- Adherence to the Charter on Human Rights establishing the freedom of movement for Bulgarian citizens and for foreigners living or traveling in the country.
- Abolition of almost all travel restrictions on Bulgarian citizens and the introduction of visa-free travel regimes with many countries.
- Ratification of conventions concerning refugees and asylum seekers, especially the Geneva Convention.
- Promotion of the cultural and educational development of ethnic Bulgarian minorities living abroad.
- Drafting of new legislation on emigration and immigration.

In the field of labor emigration, successive governments have tried to organize and regulate it in accordance with international norms and the legislation of the receiving countries. Bilateral agreements on labor migration were and are considered instruments for regulating the movement of labor, while eliminating the discrimination of legally employed Bulgarian citizens on foreign labor markets. At present, two agreements with Germany (for 2,000 workers) are in force. Similar agreements with Belgium, France, Switzerland, and Greece are expected.

12.7 Migration Prospects

Since the late 1980s a number of surveys have been carried out to quantify and evaluate Bulgaria's emigration potential. Economic hardship and political instability were identified as basic factors motivating a substantial share of Bulgaria's population to consider emigration.

Over the last few years Bulgaria's potential emigration has been high. According to NSI data for 1990 and 1991 (Kalchev and Tzvetarsky, 1991: 6–7) and the results of studies conducted by the Center for the Study of Democracy in 1990, 1991, and 1992, the potentially mobile part of the population that would be willing to emigrate comprises some 26–28% of the working-age population. According to data from the International Organization on Migration (IOM, 1993: 71), the potential migrants comprise up to 36% of the population. According to NSI data gathered at border check points (National Statistical Institute, 1992: 29) up to 5% of people aged 18–60 would be prepared to emigrate during their present trip abroad.

Males are more inclined to emigrate than females. Age also plays a role: the higher the age the lower the intention to emigrate. Every third Bulgarian aged 18–29 expresses the desire to emigrate, while of those aged 60 and above only 6.9% expressed the same intention. The greatest emigration potential can be found among people with higher education. Among those ready to leave, 3.9% have had primary education, 6.5% basic education, 11.5% secondary education, and 15.9% higher education. The proportion of those who categorically reject the emigration option under any circumstances (i.e., the categorically non-mobile) is lowest in the group with higher education (55%), followed by those with secondary education (63%), with basic education (78%), and with primary education only (82%).

The basic motive for emigration among the potential emigrants is individual welfare, stated by about 60% of those ready to emigrate. Other motives vary among the different educational or professional groups of migrants. The less well-qualified potential emigrants mention at second place the desire to live in and to get to know developed countries, while engineers, scientists, and intellectuals mention careers and self-realization at second place.

Political factors are also significant for the high potential mobility of the Bulgarian population. According to 33% of those interviewed of working age, the basic motive for emigration is the unstable political situation.

12.8 Conclusions

The migration situation in Bulgaria can be described as having decreasing emigration, increasing immigration and return migration, intensive labor migration between neighboring countries, an as yet inadequate legal framework, and a hesitant policy on migration.

Migration has become a common subject of political discussions. Opinion polls and surveys show a high emigration potential due to the economic difficulties of the country during its political and economic transition, while the ethnic tensions that caused the mass emigration of ethnic minorities to Turkey in the past seem to have lost their impact. At the same time, larger numbers of immigrants are expected to come from the CIS and some Middle East countries. New legislation is being developed and a new migration policy is making its first difficult steps.

Notes

[1] Pomaks are ethnic Bulgarian Muslims, most of whom traditionally settled in regions with a high proportion of ethnic Turks.

[2] This number refers to the overall emigrant wave in the period, but it can be used to depict emigration from Bulgaria to Turkey because most Bulgarians were not yet allowed to travel to other countries. Travel restrictions for Bulgarian citizens were lifted only in late 1990.

[3] Because no information is available, these are author's assessments based on journeys of Bulgarian citizens abroad and the difference between the numbers who departed and those who returned.

[4] Preliminary data from the December 1992 census; *Money* Newspaper, 24/1993.

[5] Illegal migrants are those who cross the border illegally, and those with expired visas. The data are collected and estimated by the Ministry of the Interior.

Chapter 13

Emigration from the Former Soviet Union: The Fourth Wave

Anatoli Vishnevsky and Zhanna Zayonchkovskaya

13.1 The First Three Waves of Emigration

Prerevolutionary Russia participated in the great intercontinental migration in the late nineteenth and early twentieth centuries. According to some estimates, between 1861 and 1915, 4.3 million people left Russia, of which almost 2.6 million during 1900–15. Two-thirds of the emigrants left for the USA (Obolenskiy, 1928: 20). Compared with the whole population of Czarist Russia, this number of emigrants was not very significant; in contrast with many other European countries, the possibility of internal agrarian colonization provided an alternative to mass emigration.

The First Wave (1917–38)

After the 1917 revolution the Soviet Union experienced several waves of mass emigration. They were largely linked to specific political circumstances and greatly differed from the prerevolutionary economic emigration pattern. It has been estimated that between 1917 and 1938 some 4–5.5 million people left the country (Heitman, 1987: 10; 1991: 2; Vishnevsky and Zayonchkovskaya, 1991: 5–7; Tsaplin, 1989: 177).

Table 13.1. Emigration from the former Soviet Union, 1948–90.

	Jews	Germans	Armenians	Greeks	Others	Total
1948–70	25,200	22,400	12,000	—	—	59,600
1971–80	248,900	64,300	34,100	—	—	347,300
1981–86	16,900	19,500	6,300	1,300	—	44,000
1987–90	301,300	308,200	31,700	23,000	20,200	684,400
Total 1948–90	592,300	414,400	84,100	24,300	20,200	1,135,300
Proportion of total (%)	52.1	36.5	7.4	2.1	1.9	100.0

Source: Heitman (1991: 2).

The Second Wave (1939–47)

The second wave of emigration occurred during and after World War II. According to some Western estimates, between 8 and 10 million people emigrated in this period, whereas recent Russian estimates put the figure at only 5.5 million. The main divergences are in the estimates of the emigration of Poles and Baltic peoples. Emigration studies were never priority research topics in the former Soviet Union and both public opinion and specialists know little if anything about it. However, they now have access to archives so their knowledge of the history of emigration will grow. However, one should not ignore the fact that emigration from the country during periods of political and military turmoil is not always recorded in the archives, so that much of the information is often irretrievably lost. During the same time about 600,000–700,000 immigrants (Ukrainians, Belarussians, Armenians, etc.) came to the USSR.

The Third Wave (1948–90)

The third wave of emigration, for the first time relatively voluntary, appears to have been much smaller (1.1 million emigrants) than the first two (*Table 13.1*). In using these estimates we have to bear in mind their approximate and illustrative nature, as is usually emphasized by the authors of publications.

Beginning in 1961, official data from the USSR State Statistics Board (see *Figure 13.1*) show that, in the 1960s during the Khrushchev regime and immediately afterward, there was some immigration to the USSR. They were mainly Armenians returning to their historical homeland, refugees from China, and a sharply increased flow of students who came to the USSR for extended periods from Asia and Africa. There

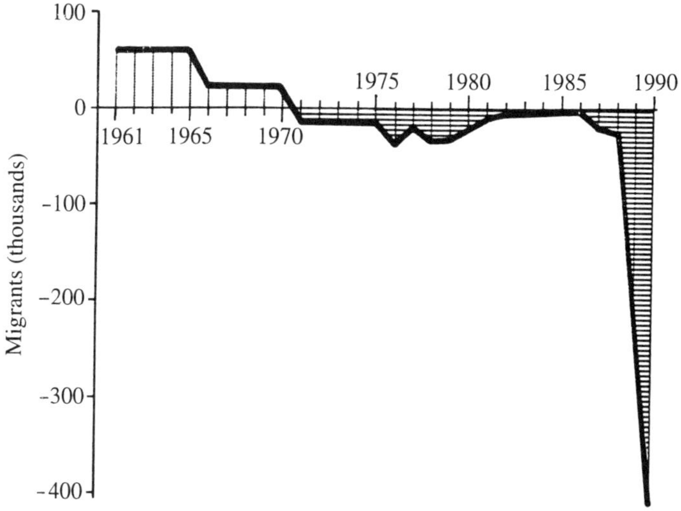

Figure 13.1. Net migration of the population of the former Soviet Union, 1961–90. Five-year averages for 1961–65 and 1966–70. Source: Vishnevsky and Zayonchkovskaya (1991).

was certainly a small outflow, too, but it was well compensated by immigration, thus making the migration balance positive.

During the later decades the inflow decreased sharply. There was also an outflow, but it was a thin stream limited by strict bans, so that the migration balance became negative. During the 1970s the figures of negative net migration were between 10,000 and 15,000 people, rising in certain years to 30,000 to 45,000, but during the 1980s emigration figures were even smaller.

A fundamental change took place in 1988 when almost free emigration of Jews, ethnic Germans, and Greeks and travel to the West by private invitation were allowed. The population quickly reacted to the greater freedom of movement. In 1988 emigration from the USSR increased 2.5 times compared with 1987 (108,000 against 39,000), again more than doubled in 1989 (235,000) and doubled again in 1990 (452,000). The reverse flow was not large. The distinctive feature of the USSR international migration exchange in recent years has been its strongly pronounced one-sidedness: a great increase in emigration while immigration has remained negligible.[1]

The main flow of emigrants in 1988–90 (about two-thirds) came, almost equally, from Russia, the Ukraine, and Kazakhstan (*Table 13.2*).

Table 13.2. Geographic origin of permanent emigrants (number of exit permits issued), in %.

Republics	1980	1988	1989	1990
Russia	19.1	19.1	20.2	22.9
Ukraine	18.5	16.4	21.3	21.1
Belarus	9.4	3.0	6.2	7.5
Moldova	10.8	2.0	3.2	4.6
Lithuania	3.0	0.6	0.8	0.8
Latvia	3.7	1.0	1.3	1.1
Estonia	1.2	1.5	0.7	0.2
Georgia	2.5	0.8	1.5	1.4
Azerbaijan	2.7	0.5	1.3	2.7
Armenia	14.9	14.6	5.2	1.2
Uzbekistan	1.9	3.3	4.3	9.3
Kyrghyzstan	2.6	9.8	7.1	4.0
Tajikistan	2.5	5.5	4.5	2.8
Turkmenistan	0.1	0.1	0.0	0.1
Kazakhstan	7.0	21.8	22.5	20.4
Total (former USSR)	36,366	108,189	234,994	452,262

Considerable flows also came from Belarus (7.5%) and Moldova (4.6%). From the European part the emigrants were mostly Jews, and from Kazakhstan and Central Asia mainly ethnic Germans. The share of emigrants from Central Asia was only 16%. The most intensive emigration flow came from the capitals and their surrounding areas. In 1989–90 about 40% of emigrants from Russia were inhabitants of Moscow and from the city and province of St. Petersburg. In 1990 emigrants from the Ukraine came mainly from the city of Kiev and Odessa province, those from Belarus came from Gomel province and the city of Minsk, and those from Kazakhstan came from Karaganda province and the city and province of Alma-Ata.

In spite of great quantitative changes during the late 1980s, qualitatively we can still identify the same third wave of emigration consisting of representatives of several national minorities who were given the right of free emigration, most of whom returned to their historical homelands or to join powerful foreign diaspora. In fact it was only due to political and economic pressure at the international level and support from abroad that the third wave of emigration had become so numerous, and this is its distinctive feature. A variety of factors motivated these emigrants to leave the country – economic, political, ethnocultural, and religious – but they all had one thing in common: politically powerful bridgeheads abroad.

For certain parts of the population of the former USSR these specific "ethnic" factors of the third wave of emigration will continue in the future, but their importance will inevitably diminish, whereas economic and political factors are already becoming apparent. The Law on Emigration from and Immigration to the USSR adopted by the Supreme Soviet in May 1991, which came into effect on 1 January 1993 in Russia and probably in other states in the new federation CIS, guarantees freedom of travel and migration as a basic human right that will enable citizens of all CIS countries, regardless of their ethnic origins, to emigrate for economic and other reasons, such as to search for work. Considering the present state of the Russian, Ukrainian, Belarussian, and other CIS economies and the overall sociopolitical crisis, there is every reason to suppose that there is the potential for increased emigration, which may become a mass movement. Many, if not all newly independent states will face a new, fourth wave of emigration.

13.2 Potential Composition of the Fourth Wave of Emigration

It is already possible to identify the components of this future wave of emigration. It may include:

1. Continuation of the third wave of ethnic emigration of people dissatisfied with their position in the legal successor states of the USSR, primarily national or religious minorities.
2. New ethnic emigration which may conventionally be called "postcolonial" and which will affect major ethnic groups, particularly Russians who are forced to leave the regions where they do not belong to the new national majority.
3. "Economic" emigration of two groups. "European" emigrants will include the skilled labor force, creating a "brain-drain" from Russia and the European republics due to worsening economic conditions or simply because of the more profitable conditions of labor abroad. "Asian" emigrants will include unskilled workers from the Asian republics in response to the population explosion, agrarian overpopulation, and low rates of development in nonagrarian sectors of the economy, when it will be impossible or inexpedient to emigrate to Russia or other European republics of the former USSR.

4. Political and ecological refugees who may arise from situations of bitter political crises or ecological catastrophes.

13.2.1 Continuation of the third wave of emigration

The new Law on Emigration affects all citizens of the former USSR including, naturally, those who constitute the main part of the third wave of emigration, which will thus merge into the fourth. In the first place it is necessary to assess the potential of that part of future emigration flows.

According to our estimates, the number of national minorities who could be regarded as potential emigrants attracted by other countries and ethnic communities living abroad hardly exceeded 8 million people in 1989. The most numerous among them, according to the 1989 census, were ethnic Germans (2 million), Jews (1.4 million; including Jews from Central Asia and Georgia, 1.5 million), and Poles (1.1 million). In addition to these ethnic groups, Chesnais (1991a: 8) included in his list 178,000 Karelians and Finns, 439,000 Koreans, 385,000 Greeks, 171,000 Hungarians, 40,000 Persians, 25,000 Czechs and Slovaks, 262,000 Gypsies, and 208,000 Turks.

Since the 1989 census no fewer than 300,000 Germans, 400,000 Jews, and about 100,000 Armenians have left the country. Hence the maximum potential that existed in 1989 and which we estimated at 8 million people has now decreased by at least 10%. Considering the emigration that took place after the 1989 census, the four most numerous groups of potential "ethnic" emigrants – Germans, Jews, Poles, and Armenians – now include about 5–5.5 million people (see *Figure 13.2*).

Each of these national minorities has its own reasons for emigration, but a number of factors may also discourage emigration. Many of them have deep roots in the places of their present residence, most were born and sometimes have lived there for several generations, have never been to their historical homeland, often do not know its language, and have no permanent contacts with it. Moreover, they are not always particularly welcomed in their historical homelands.

In this sense, an article published in *Izvestia* under the headline "March of Soviet Poles to Warsaw will not take place" is significant. As is known, large numbers of Poles were repatriated to Poland during the postwar period, particularly in 1945–46. The 1950 census in Poland showed that 2.1 million residents had arrived from those regions which

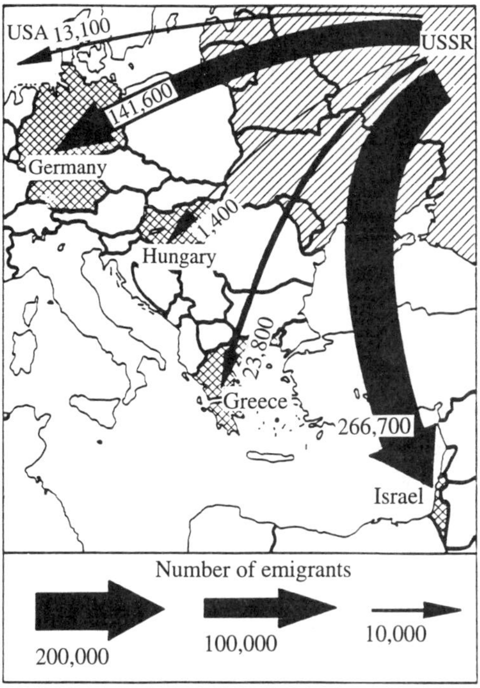

Figure 13.2. Emigration from the USSR in 1990 by countries of destination (number of exit permits issued). Source: Vishnevsky and Zayonchkovskaya (1991).

after 1939 had become part of the USSR (Marianski, 1969: 128) and in 1955–58 they were joined by 200,000 repatriated Poles. But according to the 1989 census there were still 1,126,000 Poles in the USSR, living in rather compact areas in Belarus, the Ukraine, and Lithuania, only 30.5% of whom consider Polish to be their mother tongue. In fact that they did not take advantage of repatriation in 1944–47 nor in 1956–57. No less important is the position of the Polish side. *Izvestia* quotes the Polish newspaper *Courier Polsky*:

> According to the Foreign Affairs Consular and Refugees Department it is impossible to agree to a mass emigration of Poles from the USSR in the present financial state of the country. Suppose one million Poles returned to Poland within five years; that would need from 20 to 30 trillion Polish zloty [$2–3 billion].... Emigration [to Poland] of a considerable number of Poles...would contradict the political interests of Poland. (*Izvestia*, 1991)[2]

Thus, if we talk about the continuation of the third wave of emigration, we might conclude that its actual potential seems to be much smaller than the annual 500,000 people estimated by Western experts (see Chesnais, 1991a: 11). In certain years this level may be achieved, but it is unlikely to continue for a lengthy period.

13.2.2 New ethnic emigration

The numbers of national ethnic minorities who are emigrating most actively now will inevitably decrease due to the fall in the overall number of potential emigrants in this category. However, this does not mean that such emigration will disappear completely; on the contrary, it will soon receive new impulses connected with serious changes in the migratory and also in the general political situation inside the country. The main nations – especially the Russians – are becoming new minorities in many regions and republics. Sooner or later many of them might find themselves involved in the emigration process, perhaps as a result of a process of "decolonization".

Russian territorial expansion began several centuries ago and was driven by the desire to extend the borders of the Russian Empire. With the occupation and colonization of new territories it sharply increased in the nineteenth century as a result of both military expansion and agricultural colonization. The growth of demographic pressure and increasing overpopulation that forced peoples from many European countries to cross the ocean led in Russia to "internal" colonization, for she had enough free and sparsely populated territories available within her own borders.[3] Russians and many other ethnic groups took part in the peopling of Novorossia, the regions near the Urals, Siberia, the Far East, the steppes of Kazakhstan, etc. This internal colonization saved them from the necessity to emigrate overseas; thus even now there is no sizable Russian diaspora abroad.

In the present century the emigration of Russians to the peripheral regions of the country received a strong new impetus through urbanization. Before World War I and in the years of the first Soviet five-year plan, the urbanization occurred largely within the territory of Russia and the Ukraine, but after World War II it spread to include the economic and geographical peripheries of the USSR. The citizens of the central districts of Russia were most mobile at that time, and rushed to the growing towns in Belarus, Moldova, Central Asia, Kazakhstan, and

Table 13.3. Increase in Russian populations living outside Russia, 1959–89.

Year	Number of ethnic Russians (millions) In the (former) USSR	In Russia	Outside Russia	Increase in ethnic Russian population (%) In the USSR	In Russia	Outside Russia
1959	114.1	97.9	16.2	—	—	—
1970	129.0	107.7	21.3	13.1	10.0	31.5
1979	137.4	113.5	23.9	6.5	5.4	12.2
1989	145.2	119.9	25.3	5.7	5.6	5.9

to several autonomous republics of the Russian Federation. A part of that flow was linked to the development of the natural resources of the outlying territories, such as mineral deposits, virgin lands, etc.

In the postwar period there was also an intensive flow of ethnic Russians to Latvia and Estonia, where the natural rate of increase in population in the 1960s was low and living standards were higher than in other areas of the country. That inflow resulted in serious changes in the ethnic composition of the population. In the mid-1930s Latvians made up 76.2% of the population in Latvia, Estonians 90.7% of the population in Estonia, and Russians 9.7% of the population in Latvia and 5.6% in Estonia (Marianski, 1969: 167). In 1989 the percentage of Latvians in Latvia had fallen to 52%, of Estonians in Estonia to 61.5%, while the Russian population had grown to 34% and 30%, respectively.

In the 1960s the growth of the Russian population outside the territory of Russia was 2.4 times greater than in the USSR as a whole, mostly as a result of migration. But the 1970s saw new trends. The inflow of ethnic Russians into other republics slowed down, while their number outside Russia increased by twice as much as in the USSR as a whole. In the 1980s it barely exceeded the USSR level. This means that their outflow from Russia had practically stopped and remigration was well under way (*Table 13.3*).

The migration processes of the 1960s and 1970s gradually prepared for the events of the 1980s, when the remigration of ethnic Russians into their republic replaced their territorial expansion. Strictly speaking, the process of ousting Russians began much earlier. It began in Georgia, from which the rapid outflow of Russians began in the 1960s: from 1959 to 1988 the number of Russians in Georgia fell by 18%, which means that emigration greatly exceeded the natural rate of increase of ethnic Russians. Azerbaijan was to follow. There the outflow of Russians

Table 13.4. Index of growth of Russian populations in (former) Soviet republics (USSR = 100).

Republics	1959–70	1970–79	1979–89
Russia	0.97	0.99	1.00
Ukraine	1.14	1.08	1.02
Belarus	1.26	1.14	1.02
Moldova	1.25	1.15	1.05
Lithuania	1.03	1.06	1.07
Latvia	1.12	1.09	1.04
Estonia	1.23	1.15	1.10
Georgia	0.86	0.88	0.86
Azerbaijan	0.90	0.88	0.78
Armenia	1.04	1.00	0.69
Uzbekistan	1.19	1.06	0.94
Kyrghyzstan	1.21	1.00	0.95
Tajikistan	1.16	1.08	0.93
Turkmenistan	1.05	1.05	0.91
Kazakhstan	1.23	1.02	0.98

started at the same time and their numbers began to decrease in the 1970s. Altogether, since 1959, it has decreased by 22%. The outflow of Russians from Central Asia started in the second half of the 1970s (*Table 13.4*).

Between 1979 and 1988 the remigration of ethnic Russians went on in most of the republics, although emigration to some republics continued, but at a much slower pace. The Russian population was already decreasing in Central Asia and in Transcaucasia, but emigration into the Ukraine, Belarus, the Baltic states, and Moldova continued. In 1989 Russians left only for the Ukraine and Belarus, and only a few of them went to Estonia, whereas they were returning from other republics (*Table 13.5*).

Thus, the remigration of ethnic Russians is not a new phenomenon but a tendency that began in the early 1970s. But in recent times the pace of this process has been increasingly determined by the social and political developments in the various republics of the former USSR. As a result of the many years of migratory movements from the Russian center of the country to its developing peripheries, more than 25 million ethnic Russians (17.4% of their overall number in the former USSR) are now living outside Russia, almost 70% of them concentrated in the Ukraine and Kazakhstan. The number of Russians is highest among the population of Kazakhstan, and in Latvia, Estonia, and Kyrghyzstan (see *Figure 13.3*).

Table 13.5. Migrations of Russians to and from other (former) Soviet republics, 1989 (thousands).

Republics	Arrivals to Russia from other republics	Departures from Russia for other republics	Migration balance of ethnic Russians
Ukraine	102.1	136.1	−34.0
Belarus	17.5	23.0	−5.5
Moldova	6.8	6.8	0.0
Lithuania	4.8	4.4	0.4
Latvia	7.4	6.9	0.5
Estonia	4.9	5.2	−0.3
Georgia	7.8	3.4	4.4
Azerbaijan	11.1	4.0	7.1
Armenia	4.0	1.0	3.0
Uzbekistan	21.5	15.1	6.4
Kyrghyzstan	9.0	7.4	1.6
Tajikistan	6.9	4.7	2.2
Turkmenistan	4.7	4.3	0.4
Kazakhstan	63.0	52.5	10.5
Total	271.5	274.8	−3.3

A relatively new phenomenon is the appearance of ethnic Russian refugees from the areas of severe ethnic conflict. Thus, in April 1992 some 73,500 ethnic Russians, "forced to leave the places of their permanent residence" outside Russia were officially registered in Russia. Even when Russians leave other republics not because of direct danger arising from interethnic clashes, but in a relatively calm situation, their departure often appears to have been forced. A feeling of danger is driving ethnic Russians and other Russian-speaking peoples, i.e., those representing Russian culture, out of Central Asia and certain other regions of the former USSR, as is evidenced by the strong increase in net out-migration from some of these areas.

Similar to the period of Russian settlement migration (to Siberia and Central Asia), which also brought Ukrainians, Belarussians, Jews, Armenians, Tatars, etc., to the peripheries of Czarist Russia and the Soviet Union, today the current flow of remigrating ethnic Russians has been increased by people from these other groups.[4] At present it is evident that the exodus of Russians and the accompanying groups from the CIS and Baltic states is likely to continue. It is particularly true of those states where Russians are few in number and dispersed over large areas. It is more difficult to forecast the development of events in regions with more numerous and sufficiently concentrated Russian populations, such as eastern Ukraine, northern Kazakhstan, and Estonia.

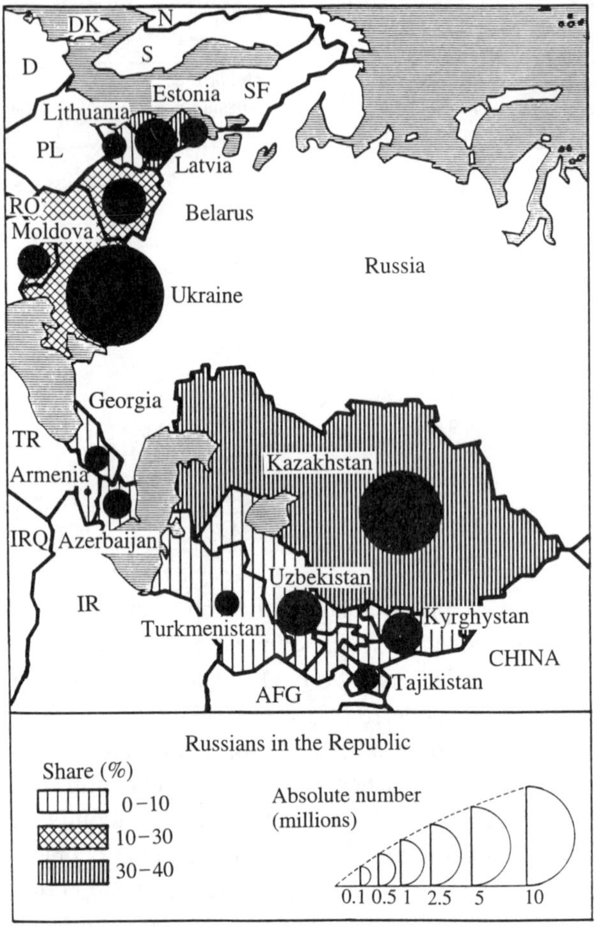

Figure 13.3. The number of Russians living outside the Russian Federation, 1989. Sources: Vishnevsky and Zayonchkovskaya (1991).

The collapse of the Soviet Union and its transformation into 15 new states has meant that 60 million people have become members of new ethnic minorities. In many cases this will lead to voluntary or forced migration – a process that will reduce the ethnic heterogeneity of the CIS and Baltic states. The largest group consists of 25 million ethnic Russians who find themselves for the first time in the position of being a national minority. Many of them are willing to return to Russia, but for the time being conditions for considerable numbers of return migrants in Russia are unfavorable. Russia is neither materially nor psychologically prepared to receive large numbers of ethnic Russians from the neighboring republics, let alone representatives of other nations. Russia and other states of the former Soviet Union even have difficulties accommodating the army contingents that are now being withdrawn from other countries.

Freedom of movement within Russia is still restricted. Moscow, St. Petersburg, most major cities, and many regional centers are trying to curb the inflow of population. The lack of a real housing market greatly complicates spatial mobility and the process of resettlement, so that many ethnic Russians who were forced to leave their former places of residence outside Russia remain homeless or without stable accommodation. In Russia most of them cannot settle in their familiar environments. In the suburbs of the bigger cities it is difficult to obtain plots of land on which to build houses, so that many of these return migrants are forced into outlying rural districts with shrinking local populations. It is clear that people used to urban life have tremendous problems in adapting to living conditions in these rural peripheries.

If the situation does not change many ethnic Russians (as well as Ukrainians, Belarussians, and other national minorities in similar situations) will start looking for opportunities either to settle in a state where their ethnic group forms a majority or to emigrate abroad. This has been confirmed by several opinion polls. According to the results of one of these polls 18% of the members of these ethnic minorities, mostly skilled workers, are planning to leave the country (*Mezhdunarodnaya Gazeta*, 1991: 159). A field survey of 945 ethnic migrants, conducted by the Center of Demography and Human Ecology of the Institute for Employment Studies (G. Vitkovskaya), showed that 27% of them would like to emigrate to another country. Of those who would like to emigrate, 42% are highly trained professionals. Comparing the intensity of the third and fourth waves of emigration, it is interesting to note that five times as many Armenian refugees desire to leave the former USSR as Russian refugees.

13.2.3 Emigration for economic reasons

"European" Emigration

Despite the prospect of new waves of "ethnic" migration, it is unlikely that they will determine the nature of the fourth wave of emigration. The economic crises that all the new nation-states of the former USSR are now experiencing will increase the potential for mass emigration to the West, i.e., emigration that is not associated with ethnic tensions and the decolonization processes mentioned above. The main motives for the expected fourth wave of emigration are economic and to a certain degree social, i.e., the opportunity for improving living standards, individual incomes, working conditions, etc.

Under prevailing conditions, those who have higher skills and a good education are the most likely to emigrate to the West. One might call this brain-drain a "European" wave of emigration because these emigrants are more likely to come from the European part of the former USSR than from the Asian part of Russia. The populations of these western regions are much better prepared to adapt to the Western way of life, they are more spatially and occupationally mobile, and they have a better knowledge of West European languages.

It is extremely difficult to assess the possible scale of this "European" type of economic migration. Until now it has not been part of the international migration of labor. The first steps are being taken now to conclude intergovernment agreements that will permit a strictly limited number of Russian, Ukrainian, Belarussian, and Baltic citizens to go to West European countries for limited periods of time. However, this involves some tens of thousands of people, whereas according to the results of several opinion polls several million people appear to be ready to leave the country as labor migrants.[5]

In 1991 Tikhonov, a researcher from the Center of Demography and Human Ecology of the Institute for Employment Studies, conducted a study of 30 experts, representatives of the state government apparatus (high-ranking ministry employees), socioeconomic sciences (heads of scientific institutions), and business (owners of enterprises and brokerage offices, members of stock exchange committees) to estimate their prospects of emigration from the territory of the former USSR. Half of the experts thought that about 2–4 million emigrants could be expected for the period 1992–97; and 20% of the experts thought emigration during this period will not exceed 2 million people, 30% expected 4–5 million emigrants. Estimates of the number of emigrants by the turn of the century were less definite, varying from 400,000 to 2 million emigrants per year, although almost half of the experts (40%) limited their estimates to 400,000–800,000 per year. Most of the experts agreed that the "ethnic" feature of emigration will weaken, and that the level of skills and education will be the basis for the next wave of emigration. Most experts think that in the future emigrants will be dominated by representatives of specific professions with high and very high professional skills.

Thus, "European" emigration of labor, which is expected both by experts and by public opinion, has the characteristic features of a brain-drain from a poor country that nevertheless has a relatively high cultural, scientific, and technological potential. This forecast fully corresponds with developments that are now taking place. According to published information, some 70,000 scientists had already left the country by 1989. In 1990 one in six Soviet emigrants was a scientist, an engineer, or a medical doctor.

"Asian" Emigration

"Asian" emigration for economic reasons may have a different nature than the "European" type. Its basic cause is agrarian overpopulation and competition in the labor market, with rapid natural increases in the population and labor force.

In the new nation-states, such competition has so far led to the ousting of minorities and foreign borns by members of indigenous and majority populations, replacing them in many jobs. In Central Asia, for example, the number of workers of indigenous nationalities in all republics almost doubled between 1977 and 1987, whereas the number of workers of other nationalities increased by only 3–9%; in Turkmenistan it decreased by 12%. In all cases the share of indigenous nationalities within the labor force exceeded their share in the overall population. There has been a sharp rise in the spatial and socioeconomic mobility of members of the indigenous and majority populations, which is being pushed by rural overpopulation. Fewer and fewer jobs are left for other nationalities.

However, the ousting of newcomers and minorities does not, of course, solve all the problems raised by overpopulation and often precedes a considerable outflow of sections of the indigenous population. The former USSR experienced a series of such population outflows, but previously they passed quite peacefully and almost unnoticed. Over a period of 20 years there has been an exodus of Armenians from Armenia, and of Moldavians, Kazan Tatars, and Northern Caucasian people from their territories. This exodus became particularly visible in the intercensal period of 1979–89, particularly from Moldova, Central Asia,

Transcaucasia, and Northern Caucasus. Most active were Moldavians, who scattered throughout the country. Russia, the Ukraine, and the Baltic states all received immigrants.[6]

Nevertheless the outflows from these regions were smaller than could have been expected from the development of main economic indicators. The main cause seems to have been the low social and spatial mobility of Central Asian populations. This leads to a paradoxical situation described, for example, in an article in *Izvestia* (15 June 1991):

> Tashkent needs workers. Local enterprises and construction works need 15,000 workers.... The aviation plant alone has about 2,000 vacancies, and the textiles group of enterprises 1,500.... This group, which has been taken on lease, is forced to shuttle temporary workers from the neighboring regions of Kazakhstan. Meanwhile, in the town itself, paradoxically as it may seem, about 25,000 of its citizens are considered to be unemployed.

Low occupational mobility, as described in this chapter, can only exist under the conditions of a rural economy with undeveloped monetary and market relations, a traditional economy preserved by the so-called socialist system. Sooner or later spatial and occupational mobility will also become an economic necessity in Central Asia. Then representatives of indigenous peoples, such as Uzbeks, Tajiks, Kirghiz, Turkmenians, and others, will to a larger extent occupy the internal labor market. But they will also start to move in larger numbers beyond the borders of their own nation-states.

Most of this labor force will be absorbed by the economic space of Russia, the Ukraine, and other parts of the former USSR; for it is easier for Uzbeks or Kazakhs to adapt themselves to the conditions of Russia or the Ukraine than to those of the West European labor market. However, other scenarios might also make sense.

Even now migratory streams are extremely sensitive to the aggravation of the crisis, to the flaring up of nationalism, ethnic clashes, and local wars, and to the decline in living standards. The analysis of the data for recent years shows that migrations have become more limited geographically. The growth of the spatial mobility of the population which had just started among the nations of Central Asia and reached a high level among Transcaucasian peoples, Moldavians, and Kazakhs has suddenly stopped. The national interchange has narrowed. All this has led to an increase in unemployment in Central Asia and eventually to the aggravation of both economic and national tensions.

Since 1988–89 competition in the labor markets and controversies over citizenship, political power, ownership, use of land, etc., have in many areas led to nationalism and ethnic conflicts and even wars, not only between Russians and the new majorities but also between local nationalities and religious groups within the new states (e.g., the conflicts in the Osh region between the Kirghiz and Uzbeks; in the Fergana Valley between the Uzbeks and Meskhetian Turks; in the Northern Caucasus between the Chechens and Ingushis; the civil wars in Moldova between the ethnic Moldavians, ethnic Russians, and Gagauz Turks; in Georgia between the Ossetes and ethnic Georgians; and the war between Armenia and Azerbaijan). Political instabilities, which have most often acquired ethnic, sometimes ethno-religious overtones, have become one of the main push factors that have forced various ethnic and religious groups to flee. At the same time, these processes make it unsafe for them to go to other neighboring states. For historical reasons the main destinations for these refugees and emigrants from Transcaucasia and Central Asia are Russia and other states in the European part of the former USSR. However, the present economic and political crises in these states may reduce the pace of this migration process, but it urges other population groups to emigrate. This applies especially to Caucasians: Armenians, Georgians, and Azerbaijanis, but also Avarians, Darjenes, Chechens, Ossetes, Ingushis, and others. These populations are highly mobile, largely urbanized, and many of them are actively looking for jobs and opportunities in urban areas. In contrast, the indigenous peoples of Central Asia are still less mobile and rarely leave their republics, despite low living standards and unemployment. However, agrarian overpopulation is quickly growing there, so that interethnic conflicts that stimulate both ethnic cleansing and gradual resettlement may change the picture.

Since Russia's big cities are no longer safe havens for potential migrants of non-Russian descent, many of them have started to look for other destinations. For example, Meskhetian Turks are now more likely to emigrate to Turkey, whereas in many other cases the orientation is most often toward the West, although emigration to countries like Iran and Afghanistan could also become an alternative.

The economic opportunities for the various groups of would-be migrants are different. All nations and nationalities in Central Asia, Kazakhstan, Georgia, Armenia, Azerbaijan, and Northern Caucasia have elite groups with high levels of professional qualifications and education. Their emigration would lead to the same kind of brain-drain as the emigration of skilled labor from the European part of Russia, the Ukraine, or the Baltic states. But these elites might not only go to the

West; some specialists will probably migrate to Turkey, Iran, and some Arab countries. For the majority of the populations of these regions the situation is different: if they were to leave their countries of origin, their emigration would be comparable to the emigration of unskilled labor from the Third World. However, such labor migration from Central Asia to the West and to some Gulf states is unlikely to take place during the coming decade, for the following reasons:

1. The mobility of the indigenous populations of Central Asia and Azerbaijan is still low and is unlikely to grow very rapidly.
2. The geographical and economic position of Central Asia and Kazakhstan will not immediately enforce stronger ties with the West and with the Gulf states.
3. The populations of these regions lack traditional relations with the West, as do the people living in former British and French colonies, that would facilitate their entry to the European labor markets. Unlike Armenians, the predominantly Muslim peoples of Central Asia have no ethnic bridgeheads in the West. Therefore if emigration from the above-mentioned regions begins, the labor markets and economic niches of Russia and the Ukraine are most likely to be explored first.
4. The requirements of the Western economy are changing: the demand for long-distance unskilled labor migrants is falling, making it even less likely that people with no knowledge of English, French, or German will find ways to establish themselves in the West.

For all of these reasons, the appearance in Europe of larger numbers of Uzbeks, Kazakhs, or Azerbaijanis seems to be very unlikely.

13.3 In Search of a Reasonable Strategy

In the past, the media in the former Soviet Union, Russia, and the West have published estimates of the potential number of East–West migrants. Most of them were based on the extrapolations of the tendencies of ethnic migration in recent years (but, as we have seen, they cannot automatically be applied to other types of migration) or on public opinion polls (which inevitably reflect the lack of experience with migration). Most estimates were, as a rule, greatly exaggerated. It was said, for example, that there would be 5, 6, or even 20 million potential emigrants just waiting for an opportunity to leave for the West. It is sometimes suggested that such estimates are purposefully aimed at frightening the West to increase and speed up financial aid to the former USSR. In reality, the serious restricting factors that exist in both the former USSR and in the potential countries of destination will undoubtedly limit East–West migration.

Shrinking economies and continuing crises are likely to force more and more people to look for better earnings, working conditions, and living standards. Moreover, political instability, if it continues for a long time, will contribute to this. On the other hand, new political and economic realities may act in the reverse direction. For instance, in some new nation-states the euphoria of independence and the growth of national sentiments may serve as counterbalances to economic push factors. The Baltic republics, which have large diaspora abroad, are even encouraging their former countrymen and their descendants to return from the USA, Canada, and Western Europe. In the larger states such as Russia and probably in the Ukraine, however, the new states and political situations are unlikely to reduce the push factors.

Emigration presupposes a certain degree of psychological readiness (and as we have seen, at present it is not very high since there are no appropriate traditions in the country), as well as a rather well-developed and complex infrastructure. For the time being, for purely technical reasons, emigration and even travel from Russia, Kazakhstan, or Central Asia to the West is almost impossible for a large majority of the population. Bus, rail, and air transportation capacities, visa-issuing embassies and consulates, frontier and customs services cannot cope with the flow of people who may want to travel or emigrate.

The lack of bridgeheads in the West also has an important impact. Usually a network of emigration linkages and a system of capillaries, facilitating the movement of people from habitual to unfamiliar economic and social environments, are necessary. Such a system is formed gradually alongside the accumulation of immigrants in the receiving countries, their self-organization, the formation of associations of compatriots, immigrant communities, etc. So far, most national groups and minorities living on the territory of the former Soviet Union cannot rely on such networks, a retaining factor that will probably reduce the build-up of the fourth wave of emigration in the years to come. The lack of support networks in the West will not only make emigration more difficult for the migrants of the fourth wave who do finally settle in the West, but their experiences will also lead to greater caution among those potential emigrants who are now expressing their readiness to leave the country. This effect will also limit the emigration flows.

The anticipation of these difficulties has already had some impact on public debates and policies aiming at the formulation of new strategies for emigration. A growing number of senior civil servants, politicians and other opinion leaders are promoting the idea that emigration should not be impeded through travel restrictions and other prohibitive measures. It would be better to shape and channel unorganized emigration at one's own risk, as is practiced by some former Soviet citizens. The new strategy of the countries of departure should be aimed at a gradual transformation of a "crisis" emigration of parts of the labor force into a "normal" one, largely temporary, at the removal of all obstacles to departure and re-entry, and at the formation of stable flows of emigration and return migration. In the view of most CIS and Baltic states, intergovernmental agreements between the sending and receiving countries should become an element of this strategy.[7]

All this, however, points not only to the complexity of problems engendered by the probable large-scale emigration from the former USSR, but also to the particular geopolitical meaning of their solution. The phenomenon of this emigration itself needs to be better comprehended. It is not sufficient to treat it as "economic" or "ethnic" emigration. It is essential to regard it, perhaps first and foremost, as an indispensable and most important step on the way to the transformation of one of the largest industrial societies on Earth from a closed into an open one, and its inclusion in the world of Western civilization. If no such transformation takes place, and if internal stresses in the former Soviet society result in its new "closure", the implications may be very serious for the entire world.

Notes

[1] For example, according to the former Ministry of Internal Affairs 235,000 people left the country for permanent residence in 1989, 452,000 in 1990, with only 2,000 people coming to the USSR for the same reason. As a result, net emigration increased 7.5 times in 1989, reaching 204,000 against 27,000 in 1988, and in 1990 it reached 413,000.

[2] Another characteristic example is an interview given by a representative of the South Korean Embassy to a correspondent of *Literaturnaya Gazeta*. When asked, "Would you like to see Soviet Korean repatriates in Seoul?", he answered, "Rather 'no' than 'yes.' We are a small country of more than 40 million people. We, of course, do not close the door to those of our countrymen who wish to return to the land of their ancestors, but we would not like to have a mass immigration of Koreans from abroad.

Soviet Koreans are citizens of the USSR and we would like them to stay in their own country" (*Literaturnaya Gazeta*, 1991: 6).

[3] The scale of this colonization was rather large; the Polish geographer Marianski (1969: 152), referred to the peopling of the steppes of the south of Russia "mass colonization. . . that can be compared only with. . . the peopling of the North American prairies."

[4] For instance, according to the results of a sample survey conducted by the State Statistics Committee of the Russian Federation, in collaboration with the Ministry of Internal Affairs, of those who came from outside Russia in 1991 and settled in new areas, 56% were Russians, 15% Ukrainians, 4.2% Armenians, 4.2% Belarussians, 3.2% Tatars, and 2.5% Azerbaijanis.

[5] Several opinion polls have been conducted by the All-Union Center for Public Opinion Study (Moscow) and by the IOM (see IOM, 1993).

[6] As a result in Russia the number of ethnic Moldavians in 1979–88 increased by 69%, against 10.5% in their own republic; ethnic Georgians and Armenians increased by 46% (against 10.3 and 13.2%, respectively, in their republics); Azerbaijanis by 220% (24%); Uzbeks and Turkmenians by 180% (34%); Kirghis by 29% (33%); and Tajiks by 210% (46%).

[7] We should not overlook other aspects of emigration from the former USSR that are acquiring international political significance. It is worth recalling the reaction of the Arabs to the massive flow of emigrants to Israel from the Soviet Union and their settlement in the West Bank and Gaza. Another example is the anxiety of Western countries concerning the possible emigration of Soviet specialists possessing atomic and other military and industrial secrets to countries such as Iraq or Libya.

Chapter 14

Migrants from the Former Soviet Union to Israel in the 1990s

Eitan F. Sabatello

14.1 Jewish Migration during the Czarist and Soviet Regimes

In the nineteenth and twentieth century Jews from the former Czarist Empire and the USSR have represented a large part of the Jewish migration worldwide. The largest wave of emigration – about 2.5 million people (see Kuznets, 1960, and sources quoted therein) – occurred between 1880 and 1920. A peak of some 200,000 per year was reached in the decade 1900–10, and was directed mainly to the Americas. But the few thousands who settled in Palestine – then a neglected Ottoman province – were instrumental in the creation of a viable Jewish community there, including the foundation of the first network of voluntary collective villages (*kibbutzim*) and of agricultural settlements (*moshavoth*).

A second sizable wave started in the early 1970s, when more than 200,000 Jews left the Soviet Union, close to 70% for Israel, and most of the rest for the USA. However the distribution by destination was uneven during the decade (see *Table 14.1*); until 1974 the majority of the 100,000 Jewish migrants went to Israel, while less than half of the 113,000 who left during 1975–79 did so. During the 1980s more than 70% of about 110,000 emigrating Jews opted for destinations other than Israel (CBS, 1991a; HIAS, 1992).

Table 14.1. Soviet Jewish immigrants to Israel and the USA, 1965–92.

Period	Total	Israel	USA	% to Israel
1965–69	8,000	7,600	400	95.4
1970–74	101,500	95,800	5,700	94.3
1975–79	112,600	54,000	58,700	47.9
1980–84	37,400	10,900	26,500	29.1
1985–89	70,300	17,900	52,300	25.4
1990	216,500	185,200	31,300	85.6
1991	182,600	147,800	34,700	81.0
1992	113,400	65,100	48,300	57.3

Sources: Israel CBS; HIAS.

Since 1989 Israel has had to face – for the second time in 40 years – the multifaceted impact of mass immigration. Created in May 1948 by a small community of barely 650,000 Jewish immigrants, the state of Israel received almost 700,000 new immigrants during the first three and a half years. These were largely integrated. During the 44 years of its existence (1948–92), Israel has received close to 2.3 million immigrants from all over the world. Its current population (at the end of 1993) of 5.3 million includes over 4.3 million Jews who are in large part first- or second-generation immigrants (39% each); 9% of the country's total population and about 10% of the Israeli Jews arrived between late 1989 and the end of 1992, including over 400,000 from the former USSR.

The current wave of more than 400,000 people (1989–92) is therefore one of the three largest waves of Jewish emigration from those areas in a century, and the largest that has ever arrived in Israel from one country, comprising 17% of the total gross immigration since independence. The quota restrictions applied by the USA since the late 1980s and the fact that emigrants from Eastern Europe are no longer eligible for political asylum in the West have greatly reduced the relative size of migratory flows there. Currently the destination of the majority of the Jewish emigrants from Russia and other CIS countries is Israel. In fact during 1990 and 1991 the size of the Soviet Jewish migration to the USA did not even reach the granted quota of 40,000 per year.

Since 1948 immigrants from the USSR have sometimes constituted a large part of the total immigration to Israel (see *Figure 14.1*) and sometimes this flow has been almost irrelevant, according to the prevailing policy of the USSR at various times. In 1990–92 the share of Soviet immigrants was well over 80%.

The distribution by age group of the Soviet migrants to Israel and to other areas during the 1970s and 1980s was somewhat different. Israel

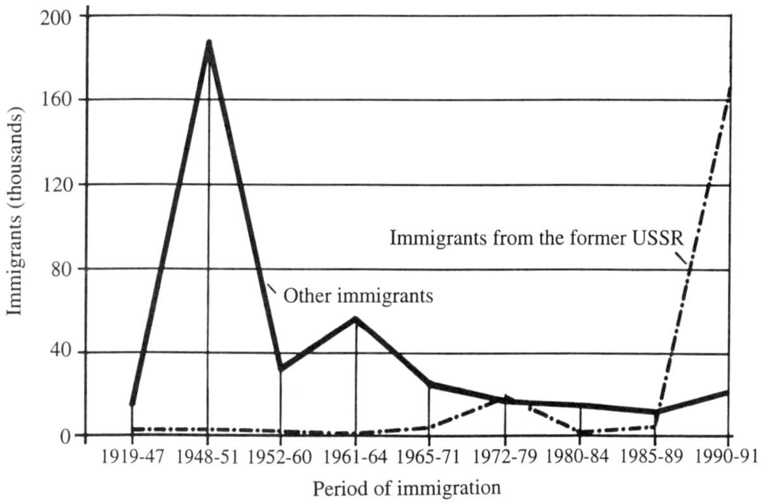

Figure 14.1. Immigrants to Israel by period of immigration and country of origin (annual average, %).

received larger percentages of both elderly and children than the USA, whereas the USA received more young adults (*Table 14.2*). Altogether, Jewish immigrants to Israel were older, on average, than those heading for the USA. Among the recent (1990s) immigrants, however, the pattern has changed in favor of younger age groups.

There are also differences in the level of education and skills of the Jewish migrants. Those arriving in Israel in the early 1970s appeared less skilled than those who went directly to the USA. By the end of the 1970s, when the number of immigrants to the USA clearly outnumbered those going to Israel, the situation was reversed (*Table 14.3*).

The last wave of USSR immigrants to Israel comprised a sizable part of the Jewish population of the former USSR and the CIS. The 1989 Soviet census registered some 1.45 million ethnic Jews; if account is taken of other Jews registered under other nationalities (such as Russian and Ukrainian) and for non-Jewish family members of Jews, then the total stock of population potentially entitled to migrate to Israel might have numbered 2–2.25 million at the time of the census. Since then about 450,000 people have left, probably more than 90% of them Jewish. At present only slightly more than 1 million Jews and a few hundred thousand persons related to Jews may still be left in the CIS (Florsheim, 1991).

Table 14.2. Soviet Jewish population in the USSR and Soviet Jewish migrants to Israel and the USA, by age group, 1971–91 (millions).

Period	0–14	15–44	45–64	65+
Soviet Jewish population[a]				
1970 (Russia only)	10	39	31	20
1979 (Russia only)	8	35	33	24
1989 (USSR)	8	33	35	24
Soviet Jewish migrants to Israel				
1971–75	23	45	22	10
1976–78	23	42	21	13
1979–80	21	40	23	16
1981–88	21	42	20	17
1989–91	23	47	18	12
Soviet Jewish migrants to the USA				
1971–75	20	53	21	6
1976–78	20	48	22	10
1979–80	19	45	22	12
1981–88	21	45	21	13
1989–91	19	44	23	14

[a]Population census; figures for 1989 are provisional estimates based on partial census data provided by Tolz (1992) and on census data for Moscow (Altshuler, 1991).
Sources: Israel CBS; HIAS.

Table 14.3. Soviet Jewish migrants to Israel and the USA, by occupational group before arrival, 1971–75 and 1989–91 (%).

Period	Academics, scientists, technicians, professionals	Managers, clerks, salesmen	Industry, service, and agricultural workers
Soviet Jewish migrants to Israel			
1971–75	43	15	42
1989–91	72	4	24
Soviet Jewish migrants to the USA			
1971–75	51	14	33
1989–91	60	10	30

Sources: Israel CBS; HIAS.

The collapse of the Soviet Union and the emergence of the new nation-states may induce an expansion of the US quota for migrants from these areas. It is difficult to predict its impact on the size of immigration to Israel. Although would-be emigrants may prefer the USA, most of them may have relatives and friends in Israel by now and might therefore opt for family reunions.

The current flow of ex-Soviet immigration to Israel has had an enormous effect on the housing market and the building industry in Israel, is inducing a revival in the use of the Russian language and culture, and is also influencing the occupational structure of the population. During the 1992 election campaign the immigrants also attracted the attention of the established political parties, since in Israel immigrants arriving (and registered) up to three months before the polls are entitled to vote.

14.2 Absorption Policy and Data System

Each person arriving or settling in Israel as an immigrant is fully recorded with his/her main sociodemographic characteristics. He/she is given an identity number (ID) and his/her file with demographic details is entered in the Population Register, and thus becomes a permanent resident. The Population Register file of an individual includes (besides the ID and family, first, and father's name): sex, year of birth, marital status, country of birth, year of immigration, address in Israel, religion, ethnic origin, and legal status (whether full citizen, permanent or intended resident). An individual's file is linked, if relevant, to those of his/her spouse and children to form a family file.

Unlike the usual practice of most European countries, a foreigner admitted as an immigrant under the Law of Return of 1950 automatically receives Israeli citizenship, unless he/she formally refuses it within three months after arrival or settlement. The Law of Return applies to all Jewish immigrants and their family members (except in specific cases indicated by law, such as people carrying dangerous contagious diseases or convicted criminals). People not entitled to settle under the provisions of the Law of Return, or those who prefer not to benefit from it, may apply for residence or citizenship, and obtain it by procedures and conditions established by the Citizenship Law, 1952.

Registration in the Population Register entitles an immigrant and his/her family to an ID card and to a series of benefits for given periods after their arrival. Until 1990 these benefits, accorded individually or to a family as a whole, and updated from time to time, ranged from allowances for initial living arrangements (in low-cost hotels for a few days or weeks) and for renting a flat (usually for one or two years), to low-interest loans to purchase one (for several years), Hebrew course fees, help and special lessons for children, health insurance, occupational orientation and retraining, income tax exemptions, and tax reductions for buying basic domestic equipment and a car. Since mid-1990 most of the short-term benefits and tax exemptions have been abolished and replaced by a lump sum payment – the "absorption basket" – that a family unit receives for one year and uses at its own discretion. Other benefits (e.g., tax reductions on cars) are adapted to changing situations.

On the basis of the records of the immigrants at registration, of their personal changes in the Population Register, and of their frontier movements (through the country's border control system), the Israel Central Bureau of Statistics (CBS) prepares statistical data on both immigrants and emigrants (CBS, 1991a). During the 1970s and early 1980s, the CBS complemented these sources with a series of special follow-up surveys. Representative samples of adult immigrants of any country of origin are interviewed at regular intervals for three to five years after their arrival. Details of background characteristics, as well as changes in their situation in housing, work adaptation, proficiency and use of Hebrew, and social and cultural integration are recorded and used for in-depth analysis and policy making. Immigrants from the USSR usually receive special attention (see, e.g., CBS, 1982).

Currently, the CBS has resumed similar, though less detailed, surveys of Soviet immigrants. Some results of the first round of this new survey, carried out in early 1991 on a sample of 1,200 immigrant households who arrived in January–June 1990, are given here (CBS, 1991b). A second round was carried out during the winter of 1991–92 on a similar sample of immigrants belonging to the larger cohort (of more than 83,000 people) who arrived in October–December 1990, with a follow-up a year later.

Other official sources of information on the immigrants' absorption processes in Israel may be traced in practically all the current or special surveys of the CBS. A typical Israeli questionnaire routinely includes questions on the year of immigration and birthplace. The Household and Population Census of 1994, similar to that of 1983 (CBS, 1989a), is another source of direct information on the living conditions of former Soviet immigrants. Many other surveys and studies on recent immigrants from the USSR have been initiated by other government, public and private agencies, or academic institutions.

14.3 Demographic Characteristics

Israel has a moderately aging population, one of the youngest of the developed countries, with only about 9% of its population aged 65 years and older. The Jews from the former USSR are considerably older; according to the 1989 census the share of elderly was close to 24%.

Table 14.4. Demographic characteristics of Soviet immigrants to Israel, 1990–92.

	1990	1991	1992
Total number	185,234	147,810	65,100
Males (%)	47.3	46.7	47.2
Age distribution			
0–14	22.8	20.6	20.0
15–65	65.1	65.7	65.4
65+	12.1	13.7	14.6
Family status (aged 15 and older)			
Never married	15.0	17.1	18.5
Married	69.3	63.8	59.3
Divorced	6.3	8.6	11.2
Widowed	9.4	10.5	11.0

Sources: Israel CBS, registration data.

Migrants from the former Soviet Union of the 1990s constitute an in-between demographic group, whose age structure at the beginning of the period 1989–92 was closer to that of the receiving population and later came closer to the sending one. For example, the proportion of those aged 65 years and older has continuously increased from 10.4% in 1989 to 14.6% in 1992 (see *Table 14.4*). The same is true for the percentages of those aged 75 and older. This may be a consequence of two not mutually exclusive factors. First, a self-selectivity initially favored the immigration of relatively young people, and later also included the older age groups; and second, the Jewish population and their relatives left behind in the CIS *per se* are becoming increasingly older.

In the long run, both factors are a result of the relatively low fertility (total fertility rate = 1.6 children per woman) prevailing among Jewish couples in the former USSR and on the low propensity of potential emigrants to leave while their children are very young (CBS, 1991c).

Women migrating to Israel tend to be significantly older than men: close to 14% in 1990 and 17% in 1992 were 65 years or older, compared with 10–12% of men. Even though it is aging, the migrant population from the USSR is still younger, on average, than the population from which it stemmed.

The age patterns of immigrants of 1990 from various former Soviet republics were somewhat different. In comparison with the overall average of 13% aged 65 and older, those from the Ukraine or Moldavia have the highest percentage of elderly (17–18%), those from Belarus and the Baltic republics are slightly above average, while only about

11% of those from Russia and close to 9% of those from the Asian republics were aged 65 or older.

Since their fertility is low and age relatively high, families (which constitute the overwhelming proportion of Soviet immigrants to Israel) are necessarily small. However, households may be considerably larger than a nuclear family, since two or more generations often live together. A typical household contains a couple with one child and one (or more) elderly parent. Single-parent nuclei of two or three generations are also rather frequent (10%), compared with their low prevalence (less than 5%) among veteran Israelis. Accordingly, in 1990–91, 87% of adult women had been married (compared with 76% in Israel), but close to 30% of them were either divorced (9–10%) or widows (15–16%).

During 1990–92 the demographic and socioeconomic patterns of the former Soviet immigrants in Israel changed somewhat. In 1990, when the flow was growing, age, marital status, education, and occupational distributions were to some extent more "favorable" than in 1991–92, when the number of newcomers gradually diminished.

14.4 Background and Current Occupational Conditions

The current wave of immigrants from the former USSR includes an unusual proportion of people with post-secondary education. About 75% of adult immigrants aged 15 years or older in 1990 and around 66% in 1991 and 1992 were recorded at registration as qualified for academic, scientific, or other professional occupations (*Table 14.5*). Jews from the European republics included similar shares of highly skilled individuals. Among those from the Asian republics this share was lower but still represented at least 60% formerly employed in the high-rank occupations. Even if border registration somewhat exaggerates the share of immigrants belonging to these categories, the large inflow of professionals, scientists, engineers, and artists potentially constitutes an exceptional brain-gain for Israel; it is therefore an important task of Israeli policy makers to minimize the possible brain-waste. However many professions do not fit the Israeli economy, as is the case for engineers in specialized or obsolete fields: in Israel there is no need for experts on building trans-Siberian railways or sub-Arctic farms. In

Table 14.5. Soviet immigrants to Israel (15 years and older) who worked before their arrival, by selected occupation 1990–92.

	1990	1991	1992
Total number aged 15+	142,900	117,400	52,000
Employed in the USSR	96,000	79,700	33,700
Labor-force participation rate	67.2	67.9	64.8
Occupations			
Scientists and academics	39.4	36.2	32.7
Of which			
Engineers and architects	25.6	23.3	20.0
Medical doctors, dentists	6.2	4.4	3.8
Other professional and technical staff, etc.	34.6	33.2	32.9

Source: Israel CBS, registration data.

some fields there is also a problem of occupational surpluses. In 1991–92, for instance, 10,000 new arrivals (3%) claimed to be physicians, representing 1% of all physicians in the former USSR.

Although this number could be somewhat reduced (as the numbers of those actually applying for doctor's licenses or refresher courses demonstrate), 6,000–7,000 of them expect to join an existing body of 14,000 Israeli medical doctors already working in the country. In the short term, it is unlikely that there will be a 50% increase in medical jobs in a small country like Israel, which is already equipped with about 190 hospitals and hundreds of first-aid clinics attached to one of the over 100 public, semipublic, or non-profit hospitals. In 1989 most of the basic health parameters of Israel were satisfactory by any Western standards, including the rate of 1 physician per 320 inhabitants.

The same may apply for the 43,000 registered immigrant engineers and architects who arrived in 1990 and 1991, most of whom hoped to join the stock of 27,000 engineers and architects already working before 1989. The same applies to the several thousands of musicians, actors, and other artists. One major exception may be the 4,000–5,000 Soviet immigrant nurses who will join a group of 40,000 veteran nurses whose turnover is high and the demand for whom usually exceeds the supply.

The problems and dilemmas of the integration of new immigrants in the Israeli labor market are only partially revealed by the sex and age rates of labor-force participation and distribution, as derived from the analysis of the sample of immigrants who arrived in January–June 1990. This may have been a somewhat special group who had the chance to

Table 14.6. Soviet immigrants of January–June 1990 aged 15 and older, by period spent in Israel (months), labor-force characteristics, and sex (%).

	Period in Israel (months)			
	6–8	9–11	12+	Total
Total in civilian labor force	51.9	57.4	59.3	56.6
Of which				
Employed	68.4	69.3	76.3	70.6
Unemployed	31.6	30.7	23.7	29.4
Not in civilian labor force	47.9	42.4	40.7	43.6
Men in civilian labor force	64.6	67.7	70.6	67.0
Of which				
Employed	74.5	77.1	85.5	78.1
Unemployed	25.5	22.9	14.5	21.9
Not in civilian labor force	35.4	32.3	29.4	32.5
Women in civilian labor force	41.1	48.4	50.5	46.8
Of which				
Employed	60.2	59.7	66.2	61.4
Unemployed	39.8	40.3	33.8	38.6
Not in civilian labor force	58.9	51.6	49.5	53.2

Note: The range of the 95% confidence interval is 1.7–4.2% in the total column, and less than 8.9 in the other columns.

come to Israel with the first wave, at a time when many job positions were still available.

Two-thirds of the adult men and 47% of the adult women in the sample had already joined the labor force (*Table 14.6*) within 6–13 months of arrival, but the unemployment rates were high – about 30% for both sexes, compared with 9% for the general population. Among these immigrants, unemployment was quite high for all age groups, but especially for women and those aged above 45 (CBS, 1991b).

Many of the few academics, professionals, etc., already employed had been unable to find jobs in which they could make use of their qualifications. For example, about 10 months after arrival only 20% of the male and only 5% of the female engineers and architects[1] were working in their professional fields, 50% of the male engineers were employed in other occupations, and 20% were still unemployed. These experiences seem to be very different from those of the Soviet immigrants who came to Israel in the early 1970s. At that time only a minority of professionals had to change to other occupational fields one year after arrival (CBS, 1982; Sabatello, 1979). Compared with the highly skilled former Soviet immigrants of 1990–91, the semiskilled

Table 14.7. Soviet immigrants of January–June 1990, aged 15 and older, employed in Israel by occupation in Israel and before immigration, and by sex (%).

	Employed in Israel			Employed before immigration		
	Men	Women	Total	Men	Women	Total
Total number of immigrants[a]	9,100	5,800	14,900	13,700	13,200	26,900
Scientists and academic staff	9.0	8.7	8.9	30.5	37.6	34.0
Other professional and technical staff, etc.	10.5	18.1	13.4	16.3	27.4	21.8
Administrators and managers	—	—	—	11.3	4.1	7.7
Clerical workers	(1.4)	6.9	3.5	2.4	13.4	7.8
Sales workers	(2.3)	—	2.2	3.4	4.5	4.0
Service workers	12.4	36.4	21.8	2.9	5.8	4.3
Agricultural workers	(1.9)	(2.3)	(2.0)	—	—	—
Skilled workers in industry, etc.	48.4	18.1	36.6	32.5	6.4	19.6
Other workers in industry and unskilled workers	13.3	7.4	11.0			(0.8)

[a]Including those whose occupations are not known. The 95% confidence interval of each cell is less than 5.2%. Values in parentheses are estimates with relatively high sampling errors.

were more likely to be employed at all and to have found a job close to their former one (CBS, 1991b).

Ten months after arrival in Israel the occupational structure of the immigrants differed substantially from the positions and jobs they had held before they left the USSR (*Table 14.7*). The differences mostly reflect the selective entrance into the Israeli labor market. Many immigrants were obliged to accept jobs below the level of their former occupation. In these low-level jobs they often substituted for foreign labor force, mainly Palestinians from the West Bank and Gaza Strip. However, immigrants who had come to Israel (even slightly) less recently obtained positions more closely related to their skills.

14.5 Re-emigration of Immigrants

In Israel emigration has been much lower than immigration but not negligible. Since independence about 10% of all immigrants have left the country, usually within the first few years after arrival; as a rule, the larger the inflow within a given period, the larger will be the outflow a few years later. Israel's "border monitoring register"[2] at any time allows an assessment of who has left the country, who has come back, and who is still abroad. A stay abroad for a continuous period of more than one year is a good proxy for long-term emigration (CBS, 1991d). For the new immigrants, a shorter period of continuous absence, such as three months, may be enough to establish their intentions not to settle in Israel (CBS, 1989b). In the last decade this system ensured that an annual net addition of 10,000–15,000 residents joined those staying abroad for more than one year.

In the 1970s, when a previous wave of immigrants had arrived from the USSR, the continuous immigrant absorption survey was used to assess emigration.

Focusing on the immigrants of the 1970s from the former USSR and other former Communist countries we can say that 3–7% of the adult immigrants from Eastern Europe again went abroad (for more than three months) within three years after arrival. After five years, the rate was 9–11%, depending on the migratory cohort considered. Highly skilled immigrants were more likely to emigrate than others (CBS, 1989b). These rates are significantly lower than those for the immigrants to Israel from Western countries.

For the more recent inflow of the 1990s from the USSR, it is of course too early to seriously check re-emigration trends. We can only say that assumptions made to prepare 1990-based projections of the Israeli population until 2005 (CBS, 1992) are based on the past trends of emigration among the East European and Soviet immigrants, as well as the educational–occupational mix of the current immigrant flow. Accordingly, an emigration rate of up to 15% of the several hundreds of thousands of immigrants expected to arrive during 1990–95 is anticipated. Most of these emigrants will not remigrate to a CIS country but will try to settle in Western Europe and North America.

14.6 Conclusions

Immigrant registration statistics in Israel indicate not only the magnitude of the recent wave of immigration but also the socioeconomic characteristics of the former Soviet newcomers of the 1990s. For the moment the crucial question is how to integrate these immigrants and how to make use of the potential brain-gain they represent. Between 1989 and 1992 Soviet immigration increased the Israeli population by 9%. Of these new immigrants, 65–70% are highly skilled professionals, technicians, people with scientific and other academic backgrounds, increasing the total numbers of people in Israel with such skills by no less than 30%. It seems almost inevitable that some of those who worked in highly skilled jobs in the former Soviet Union will be obliged to accept less qualified jobs in Israel, certainly in the short term. This would apply to a larger extent than average to those who were over 40 or 50 at arrival, to women, and to all those for whom suitable retraining is difficult or impossible. This, at least, was the experience of Soviet immigrants of the 1970s. Although their numbers, the pace of their arrival in the country and their impact on the existing Israeli labor force were smaller, these immigrants were more "absorbable" within a relatively short time than the current inflow.

Notes

[1] In the survey, occupations could be more accurately investigated and recorded than at border registration (see above).

[2] Each resident leaving the country for any purpose must fill in an "Exit/Return" form, which is fed into a computerized border monitoring register.

References

Airey, C., 1984, Social and moral values, in R. Jowell and C. Airey, eds., *British Social Attitudes: The 1984 Report*, Gower, Aldershot.

Altshuler, M., 1991, Socio-demographic profile of Moscow Jews, in L. Dymerskaya-Tsigelman and I.E. Cohen, eds., *Jews and Jewish Topics in the Soviet Union and Eastern Europe*, Center for Research and Documentation of East European Jewry **3**(16), Hebrew University of Jerusalem.

Bade, K. J., ed., 1992, *Migration in Geschichte und Gegenwart*, Beck, Munich.

Baletić, Z., and Baučić, I., 1979, *Population, Labour Force and Employment in Yugoslavia*, Research Report 54, Vienna Institute for International Economic Comparisons, Vienna.

Barsotti, O., ed., 1988, *La presenza straniera in Italia: il caso della Toscana*, Angeli, Milan.

Barsotti, O., and Lecchini, L., 1991, *Les parcours migratoires en fonction de la nationalité*, Paper presented at the European Population Conference, 21–25 October, Paris.

Basok, T., and Brym, R.J., eds., 1991, *Soviet-Jewish Emigration and Resettlement in the 1990s*, York Lanes Press, Toronto.

Bauböck, R., 1991, Einwanderungs- und Minderheitenpolitik: Ein Plädoyer für neue Grundsätze, *Österreichische Zeitschrift für Soziologie* **3**:42–56.

Baučić, I., 1973, Radnici u inozemstvu prema popisu stanovništva Jugoslavije 1971. godine (Yugoslav workers abroad according to the 1971 population census), *Migracije radnika*, knj. 4, Radovi instituta za geografiju Sveučilišta u Zagrebu, Zagreb.

Bethlehem, S., 1981, *Heimatvertreibung, DDR-Flucht, Gastarbeiterzuwanderung. Wanderungsströme und Wanderungspolitik in der Bundesrepublik Deutschland*, Klett-Cotta, Stuttgart.

Bezlov, T., 1991, Political attitudes in the pre-election situation, *Cultura Newspaper* **58**.

Bhagwati, J.N., 1984, Incentives and disincentives: International migration, *Weltwirtschaftliches Archiv* **4**:678–701.

Biffl, G., 1986, Der Strukturwandel der Ausländerbeschäftigung, in H. Wimmer, ed., *Ausländische Arbeitskräfte in Österreich*, Campus, Frankfurt/New York.

Biffl, G., 1990, Wandel in der Ausländerpolitik als Folge der Öffnung Osteuropas, *WIFO-Monatsberichte* **10**:557–61.

BIGA, 1989, *Possible Swiss Strategies for a Refugee and Asylum Policy in the 1990s*, Bundesamt für Industrie, Gewerbe und Arbeit, Berne.

Birrell, R., and Birrell, T., 1990, *An Issue of People*, 2nd ed., Longman/Cheshire, Melbourne.

Black, R., and Vaughan, R., eds., 1993, *Geography and Refugees: Patterns and Processes of Change*, Belhaven Press, London/New York.

Blattner, N., Schwarz, H., and Sheldon, G., 1985, Die Ausländerbeschäftigung als Determinante von Wirtschaftswachstum und Produktivität in einem Industrieland: Das Beispiel der Schweiz, in H. Giersch, ed., *Probleme und Perspektiven der weltwirtschaftlichen Entwicklung, Jahrestagung des Vereins für Socialpolitik*, Duncker & Humblot, Berlin.

Böhning, W.R., 1991, *International Migration to Western Europe: What to Do?* Paper presented at the European Population Conference, 21–25 October, Paris.

Bolkestein, F., 1991, Integratie van minderheden moet met lef worden aangepakt, *De Volkskrant*, 12 September.

Brubaker, R., 1991, *Immigration and Ethnic Questions in Eastern Europe: Historical and Comparative Perspectives*, Paper presented at the Conference on the New Europe and International Migration, 25–27 November, Turin.

Bruni, M., and Pinto, P., 1990, Mediterraneo, le due sponde dell'immigrazione, *Politica ed Economia* **4**.

Bundesamt für Statistik, 1990, *Statistisches Jahrbuch der Schweiz 1990*, NZZ Verlag, Zurich.

Bundesanstalt für Arbeit, 1991, *Amtliche Nachrichten der Bundesanstalt für Arbeit*, Nuremberg.

Bundesblatt, 1988, Bericht über die Stellung der Schweiz im europäischen Integrationsprozess vom 24 August, *Bundesblatt* IV/1988: 121 *et seq.*, Berne.

Bundesblatt, 1990, Informationsbericht des Bundesrates über die Stellung der Schweiz im europäischen Integrationsbericht vom 26 November, *Bundesblatt* IV/1990: 291 *et seq.*, Berne.

Bundesblatt, 1991, Bericht des Bundesrates zur Ausländer und Flüchtlingspolitik vom 15 Mai, *Bundesblatt* III/1991: 291 *et seq.*, Berne.

Calvanese, F., 1989, *La presenza straniera in Campania: specificita locali e tendenze generali del fenomeno*, Paper presented at the International Conference on Emigration and Migration Policy of the 1980s, 16–18 May, Salerno.

Castles, S., *et al.*, 1990, *Mistaken Identity: Multiculturalism and the Demise of Nationalism in Australia*, 2nd ed., Pluto Press, Sydney.

CBS, 1982, *Immigrants from the USSR: The First Five Years in Israel*, Special Series 682, Israel Central Bureau of Statistics, Jerusalem.

CBS, 1988, Evaluation de l'émigration d'Israel: mesure actuelles et perspectives, AIDELF, ed., *Les migrations internationales*, Israel Central Bureau of Statistics, Paris.

CBS, 1989a, *Immigrants from USSR 1970–1983*, Special Series 846, Israel Central Bureau of Statistics, Jerusalem.

CBS, 1989b, Immigrants who left Israel and did not return (immigrants 1969/70–1986), *Supplement to the Monthly Bulletin of Statistics* **2**:3–26, Israel Central Bureau of Statistics, Jerusalem.

CBS, 1991a, *Statistical Abstract of Israel* **42**, Israel Central Bureau of Statistics, Jerusalem.

CBS, 1991b, Employment of immigrants from the USSR who arrived in Israel in January–June 1990, *Supplement to the Monthly Bulletin of Statistics* **9**:111–46, Israel Central Bureau of Statistics, Jerusalem.

CBS, 1991c, *Immigration to Israel 1990*, Special Series 900, Israel Central Bureau of Statistics, Jerusalem.

CBS, 1991d, Indicators of the number of Israeli residents abroad, *Supplement to the Monthly Bulletin of Statistics* **11**:23–44, Israel Central Bureau of Statistics, Jerusalem.

CBS, 1992, *Projections of Population of Israel up to 2005* (based on the population in 1990), Special Series 913, Israel Central Bureau of Statistics, Jerusalem.

CENSIS, 1990, *Migrare ed accogliere*, pp. 86–7, Centro studi investimenti sociali, Rome.

Centar za demografska istraživanja, 1971, *Migracije stanovništva Jugoslavije* (*Migrations of the Yugoslav Population*), Institut društvenih nauka, Belgrade.

Central Statistical Office, 1989, *Demographic Yearbook 1989*, Warsaw.

Central Statistical Office, 1991, *Demographic Yearbook 1991*, Statistical Yearbooks, Warsaw.

Chesnais, J.-C., 1991a, *L'Emigration soviétique: passé, présent et avenir*, Paper presented at the International Conference on Migration, 13–15 March, Rome, OCDE/GD (91)24, Paris.

Chesnais, J.-C., 1991b, *Migration from Eastern to Western Europe, Past (1946–1989) and Future (1990–2000)*, Paper presented at the Conference of Ministers on the Movement of Persons from Central and East European Countries (Council of Europe, Vienna, 24–25 January), Strasbourg.

Citizens' Forum, 1991, *Citizens' Forum on Canada's Future: Report to the People and Government of Canada*, Canadian Government Publishing Centre, Ottawa.

Coleman, D.A., 1985, Inter-ethnic marriage in Great Britain, *Population Trends* **40**:4–10.

Coleman, D.A., 1987, United Kingdom statistics on immigration: Development and limitations, *International Migration Review* **21**(4):1138–69.

Coleman, D.A., 1992a, Population projections: What they can tell us about the need for international migration, *International Migration* 26/2: *The New Europe and International Migration* (Special Issue: Proc. symposium at the Giovanni Agnelli Foundation, Turin 1991): 413–61.

Coleman, D.A., 1992b, Ethnic marriage, in A.H. Bittles and D.F. Roberts, eds., *Minority Populations: Genetics, Demography and Health*, London, Macmillan.

Coleman, D.A., in press a, *International Migration in Europe: Adjustment and Integration Processes and Policies*, M. Macura and D.A. Coleman, eds., Proc. UN ECE/UN FPA Expert Group Meeting on International Migration, July, Geneva.

Coleman, D.A., in press b, Trends in fertility and intermarriage among immigrant populations in Western Europe as measures of integration, *Journal of Biosocial Science* (submitted for publication 1991).

Coleman, D.A., and Salt, J., 1992, *The British Population: Patterns, Trends and Processes*, Oxford University Press, Oxford.

Council of Europe, 1991, *Recent Demographic Developments in Europe*, Council of Europe Press, Strasbourg.

Council of Europe, 1993, *Recent Demographic Developments in Europe and North America 1992*, Council of Europe Press, Strasbourg.

Darski, L.E., 1991, Fertility in the USSR: Basic trends, EAPS/IUSSP/INED, in *Proc. European Population Conference*, Paris (mimeo).

Delcroix, C., 1991, Politique d'intégration locale aux Pays-Bas, in D. Lapeyronnie, ed., *Les politiques locales d'intégration des minorités immigrées en Europe et aux Etats-Unis*, ADRI, Paris.

Dell'Aringa, C., and Neri, F., 1987, Illegal immigrants and the informal economy in Italy, *Labour* **1**(2):107–26.

Department of International Economic and Social Affairs, 1986, *Migrant Workers: The Social Situation of Migrant Workers and their Families*, Center for Social Development and Humanitarian Affairs, New York.

Dhima, G., 1991, *Politische Ökonomie der schweizerischen Ausländerregelung, eine empirische Untersuchung über die schweizerische Migrationspolitik und Vorschläge für Ihre künftige Gestaltung*, Verlag Rüegger, Chur/Zurich.

Di Comite, L., Ancona, G., and Dell'Atti, A., 1985, L'immigrazione straniera in Puglia, *Affari Sociali Internazionali* **3**.

Dimova, L. *et al.*, 1990, Emigration is increasing, *Troud Newspaper*, 10 October.

Dohse, K., 1981, *Ausländische Arbeiter und bürgerlicher Staat: Genese und Funktion von staatlicher Ausländerpolitik und Ausländerrecht*, Anton Hain, Königstein/Ts, Germany.

Elzner, C., Mitschele, A., and Quack, S., 1992, *Probleme und Strategien der beruflichen Integration von Aussiedlerinnen in der BRD: Studie im Auftrag der Berliner Senatsverwaltung für Arbeit und Frauen*, Berlin (mimeo).

Entzinger, H., 1985, The Netherlands, in T. Hammar, ed., *European Immigration Policy*, Cambridge University Press, Cambridge.

Entzinger, H.B., and Stijnen, P.J.J., eds., 1990, *Etnische minderheden in Nederland*, Meppel/Heerlen, Boom/Open University, Amsterdam.

Eversley, D.E.C., and Sukdeo, F., 1969, *The Dependents of the Coloured Commonwealth Population of England and Wales*, Institute of Race Relations, London.

Fassmann, H., 1985, A survey of patterns and structures of migration in Austria, 1850–1900, in D. Hoerder, ed., *Labor Migration in the Atlantic Economies: The European and North American Working Classes During the Period of Industrialization*, Contributions in Labour History 16, Westport, London.

Fassmann, H., 1991, Einwanderung, Auswanderung und Binnenwanderung in Österreich-Ungarn um 1910, *Demographische Informationen 1990/1991*, Institute for Demography, Austrian Academy of Sciences, Vienna.

Fassmann, H., and Münz, R., 1990, Migration und Bevölkerungspolitik: Österreich im internationalen Vergleich, in B. Felderer, ed., *Bevölkerung und Wirtschaft, Jahrestagung des Vereins für Socialpolitik 1989*, Duncker & Humblot, Berlin.

Fassmann, H., and Münz, R., 1992, *Einwanderungland Österreich? Gastarbeiter – Flüchtlinge – Immigranten*, Dachs J&V Edition, Vienna.

Fassmann, H., and Münz, R., 1993, Österreich: Einwanderungsland wider Willen, *Migration* **1**:11–38.

Fassmann, H., Findl, P., and Münz, R., 1991, *Die Auswirkungen der internationalen Wanderungen auf Österreich. Szenarien zur regionalen Bevölkerungsentwicklung 1991–2031*, ÖROK-Schriftenreihe 89, Vienna.

Federal Ministry for Foreign Affairs, 1990, *Foreign Policy Report 1990*, Vienna.

Feichtinger, G., and Steinmann, G., 1992, Immigrants into a population with fertility below replacement level: The case of Germany, *Population Studies* **46**:275–84.

Ferruzza, A., and Ricci, M., 1991, *Socio-demographic Characteristics of the Immigrants in Italy: A Multivariate Analysis, Istat*, Paper presented at the European Population Conference, Paris.

Findl, P., Holzmann, R., and Münz, R., 1987, *Bevölkerung und Sozialstaat*, Manz, Vienna.

Findlay, A., and Stewart, A., 1985, *The New Nomads: A Survey of British Expatriates Returning from the Middle East*, Population Geography Study Group Conference, Liverpool University.

Fischer, P.A., 1991, Migration, its determinants and integration: Some presumptions about the Nordic Experience, in J. Korkiasaari and I. Söderling, eds., *Migrationen och det framtide Norden*, Nordisk Ministerrad, Copenhagen.

Fischer, P.A., and Straubhaar, T., 1991, *Integration und Migration in Nordeuropa: Freizügigkeit im Gemeinsamen Nordischen Arbeitsmarkt (Free Movement of Labour within the Nordic Common Labour Market*; with an English Summary), Intermediate report of the project "Freizügigkeit im Gemeinsamen Nordischen Arbeitsmarkt", Institute of Economics, University of Berne.

Florsheim, J., 1991, Immigration to Israel from the Soviet Union in 1990, in L. Dymerskaya-Tsigelman and I.E. Cohen, eds., *Jews and Jewish Topics in the Soviet Union and Eastern Europe*, Center for Research and Documentation of East European Jewry 2(15), Hebrew University of Jerusalem.

Furcht, A., 1989, La nuova immigrazione e problemi economici, sociali e politici: alcune osservazioni, in C. Maccheroni and A. Mauri, eds., *Le immigrazioni dall'Africa mediterranea verso l'Italia*, Giuffre, Milan.

GCP, 1989, *Demographic Situation of Poland*, 1989 Report, Governmental Commission on Population, Warsaw.

Gnehm, A., 1966, *Ausländische Arbeitskräfte – Ihre Bedeutung für Konjunktur und Wachstum dargestellt am Beispiel der Schweiz*, Paul Haupt Verlag, Berne.

Gokder, A., 1992, *Report on the Migration Situation in Turkey*, OECD, SOPEMI, Paris.

Hagmann, H.M, 1991, La Suisse/Switzerland, in J.L. Rallu and A. Blum, eds., *European Population I: Country Analyses*, John Libbey, Montrouge/London/Rome.

Hammar, T., 1990, *Democracy and the Nation State: Aliens, Denizens and Citizens in a World of International Migration*, Avebury, Aldershot.

Hárs, A., 1992, Migráció és munkaeröpiac (Migration and Labor Market), Budapest (unpublished).

Haskey, J., 1990, The ethnic minority populations of Great Britain: Estimates by ethnic group and country of birth, *Population Trends* **60**:35–8.

Haug, W., 1980, *...und es kamen Menschen: Ausländerpolitik und Fremdarbeit in der Schweiz 1914 bis 1980*, Z-Verlag, Basel.

Hauser, H., 1991, *EWR-Vertrag, EG-Beitritt, Alleingang: Wirtschaftliche Konsequenzen für die Schweiz* (with the collaboration of S. Bradke), Gutachten zu Handen des Bundesrates, Bundesamt für Konjunkturfragen, Berne.

Heitman, S., 1987, The third Soviet emigration: Jewish, German and Armenian emigration from the USSR since World War II, *Berichte des Bundesinstituts für ostwissenschaftlische und internationale Studien* **21**:1–108.

Heitman, S., 1991, Soviet emigration in 1990: A new "fourth wave?", *Innovation* **3/4**:1–15.

Herbert, U., 1986, *Geschichte der Ausländerbeschäftigung in Deutschland 1880–1980: Saisonarbeiter, Zwangsarbeiter, Gastarbeiter*, Dietz, Berlin.

Heršak, E., 1983, *Migracijska razmjena izmedju Italije i Jugoslavije (Migration Change Between Italy and Yugoslavia)*, Migracije, Centar za istraživanje migracija, Zagreb.

HIAS, 1992, *Statistical Abstracts*, New York.

Hoffmann-Nowotny, H.J., and Killias, M., 1979, Labor importing countries: Switzerland, in R.E. Krane, ed., *International Labor Migration in Europe*, Praeger, London/New York.

Hollifield, J.F., 1992, *Immigrants, Markets, and States: The Political Economy of Postwar Europe*, Cambridge, MA/London.

Home Affairs Committee, 1982, *Fifth Report from the Home Affairs Committee: Immigration from the Indian Sub-Continent*, HMSO, London.

Home Office, 1977a, *British Nationality Law: Discussion of Possible Changes*, HMSO, London.

Home Office, 1977b, *A Register of Dependants: Report of the Parliamentary Group on the Feasibility and Usefulness of a Register of Dependants*, HMSO, London.

Home Office, 1991, *Immigration and Nationality Department: A Report on the Work of the Department*, HMSO, London.

Horvath, T., 1988, Die Rückkehrer, in T. Horvath and R. Münz, eds., *Migration und Arbeitsmarkt*, Eisenstadt, Austria.

Huber, K., 1963, *Die ausländischen Arbeitskräfte in der Schweiz*, Vogt-Schild, Solothurn.

International Migration, 1989, An assessment for the 90s, *International Migration Review* (Special Silver Anniversary Issue) 87, Center for Migration Studies, New York.

IOM, 1993, *Profiles and Motives of Potential Migrants*, An IOM study undertaken in four countries: Albania, Bulgaria, Russia, and Ukraine, International Organization on Migration, Geneva.

ISTAT, 1990, *Gli immigrati presenti in Italia: una stima per l'anno 1989*, Rome.

John, M., 1991, Die Zuwanderung im Mitteleuropäischen Raum, Informationen zur Politischen Bildung 2, *Flucht und Migration*, pp. 19–32.

Jones, C., 1977, *Immigration and Social Policy in Britain*, Tavistock, London.

Jones, K., and Smith, A.D., 1979, *The Economic Impact of Commonwealth Immigration*, National Institute for Economic and Social Research, Cambridge.

Jones, P.R., 1982, Some sources of current migration, in D.A. Coleman, ed., *The Demography of Immigrants and Minority Groups in the UK*, Academic Press, London.

Jones, P.R., and Shah, S., 1980, Arranged marriages: A sample survey of the Asian case, *New Community* **8**(3):339–43.

Kalchev, J., and Tzvetarsky, S., 1991, The potential emigration of Bulgarian citizens travelling abroad, *National Institute of Statistics Publication*, Sofia.

Kayser, B., 1977, The effects of international migration on the geographical distribution of populations in Europe, *Population Studies* **2**, Council of Europe, Strasbourg.

King, R., ed., 1993, *Mass Migration in Europe: The Legacy and the Future*, Belhaven Press, London.

Kirk, D., 1946, *Europe's Population in the Interwar Years*, Demographic Monographs 3, Gordon & Breach, London.

Kirwan, F.X., and Nairn, A.G., 1983, Migrant employment and the recession: The case of the Irish in Britain, *International Migration Review* **17**:672–81.

Komarica, Z., 1970, *Jugoslavija u suvremenim evropskim migracijama* (*Yugoslavia in the Current European Migrations*), Ekonomski institut Zagreb, Zagreb.

Komitee für ein ausländerfreundliches Österreich, ed., 1984, *O du gastlich Land. Vom Leben der Ausländer/innen in Österreich*, Vienna.

Korcelli, P., 1991, International migration in Europe: Polish perspectives for the 1990s, Paper presented at the Conference on the New Europe and International Migration, 25–27 November, Turin.

Körner, H., 1976, *Der Zustrom von Arbeitskräften in die Bundesrepublik Deutschland 1950–1972, Auswirkungen auf die Funktionsweise des Arbeitsmarktes*, Peter Lang, Frankfurt/Munich.

Kosinski, L., 1963, Demographic processes in the recovered territories from 1945 to 1960 (in Polish), *Prace Geograficzne* **40**, Polish Scientific Publishers, Warsaw.

Krane, E.R., ed., 1979, *International Labor Migration in Europe*, Praeger, London/New York.

Kunz, K.L., 1989, Ausländerkriminalität in der Schweiz – Umfang, Struktur und Erklärungsversuch, Schweiz, *Zeitschrift für Strafrecht* **106**:373–92.

Kupiszewski, M., 1992, *Sources and Usefulness of Information on Mobility in Poland*, Working Paper 10, School of Geography, University of Leeds.

Kuznets, S., 1960, Economic structure and life of the Jews, in L. Finkelstein, ed., *The Jews*, Harper & Brothers, New York.

Latuch, M., 1989, *Dilemmas and Problems of Contemporary Migration of Poles Abroad*, Monografie i Opracowania 287, Academy of Planning and Statistics, Warsaw.

Lee, E.S., 1966, A theory of migration, *Demography* **3**(1):47-57.

Leskel, J., 1990, *EFTA Countries' Foreign Direct Investment in the European Free Trade Association: EFTA Trade 1990*, EFTA, Geneva.

Lewis, A.W., 1954, *Development with Unlimited Supplies of Labour*, Manchester School of Economic and Social Studies 22, Manchester.

Lijphart, A., 1975, *The Politics of Accommodation: Pluralism and Democracy in the Netherlands*, University of California Press, Berkeley.

Linke, W., 1976, The demographic characteristics and the marriage and fertility patterns of migrant populations, *Population Studies* **1**, Council of Europe, Strasbourg.

Lucassen, L., and Kubben, A.J.F., 1992, *Het partij le gelijk*, Leiden, COMT.

Lucassen, J., and Penninx, R., 1985, *Nieuwkomers: Immigranten en hun nakomelingen in Nederland 1550–1985*, Meulenhoff, Amsterdam.

Mackensen, R., 1991, *Wanderungsbewegungen in Europa aus der Sicht der Bundesrepublik Deutschland*, Gesellschaft für Regionalforschung, Seminarberichte 30, Heidelberg.

Maillat, D., 1987, Long-term trends of international migration flows: Experience of European receiving countries, in *The Future of Migration*, OECD, Paris.

Majava, A., 1991, Towards an equitable sharing of the benefits of international migration, *Yearbook of Population Research in Finland* **29**:93–8, Helsinki.
Malchov, B., Tayebi, K., and Brand, U., 1990, *Die fremden Deutschen: Aussiedler in der Bundesrepublik*, Hamburg.
Mammey, U., 1990, *The Demographic and Socio-Economic Impact of the Recent European East–West Migrations in Germany*, Bundesinstitut für Bevölkerungsforschung, Wiesbaden (mimeo).
Marianski, A., 1969, *Sovremennye migratsii naseleniya* (*Contemporary Migrations of Population*), Moscow (translated from Polish).
Matuschek, H., ed., 1991, *Minderjährige auf der Flucht. Situation und Probleme unbegleiteter minderjähriger Asylwerberinnen in Österreich*, Vienna.
Mauron, T., 1991, *Rapport du Correspondant Suisse*, Report for the Continuous Reporting System for Migration in the OECD (SOPEMI), Berne.
Meningen over Medelanders, 1992, *Meningen over Medelanders: Integratie of assimilatie?*, M&P, Weert.
Mikulić, B., 1987, Aktuelni problemi povratka i zapošljavanja vanjskih migranata Bosne i Hercegovine (Current problems of return migration and employment of temporary economic emigrants from Bosnia and Herzegovina), *Ekonomski glasnik* **37**(1–2):51–75.
Minderhedennota, 1983, Ministerie van Binnenlandse Zaken, the Hague.
Morokvasić, M., 1993, Flucht und Vertreibung im ehemaligen Jugoslawien, *Demographie Aktuell* **2**, Berlin.
Mühlgassner, D., 1984, Die Sonderstellung Österreichs in Europa: Aufnahme- und Abgabeland von Gastarbeitern, in E. Lichtenberger, ed. (with the collaboration of H. Fassmann), *Gastarbeiter – Leben in zwei Gesellschaften*, Austrian Academy of Sciences, Vienna.
Mulina, T., Macura M., and Rašević M., 1981, *Stanovništvo i zaposlenostu dugoročnom razvoju Jugoslavije* (*Population and Employment in the Long-Range Development of Yugoslavia*), Ekonomski Institut, Belgrade.
Muus, P.J., 1991, *Migration, Minorities and Policy in the Netherlands: Recent Trends and Developments* (SOPEMI Netherlands, 1991), University of Amsterdam, Centre for Migration Research.
Muus, P., and Cruijsen, H., 1991, *International Migration in the European Community*, Paper presented at the International EUROSTAT Conference on Human Resources in Europe, Luxembourg.
Nabholz, R., and Artho, M., 1992, *Auswanderung aus der Schweiz als Folge einer Freizügigkeit im EG-Raum*, Licentiate thesis at the University of Berne (mimeo).
Nanten, P., 1992, Official statistics and problems of inappropriate ethnic categorization, *Policy and Politics* **20**(4):277–85.
National Statistical Institute, 1992, *Domestic and Exterior Migration of the Population at the End of the 1990s*, Sofia.
Nederlands Gesprek Centrum, 1992, *De toekomstkansen van allochtone jongeren*, Ministerie van Binnenlandse Zaken, Maatschappelijk debat over integratie, the Hague.
Neuhoff, H., 1979, Der Lastenausgleich aus der Sicht der Vertriebenen, in H.J. Merkatz, *Aus Trümmern wurden Fundamente: Vertriebene, Flüchtlinge, Aussiedler. Drei Jahrzehnte Integration*, Walter Rau, Düsseldorf.
Obolenskiy, V.V. (Osinskiy), 1928, *Mezhdunarodnyie i mezhkontinentalnyie migratsii v dorevolutsionnoi Rossii i v SSSR* (*International and intercontinental migrations in pre-revolutionary Russia and the USSR*), Moscow.
OECD, 1988, *The Social Policy Implications of Ageing Populations*, Paris.
OECD, 1991a, *Labour Force Statistics, 1968–88* (annual), Paris.
OECD, 1991b, *OECD Economic Surveys 1990/91: Switzerland*, Paris.

OECD, 1991c, *National Accounts, Main Aggregates* **1**, Paris.

OECD, 1991d, *Quarterly Labour Force Statistics* **2**, Paris.

OECD, 1991e, *The Swiss Delegation's Contribution*, Paper presented at the International Conference on Migration, 13–15 March, Rome.

OECD, 1991f, *Historical Statistics 1960–89*, OECD Economic Outlook, Paris.

OECD, 1991g, SOPEMI 1990, *Continuous Reporting System on Migration*, Directorate for Social Affairs, Manpower and Education, OECD, Paris.

OECD/SOPEMI, 1992, *Trends in International Migration*, Paris.

O'Grada, C., 1985, *On Two Aspects of Post-War Irish Immigration*, Centre for Economic Policy Research, London.

Okolski, M., 1991a, *Migration and Skilled Labour Mobility*, OECD, Paris.

Okolski, M., 1991b, *Migratory Movements from Countries of Central and Eastern Europe*, Paper presented at the Conference of Ministers on the Movement of Persons from Central and East European Countries, Vienna, 24–25 January, Council of Europe, Strasbourg.

OPCS, 1988, *International Migration 1986*, Series MN No. 13, HMSO, London.

OPCS, 1992, *International Migration 1990*, Series MN No. 17, HMSO, London.

Opitz, P. J., 1991, *Das Weltflüchtlingsproblem zu Beginn der 90er Jahre*, Munich.

Oversea Migration Board, 1954, *First Annual Report of the Oversea Migration Board*, HMSO, London.

Pavlik Z., Rychtaříková, J., and Šubrtová, A., 1986, *Základy demografie* (*The Foundations of Demography*), Academia, Prague.

Peach, G.C.K., 1968, *West Indian Migration to Britain*, Oxford University Press, Oxford.

Peach, G.C.K., 1979, British unemployment cycles and West Indian immigration 1955–74, *New Community* **7**:40–4.

Peach, G.C.K., 1981, Ins and outs of Home Office and IPS immigration data, *New Community* **9**:117–19.

Peach, G.C.K., 1991, *The Caribbean in Europe: Contrasting Patterns of Migration and Settlement in Britain, France, and the Netherlands*, Centre for Research in Ethnic Relations, Warwick, UK.

Penninx, R., 1984, Immigrant populations and demographic development in the member states of the Council of Europe, *Population Studies* **13**, Council of Europe, Strasbourg.

Petrov, D., and Nikolov, T., 1988, *Bulgarians in South America*, National Statistical Institute, Sofia.

Potts, L., 1988, *Weltmarkt für Arbeitskraft: Von der Kolonisation Amerikas bis zu den Migrationen der Gegenwart*, Junius Verlag, Hamburg.

Prins, C.J.M., 1991, *Registertelling naar nationaliteit en geboorteland, 1 januari 1990*, Maandstatistiek van de bevolking (CBS), 1 January.

Pugliese, E., 1990, Gli immigrati nel mercato del lavoro, *Polis* **IV**(1).

Puskás, J., 1981, A magyarországi kivándorlás sajátosságai a két világháboru között (1920–1940) (Characteristics of emigration from Hungary between the two world wars; 1920–1940), *Magyar Tudomány* **10**:735–45.

Randé, J., 1987, Magyarok külföldön (Hungarians abroad), *Külpolitika* **5**:114–26.

Ravenstein, E.G., 1885, The laws of migration, *Journal of the Royal Statistical Society* **48**:167–337.

Ravenstein, E.G., 1889, The laws of migration, *Journal of the Royal Statistical Society* **52**:241–301.

Reichling, G., 1986, *Die deutschen Vertriebenen in Zahlen*, Teil I: *Umsiedler, Verschleppte, Vertriebene, Aussiedler 1940–1985*, Kulturstiftung der deutschen Vertriebenen, Bonn.

Robertson, D.B., 1992, The Cost of Commonwealth, in D.A. Coleman, ed., *Dis-United Kingdom? The Political Economy of Cultural Pluralism*, Institute of Economic Affairs, London.

Rogers, A., and Castro, L., 1981, *Model Migration Schedules*, RR–81–30, International Institute for Applied Systems Analysis, Laxenburg, Austria.

Royal Society, 1987, *The Migration of Scientists and Engineers to and from the UK*, Royal Society and Fellowship of Engineering, London.

Rykiel, Z., 1989, Intermarriage and Social Integration in the Katowice Region, *Prace Geograficzne* **152**, Institute of Geography and Spatial Organization, Polish Academy of Sciences, Warsaw.

Sabatello, E.F., 1979, Patterns of occupational mobility among the new immigrants to Israel, *International Migrations* **17**(3–4):267–78.

Sakson, A., 1986, *Migration of the Population of Warmia and Mazury to the FRG*, Monografie i Opracowania 212, Academy of Planning and Statistics, Warsaw.

Salt, J., 1991, *International Migration and the United Kingdom*, Migration Research Unit, University College London.

Salt, J., 1992, *International Migration and the United Kingdom*, Report of the UK SOPEMI Correspondent to the OECD, 1992, London, Migration Research Unit, University College London.

Salt, J., and Clout, H., ed., 1976, *Migration in Post-War Europe*, Oxford University Press, Oxford.

Saopštenje (*Informations*), various years, Savezni zavod za statistiku, Belgrade.

Sauvy, A., 1969, *The Economic and Political Consquences of Selective Migrations from One Country to Another: Population Growth and Brain Drain*, Edinburgh University Press.

Schwarz, H., 1988, *Volkswirtschaftliche Wirkungen der Ausländerbeschäftigung in der Schweiz*, Verlag Rüegger, Chur/Zurich.

Seifert, W., 1991, *Ausländer in der Bundesrepublik: Soziale und ökonomische Mobilität*, Wissenschaftszentrum Berlin für Sozialforschung.

SGJ, various years, *Statisički godišnjak Jugoslavije* (*Statistical Yearbook of Yugoslavia*), Savezni zavod za statistiku, Belgrade.

Siebert, H., and Koop, M.J., 1991, Institutional competition: A concept for Europe? *Aussenwirtschaft* **45**.

Social and Cultural Planning Office, 1986, *Ethnic Minorities: Social and Cultural Report*, Rijswijk, the Netherlands, pp. 367–99.

Social and Cultural Planning Office, 1992, *Sociale en Culturele Verkenningen 1992*, Rijswijk, the Netherlands.

Statistical Office of the European Community, 1987, *Demographic and Labor Force Analysis Based on Eurostat Data Bank*, Luxembourg.

Straubhaar, T., 1988, *On the Economics of International Labour Migration*, Verlag Paul Haupt, Berne/Stuttgart.

Straubhaar, T., 1991a, *Schweizerische Ausländerpolitik im Strukturwandel*, Strukturberichterstattung, Bundesamt für Konjunkturforschung, Berne.

Straubhaar, T., 1991b, Migration pressure, in W.R. Böhning, P.V. Schaeffer, and T. Straubhaar, eds., *Migration Pressure: What is it? What Can One Do About It?* Working Paper, International Migration for Employment, ILO, Geneva.

Straubhaar, T., and Lüthi, A., 1990, EG-Freizügigkeit und schweizerische Ausländerpolitik, *Schweizerische Zeitschrift für Volkswirtschaft und Statistik* **126**:293–309.

Tabah, L., 1989, *World Demographic Trends and Their Consequences for Europe*, Council of Europe, Strasbourg.

Tanić, Z., 1979, Yugoslavia, in R.E. Krane, ed., *International Labor Migration in Europe*, Praeger, London/New York.

Tannahill, J.A., 1958, *European Volunteer Workers in Britain*, Manchester University Press, Manchester.

Tapinos, G.P., 1991, *Les Migrations Extra-Communautaires et l'avenir des populations Etrangéres*, Paper presented at the International EUROSTAT Conference on Human Resources in Europe, Luxembourg.

Todaro, M.P., and Harris, J.R., 1970, Migration, unemployment and development, *American Economic Review* **60**(3).

Tolz, M., 1992, Balance of births and deaths among Soviet Jewry, in L. Dymerskaya-Tsigelman and I.E. Cohen, eds., *Jews and Jewish Topics in the Soviet Union and Eastern Europe*, Center for Research and Documentation of East European Jewry **2**(18), The Hebrew University of Jerusalem.

Tóth, J., 1991, A politikai migrációtól a migrációs politikáig (From political migration to migration policy), *Mozgó világ* **11**:111–15.

Tsaplin, V., 1989, Statistika zhertv stalinizma v 30e gody (Statistics on the victims of Stalinism in the 1930s), *Voprosy istorii* **4**.

Tuchtfeldt, E., 1978, Die schweizerische Arbeitsmarktentwicklung – Ein Sonderfall? in O. Issing, ed., *Aktuelle Probleme der Arbeitslosigkeit*, Duncker & Humboldt, Berlin.

United Nations, 1970, Methods of Measuring Internal Migration, Manual VI, *Population Studies* **47**, New York.

United Nations, 1986, *Migrant Workers 2: The Social Situation of Migrant Workers and Their Families*, Department of International Economic and Social Affairs; Center for Social Development and Humanitarian Affairs, New York.

United Nations/ECE, 1991, *Long-term Migration among the Member Countries of the EC and Selected Other Countries and Areas*, Geneva, unpublished.

United Nations/ECE, 1993, *Rapid Information*, Vol. 2, Geneva.

Vaccina, F., 1983, Alcuni aspetti della immigrazione tunisina a Mazzara del Vallo, *Studi Emigrazione* **71**.

Vasileva, D., 1992, Bulgarian Turkish emigration and return, *International Migration Review* **26**.

Venturini, A., 1990, Il ruolo delle immigrazioni nel mercato del lavoro delle societa industrializzate: complementarieta, sostituzione o trasformazione, in G. Ancona, ed., *Migrazioni mediterranee e mercato del lavoro*, Cacucci, Bari.

Vicarelli, G., 1990, I lavoratori stranieri nelle Marche: immigrazione e regolazione sociale in un'area a economia diffusa, in E. Moretti and A. Cortese, eds., *La presenza straniera in Italia: il caso delle Marche*, Angeli, Milan.

Vishnevsky, A., and Zayonchkovskaya, J., 1991, L'émigration de l'ex-Union soviétique: premices et inconnues, *Revue Européenne des Migrations Internationales* **7**(3).

Vizzini, S., 1983, Su alcuni aspetti demografici ed economici dell'immigrazione araba a Mazzara del Vallo, *Studi Emigrazione* **71**.

Vogler-Ludwig, K., 1988, Europäischer Binnenmarkt und Beschäftigung. Ein Problemaufriss, *Beiträge zur Arbeitsmarkt- und Berufsforschung* **127**, Nuremberg.

Wimmer, H., ed., 1986, *Ausländische Arbeitskräfte in Österreich*, Campus, Frankfurt/New York.

WRR, 1979, *Ethnic Minorities*, Dutch Scientific Council for Government Policy, the Hague.

WRR, 1989, *Immigrant Policy*, Dutch Scientific Council for Government Policy, the Hague (English version published in 1990).

Yugoslav Statistical Office, 1971, Lica na privremenom radu u inostranstvu (Temporary Emigrant Workers), *Statistical Bulletin* **679**.

Index